A Primer on
Macroeconomics

A Primer on Macroeconomics

Thomas Beveridge

A Primer on Macroeconomics
Copyright © Business Expert Press, 2013.

First published in 2013 by
Business Expert Press, LLC
222 East 46th Street, New York, NY 10017
www.businessexpertpress.com

ISBN-13: 978-1-60649-423-3 (paperback)

ISBN-13: 978-1-60649-424-0 (e-book)

Business Expert Press Economics and Finance
collection

Collection ISSN: 2163-761X (print)
Collection ISSN: 2163-7628 (electronic)

Cover and interior design by Exeter Premedia Services Private Ltd.,
Chennai, India

First edition: 2013

10 9 8 7 6 5 4 3 2 1

Printed in the United States of America.

Abstract

Economics, far from being the "dismal science," offers us valuable lessons that can be applied to our everyday experiences. At its heart, economics is the science of choice and a study of economic principles that allows us to achieve a more informed understanding of how we make our choices, whether these choices occur in our everyday life, in our work environment, or at the national or international level.

The present text represents a common sense approach to basic macroeconomics. It is directed toward all students, but particularly those within business school settings, including students beginning an advanced business degree course of study. It will deliver clear statements of essential economic principles, supported by easy-to-understand examples, and uncluttered by extraneous material; the goal being to provide a concise readable primer that covers the substance of macroeconomic theory.

The text begins by explaining key economic principles and defining important terms used in macroeconomic discussion. It uses a single unifying tool—aggregate demand and aggregate supply analysis—to probe differing perspectives on macroeconomic policies

Keywords

comparative advantage, opportunity cost, demand and supply, equilibrium, GDP, business cycle, aggregate price level, inflation rate, unemployment rate, expenditure multiplier, fiscal and monetary policies, crowding-out effect, money multiplier, international trade issues, stabilization

Contents

Preface

This *Primer on Macroeconomics* has been long in the writing. It has been shaped by after-class discussions with students over many years while we tried to break down economics into understandable concepts and examples. A former student, Dr. Jeff Edwards, now Chairman of the Economic Department at North Carolina A&T State University, requested that I write an introductory text, and advised "Make it like your lectures."

No book, at least no book that I'm capable of writing, can capture the immediacy and intimacy of a classroom environment but, equally, no classroom environment permits the opportunity to dwell on detail quite as effectively as the pages of a book. As with everything in economics, there are trade-offs.

I've devised this *Primer* to help you to master the concepts in what may to be your first, and perhaps only, economics course. I've given you opportunities to apply these concepts in real-world situations. Most economists stress the need for competence in three major areas—the application of economic concepts to real-world situations, the interpretation of graphs, and the analysis of numerical problems. This *Primer* allows you to develop these important skills. In addition, you may visit my website www.tbeveridge.com where additional learning support is available to you in the form of a chapter-by-chapter study guide, with exercises, applications and examples, and further learning experiences and tips. Feel free to contact me with questions and requests, and I'll be happy to respond as time permits.

Throughout the text, I've attempted to maintain the sense of a dialogue—there are frequent "Think it through" pauses, during which you can review and check your grasp of the topic under discussion.

I hope that this book will ignite in you a passion for economics that will blaze for a lifetime. Economics surrounds us—it fills the airwaves, our daily lives, our hopes, and dreams. Learning how to apply economic concepts to our world creates a better and more durable understanding and a reasonable goal for a noneconomics major is to have sufficient insight to evaluate the economic content of articles in *The Wall Street Journal* or *The Economist* or the views expressed by commentators on CNN or Fox.

This *Primer* has been written with the hope that, long after you have turned the final page, you will retain a deeper understanding of economic issues and the tools to analyze the exciting and challenging concerns that we all must address in our contemporary world.

Best wishes to you in your study of economics. You will find it a rewarding and worthwhile experience, and I trust that this *Primer* will stimulate you in your endeavors.

Acknowledgments

Through the years, many students have asked me questions and, by doing so, have given me deeper insights into the difficulties that arise when Economics is first approached. I am grateful to all of them. Much of the material included in this book springs from such "after class" discussions.

The efforts of reviewers Phil Romero and Jeff Edwards have added greatly to the quality of the final product. A former student, Jonas Feit, now thriving at North Carolina State University, critiqued early drafts. Cindy Durand of Business Expert Press deserves credit for keeping things moving smoothly. Denver Harris has been stalwart and reliable in converting a misshapen poorly-written manuscript into an orderly text. Needless to say, any remaining *lapsi calami* are my responsibility.

This *Primer* is dedicated, with love, to the memory of my parents, Pam (my long-suffering wife), Andrew (whose surprises are no longer shocks but delights), and to the dogs and cats, and especially for Cody, for whom all lunches are free.

Thomas Beveridge
Hillsborough, North Carolina

CHAPTER 1

Scarcity and Choice

By the end of this chapter you will be able to:

1. Identify the three fundamental economic questions.
2. Explain why a production possibility frontier has a negative slope and why that slope depicts the concept of opportunity cost.
3. Interpret what is depicted by a production possibility frontier.
4. Explain why increasing opportunity costs occur in the real world and how this relates to the production possibility frontier diagram.
5. Use the production possibility frontier to identify how economic growth might occur.
6. Distinguish between productive efficiency and allocative efficiency.
7. Distinguish between absolute advantage and comparative advantage.
8. Use comparative advantage to explain the theory that individuals or countries can gain from specialization and exchange.

Economics: The Scientific Study of Rational Choice

Imagine you're in a restaurant and the server has just handed you the menu. You are preparing to make a choice. You have entered the realm of economics. At its most fundamental, economics is about choice. We may define economics as the scientific study of rational choice. Although that assumption of rationality has recently come under some attack, it remains a good working assumption. We make choices and consider trade-offs as we strive to achieve the best outcomes possible in our own self-interest. Individually and as a society, we must make choices because, although we have unlimited wants, we have limited (scarce) resources to meet those wants.

Scarcity

In economics, an item is considered "scarce" if, when its price is zero, then there is not enough of the item available to satisfy our requirements. If a good has a positive price tag then it's scarce. Can you think of any "free" (nonscarce) goods? Is clean air a free good or is it scarce?

Resources

Economists define four types of scarce resource.

Natural resources include any usable naturally occurring resources. Farmland, a navigable river, or lobsters off the coast of Maine are examples of natural resources.

Capital resources are reusable tools—goods that are produced to make other goods. Private capital includes a carpenter's chisel, a sales rep's car, or a warehouse, whereas social capital includes the nation's roads, bridges, and docks.

Human resources ("labor") include all of the mental and physical attributes of the labor force, such as the shooting ability of LeBron James, the physical stamina of a fruit picker, or the specialized skills and knowledge of a brain surgeon. As an aside, if a worker trains and acquires new skills, this acquisition is termed "human capital." Education of any kind that increases our abilities is an investment in human capital.

Finally, **enterprise** ("entrepreneurial ability") is the risk-taking talent needed to recognize unfulfilled market opportunities and organize production to meet those needs.

The rewards for the use of these four classes of resource are rent, interest, wages and salaries, and profit, respectively. The farmer who lets a neighbor use his tractor during harvest would receive an interest payment, but if he lets him use some unneeded acreage, then the payment is rent. The farm laborer receives a wage or salary. The farmer (the owner of an enterprise) hopes to earn a profit for himself.

Comment: In economics, unlike in accounting, profit (more properly, a "normal" profit, which is a reasonable rate of return for the entrepreneur) is treated the same as wages and salaries, rent, and interest. Just as those other payments represent costs of doing business, so does profit. We will return to this point later in the chapter.

Caution #1: Although money can be used to buy or hire productive resources, it in itself is not a productive resource. A trunk filled with dollars washed up on Robinson Crusoe's island would do him no good at all. It has no productive value.

Caution #2: Terms used in economics may not mean the same as in regular speech. "Rent" is a good example. Apartment-dwellers pay "rent" to their "landlord," but not much of that payment is for the use of a natural resource (the space the apartment occupies); most of it is for the structure itself, and for the wiring and plumbing and other man-made (capital) features being used. "Investment" is yet another such term—for an economist, "investment" is the accumulation of additional capital (not the accumulation of money or other financial assets).

THINK IT THROUGH: Every productive activity involves some combination of those four categories of scarce resource. Think of your own work environment and identify examples of each of the four types of resource. It is almost impossible to specify a productive activity that does not involve human resources, natural resources, capital, and enterprise. Try it!

The Economic Challenge and Three Fundamental Questions

The economic challenge, then, is to find the way to best satisfy our unlimited wants with our limited resources. The three fundamental questions that must be answered by any economy are: "What to Produce?", "How to Produce?", and "How to Distribute Production?". Every economy must transform its scarce natural, capital, and human resources into usable production through the application of enterprise. In a complex society, the opportunity to cooperate and specialize offers great scope for increased production—but decisions must be made regarding the extent of cooperation, who specializes in what, and how goods are distributed. Even Robinson Crusoe and Friday on their island must come up with answers to these questions. Wants are limitless, but resources are scarce. We are compelled to make choices.

As a restaurant owner, because you cannot offer everything, you must decide *which* items will be on your menu (what to produce). You must also determine *how* your service will be produced (*cordon-bleu* chef or a microwave; self-service or servers and so on). Finally, you must come up with a method of allocating your production among your potential customers (first-come first-serve or reservations; all you can eat or *à la carte*).

The trick is to choose the most effective technique in order to produce "the right stuff." In our economy, although there is a role for the public provision of certain goods and services such as national defense or our justice system, we mainly use private markets to answer the three fundamental questions. We produce items that can earn a profit as cheaply as possible (in order to make the most profit) and provide them to those who are able to pay the price.

THINK IT THROUGH: When the *Titanic* sank in 1912, there were limited spaces available in the lifeboats. The collision with the iceberg posed an immediate "distribution" question—who gets the lifeboat seats? The traditional solution of "Women and children first!" was largely adhered to (most babies and children and a high proportion of women survived) although upper-class males seem to have been given priority over steerage passengers. If "Women and children first" were not used to allocate lifeboat seats, what other methods would have been effective in such a crisis situation?

THINK IT THROUGH: Can you think of other "rules" that our society has developed to apportion our limited goods and services?

Opportunity Cost

Choice is at the heart of economics. Any time we make a choice, there is a cost. Economists use the term "opportunity cost." **Opportunity cost** is the *value of the next most preferred alternative given up when you make a choice.* This idea of opportunity cost is both simple and profound—there's no such thing as a free lunch, as the saying goes. In the restaurant, if you order shrimp lo mein, then you give up the opportunity to have other items on the menu. If the shrimp had not been available, then the value you place on the item you would have chosen instead is the opportunity cost of the shrimp.

Remember: Whenever you make a choice, you are choosing to accept one option (A) but you are also choosing to give up all the other options

(B, C, and so on). Opportunity cost is the value you place of the second-best option. The value of the option selected should exceed its opportunity cost otherwise you've not made a rational choice. Note that our opportunity cost definition doesn't refer explicitly to a financial cost. Even if a friend is paying the tab, it's still not a free lunch for you because you are making choices. Choosing the New York strip means that you can't choose your next-favorite option.

Production Possibility Frontier

The production possibility frontier (PPF) diagram can be used to depict choice and opportunity cost. A PPF diagram shows precisely what its name suggests—the frontier (or boundary) between what it's possible to produce and what it's not possible to produce, given the most effective use of our resources and our technology. We know already what our resources consist of (human resources, natural resources, capital, and enterprise), but what is "technology?" **Technology** is our method of combining our resources. If we develop a method of combining our resources that increases output, then this is a technological advance. A better crop rotation system in farming would be an example. Can you think of others?

In a world where two goods are produced (say, guns and butter) and where all resources are fully employed, if we allocate more of our resources to produce guns then fewer resources are available to produce butter and less butter will be produced—there is a trade-off. The opportunity cost of choosing to produce more guns is the butter we can no longer produce.

Following from this conclusion, it is clear that the PPF must have a negative slope. More guns mean less butter.

Suppose we have a small firm that produces two goods—wooden chairs and tables. We have workers and other resources. Each hour, using the best available production methods (technology), there can be only a finite quantity of chairs we can produce. Let's say six chairs. We can plot this option (6 chairs, 0 tables) on the vertical axis of Figure 1-1 at point A. Similarly, there are only so many tables we can produce—perhaps three tables. We can plot this option (0 chairs, 3 tables) on the horizontal axis at point D. If we're currently producing six chairs then, if we increase the production of tables, we will have to pull resources away

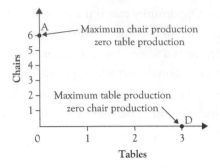

Figure 1-1. Constructing a production possibility frontier.

from chair production. Chair production will decrease as table production increases—there is a negative relationship between them.

So far, we have the two endpoints of the PPF and we know that it must have a negative slope. The frontier's slope represents the rate at which one good is given up as more of the other good is produced. This rate, known formally as the "marginal rate of transformation," describes opportunity cost. For example, if we produce one more table, the opportunity cost is the number of chairs we will no longer be able to produce.

The Law of Increasing Cost

This rate of trade-off is unlikely to remain constant as we increase the production of chairs because not all resources are equally well suited to different activities. Think back to high school and the choosing of teams for basketball. Just as some players were better than others and would be chosen first, some resources will be more productive in chair production than others and will be preferred.

Suppose we have three workers—Abe, Bill, and Calvin—whose hourly outputs are listed as follows.

	Tables		Chairs	Opportunity cost of one	
				Table	Chair
Abe	1	or	1	1 chair	1 table
Bill	1	or	2	2 chairs	1/2 table
Calvin	1	or	3	3 chairs	1/3 table

Who would you choose first to produce tables? And who would be your next choice? You should choose Abe first to produce tables, then Bill, and, finally, Calvin because Abe can produce tables at the lowest (opportunity) cost. With Abe, the table he produces "costs" one chair, but, if Calvin produces a table, then we must give up the three chairs he could otherwise have produced. Looked at differently, we should keep Calvin producing chairs as long as possible because he is so good at chair production.

Note that, as we expand production of tables, the opportunity cost of tables increases. The first table (Abe's) costs one chair, Bill's costs two chairs, and Calvin's costs three chairs. The production alternatives are given as follows.

Production alternative	Tables	Chairs
A	0	6
B	1	5
C	2	3
D	3	0

We can plot these alternatives. Graphically, as shown in Figure 1-2, the PPF bends outward. The slope of the PPF depicts the increasing opportunity cost we have discussed.

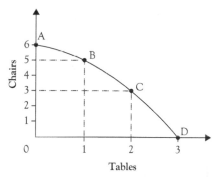

Figure 1-2. Production possibility frontier.

THINK IT THROUGH: Verify that, if the workers are all producing tables, and we switch them over to producing chairs, we should switch Calvin first, then Bill, and, finally, Abe. Opportunity cost again increases as we expand the production of chairs.

Comment on Reciprocals: Note that, for Calvin, the opportunity cost of producing one table is three chairs and the opportunity cost of one chair is a third of a table. The opportunity costs are reciprocals of each other. If Calvin is the least costly at producing chairs then he necessarily must be the most costly at producing tables. This is a general result and we'll use it later in this chapter when we look at comparative advantage.

Marginal Cost

Let's press this example a little further. Economists, as we shall see later, are deeply concerned with "marginal" analysis. "Marginal" is just a fancy term economists use, meaning "extra" or "additional." **Marginal cost** is the additional cost incurred when an extra unit of a good is produced. (Similarly, marginal benefit is the additional benefit that is received when an extra unit of a good is consumed.) Superficially, we think of "the additional cost incurred when an extra unit of a good is produced" in dollars and cents terms but, more profoundly, it is the opportunity cost. Alone on his island, Robinson Crusoe has no money, but, because he makes choices, he incurs costs. Choosing to produce more chairs results in increasing costs. The extra cost of the first table was one chair, but the second table costs two chairs, and the third table's cost was higher still. Typically, because of the law of increasing cost, we'd predict that the marginal cost would increase as more tables are produced.

THINK IT THROUGH: If the cost of producing additional tables increases, what must happen to the price of tables in order to encourage the producer to boost output?

Constant Costs

An outward-bending PPF depicts increasing cost. However, if the PPF is a straight downward-sloping line, then the opportunity cost is constant. This would happen if resources were identical in abilities. If the PPF were to bend inward, then this would tell us that opportunity cost is decreasing—in real-world terms, improbable.

Any PPF diagram has three regions—the frontier itself, inside the frontier, and beyond the frontier. Consider Figure 1-3. Any point on the frontier (such as point K) represents a point of maximum production; any point inside the frontier (such as point L) indicates underproduction; and

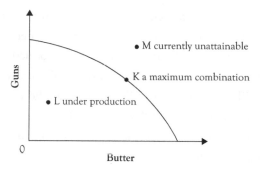

Figure 1-3. The components of a production possibility frontier.

any point beyond the frontier (such as point M) is an option that is not attainable given our current resources and technology.

Although increasing costs are typical in the real world, from now on we will assume that producers face constant opportunity costs, because this will allow us to draw the simpler straight-line PPFs.

Note: If we have constant costs, then marginal cost is constant, rather than increasing, as output increases.

Relaxing the Diagram's Assumptions

The PPF is drawn based on a given set of resources and a given best way of combining them. If we get more resources or better resources, or an improved way of combining our given resources, then there will be a general increase in what it is possible to produce. In such a case, the PPF will shift outword from PPF1 to PPF2, as shown in Figure 1-4. A decrease in the quantity or quality of resources will shift the whole curve inwards as what it is possible to produce is diminished.

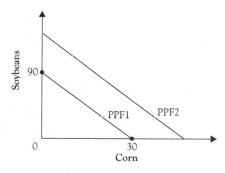

Figure 1-4. A general increase in the production possibility frontier.

A resource or technology change could be specific to only one good. In farming, for example, a strain of corn with a higher yield might be developed. In this case, although the maximum production of soybeans would be unaltered, the maximum production of corn would increase, causing the PPF to pivot from PPF1 to PPF2, as shown in Figure 1-5. Observe that the slope of the PPF has changed. Because the slope of the frontier depicts opportunity cost, the opportunity cost of corn (and thus soybeans) must have changed.

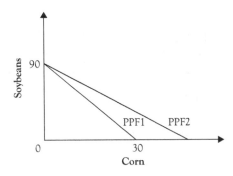

Figure 1-5. A good-specific increase in the production possibility frontier.

Consider the slope of PPF1 and its endpoints. If we choose to produce only corn then we can produce 30 units of corn, but we must give up the 90 units of soybeans that could have been produced. Each unit of corn "costs" three units of soybeans. Now consider the slope of PPF2. If we choose to produce only corn then we can produce 45 units of corn, but we must give up the 90 units of soybeans. Each unit of corn now "costs" only two units of soybeans. The opportunity cost of corn has decreased. Verify for yourself that the opportunity cost of a unit of soybeans has increased from one-third of a unit of corn to one-half of a unit of corn.

THINK IT THROUGH: What happened to Europe's PPF during the Black Death? What was the effect on American production of the introduction of the Internet in the 1990s? Finally, in 1945, the Manhattan Project developed the atomic bomb. In terms of "guns and butter," how did the Allies' PPF change? Show each of these cases with a PPF diagram.

Using the Production Possibility Frontier Diagram

We have now developed an understanding of the general meaning of the PPF and the assumptions behind it. But how can it be used? The analysis can be used in several ways, for instance, when thinking about the consequences of choice, different concepts of efficiency, the distinction between microeconomics and macroeconomics, and the basis for trade.

The PPF illustrates choice. Along the frontier, where we have full employment of resources, if we choose to produce more guns, the consequence is that we must settle for less butter. The slope of the frontier shows the rate of trade-off and reminds us that "there's no such thing as a free lunch."

Comment: Note, though, that if we have unemployed resources, we may be able to produce more guns without giving up any butter. There need be no opportunity cost in this situation.

Efficiency: The PPF can also be used to distinguish between two differing concepts of efficiency. Consider Figure 1-6.

Any point on the frontier is a point of maximum **productive efficiency**. In this sense of producing at maximum capacity, points A, B, C, and D are all equally "efficient." Point E is inefficient because some of our scarce resources are being squandered—we could be producing at a higher level.

However, there's more to life than simply producing lots of stuff. Our economy ought to produce "the right stuff." Consider the figure once more. Are points A, B, C, and D equal in terms of satisfying our wants?

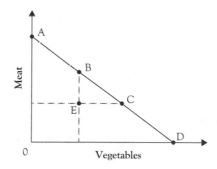

Figure 1-6. Productive efficiency and allocative efficiency.

Clearly not! If we are a society of vegans then point A (all meat, no vegetables) is a less desirable option than point D. Not all points on the frontier are equivalent in terms of **allocative efficiency** (producing the mixture of goods that society prefers the most). In fact, point A is less desirable than point E (where we get at less some vegetables).

The two "efficiency" concepts are distinct. In terms of productive efficiency, any point on the PPF is superior to any point inside the frontier. However, in terms of allocative efficiency, a given point inside the frontier may be preferred to some points on the frontier. (As a general rule though, there must be at least one point on the frontier that is superior to any point inside. Point C, for example, is preferred to point E because society gets more vegetables without losing any meat.)

Comment: Intuitively, productive efficiency may be thought of as "activity" while allocative efficiency may be thought of as "achievement."

Microeconomics Versus Macroeconomics: Microeconomics generally starts from the assumption that society is already at a point on its PPF and can be thought of as examining how we might move the production mix to a point of greater allocative efficiency along the line. Macroeconomics, which considers the consequences of unemployment or lackluster growth, may be thought of as exploring how we might either move toward the frontier or, indeed, shift the frontier itself.

Comparative Advantage and the Basis for Trade

The PPF and opportunity cost can be used to examine the basis for specialization and trade. The roots of this analysis reach back to the early nineteenth century and the British economist, David Ricardo, who developed the Law of Comparative Advantage that we shall examine in more detail in Chapter 8.

Briefly, assuming two participants (Jack and Jill), two goods (bread and wine), and constant costs (straight-line PPFs), if Jack and Jill's opportunity costs differ, then it must be the case that each individual must have a *"comparative advantage"* in the production of one of the two goods. The one exception to this would be if the opportunity costs were identical. We can make this analysis a little easier if we realize that the comparative advantage referred to is an opportunity cost advantage. If, relatively, Jack

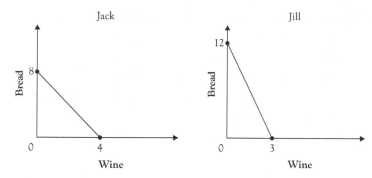

Figure 1-7. The graphical basis for trade.

can produce wine at a lower opportunity cost than Jill, (that is, Jack has a comparative cost advantage in wine production), then Jill must be able to produce bread at a lower opportunity cost than Jack (that is, a comparative cost advantage in bread production).

This may seem a curious conclusion. An obvious objection to raise would be "But what if Jack can produce both goods more cheaply than Jill?" Such a situation is impossible. Recall the tables and chairs example where we concluded that each worker's opportunity cost of producing a chair is the reciprocal of his opportunity cost of producing a table. Relatively, the greater the cost advantage a worker has in the production of one good, the greater the cost disadvantage he has in the production of the other good.

Consider Figure 1-7. Jack, specializing only in bread production, can bake eight loaves each day, while Jill, similarly devoted to bread production, can bake twelve loaves each day. Jill can produce more loaves perhaps because of superior skill, better ingredients, or a more reliable oven. Fully devoted to wine production, Jack can produce four bottles each day, but Jill (less skilled perhaps, or with less good grapes) can produce only three. Recall that the slope of the PPF depicts opportunity cost so the straight lines indicate that the opportunity costs are constant for each individual. The differing slopes indicate that the opportunity costs between individuals are different.

The **Law of Comparative (Cost) Advantage** states that Jack and Jill will benefit from specialization and trade if their opportunity costs (and the slopes of the frontiers) differ.

We must determine who should produce what good by comparing opportunity costs. For Jack, the opportunity cost of producing eight loaves is the four bottles of wine he is no longer able to produce—one loaf costs half a bottle of wine. Using the reciprocal trick, one bottle of wine "costs" two loaves. For Jill, the opportunity cost of producing twelve loaves is the three bottles of wine she can no longer produce—one loaf costs a fourth of a bottle of wine. Using the reciprocal trick, one bottle of wine "costs" four loaves.

Jack can produce wine cheaper (he has a comparative advantage in wine) while Jill can produce bread cheaper (she has a comparative advantage in bread). As long as the slopes of the PPFs differ, then it must be true that one producer has a comparative advantage in one good and the other producer has the comparative advantage in the other good. Again, because of reciprocity, no individual can have a comparative advantage in both goods.

Caution: "But," you say, "this result is obvious. Jack is better at wine production because he can produce more wine than Jill, and Jill is better at bread production because she can produce more loaves than Jack!" This is false logic. You have fallen into the trap of absolute advantage. In absolute terms, while it is true that Jack is superior to Jill in wine production and Jill trumps Jack in bread production, this fact has no bearing on how the two parties should specialize.

The fallacy is easy to show. Suppose that Jack can produce more wine and more bread than Jill. Does this mean that Jack should produce everything and that Jill should produce nothing? Clearly not. In the real world, there are large countries with many resources and small countries with few, but the small countries can still gain from trade and can contribute to general prosperity despite an absolute disadvantage in all goods.

We can summarize the results thus far.

Opportunity cost of	Jack	Jill	Comparative advantage
one loaf of bread	1/2 bottle	1/4 bottle	Jill
one bottle of wine	2 loaves	4 loaves	Jack

Jack and Jill decide to specialize according to comparative advantage and trade with each other. Is mutually beneficial trade possible? Let's assume that Jack and Jill barter their trade goods, wine and bread, respectively. If the "price" of a bottle of wine is two loaves then Jack will not gain from trade (as his cost of production of a bottle of wine is also two loaves) but Jill will gain from trade. (Can you verify this?) If the "price" of a bottle of wine rises to four loaves then Jack gains from trade but Jill will not gain because, if the price of wine is four loaves then the price of bread is a quarter of a bottle of wine, which equals Jill's cost of production—her cost and the price at which she is trading are equal.

Between these two prices for a bottle of wine (two loaves and four loaves) lies a range of prices that will benefit both traders. Consider the situation where one wine is traded for three loaves. Jack, producing wine at a cost of two loaves, will gain because the price exceeds his cost. Similarly, but less obviously, Jill, producing bread at a cost of a quarter of a bottle of wine per loaf, will also gain because the price of a loaf (one-third of a bottle of wine) is also higher than her cost. Both benefit.

There is no requirement that both benefit equally—it depends on relative negotiating abilities, for example. As long as the price lies between the limits where one party or the other does not gain (one wine sells for two loaves and one wine sells for four loaves) trade will be mutually beneficial. More on trade in Chapter 8.

Caution: We have concluded that the Law of Comparative Advantage persuades us that trade can be beneficial. Before moving on, it's worth noting that the analysis depends on the assumption that each person (or economy) is fully employed. If that is not the case, then the basis for trade (being on the PPF and, from there, opportunity cost) evaporates. Our opportunity cost calculations are valid only along the frontier itself. A nation struggling through a recession might still find it to be in its own best interests to restrict imports.

Review: In this chapter we have discovered that "there is no such thing as a free lunch," in the sense that, any time a choice is made an alternative is chosen, but another alternative is given up. The value placed on the next-best alternative that is given up when a choice is made is its *opportunity cost*—perhaps the single most important idea in economics. When we look at "cost" in future chapters, keep in mind that, at its most profound level, it is opportunity cost that is involved.

CHAPTER 2

Demand and Supply

By the end of this chapter you will be able to:

1. State and explain the law of demand and the law of supply.
2. Draw and interpret demand and supply graphs.
3. Distinguish between a shift of a demand or supply curve and a movement along a curve, and show these cases correctly on a graph.
4. Determine equilibrium price and quantity and explain how the market adjusts when demand or supply changes.
5. Define shortage and surplus and predict their effects on the market price.
6. Specify the determinants of demand and supply and indicate how each must change for demand and supply to increase or decrease.
7. Distinguish between two goods that are substitutes and two goods that are complements.
8. Distinguish between normal and inferior goods.
9. Use demand and supply to interpret changes in the international value of the dollar.

George Bernard Shaw once jokingly remarked that if you taught a parrot to squawk the phrase "demand and supply" then you had trained an economist. Certainly it's true that demand and supply analysis is the lingua franca of economics.

Chapter Preview: Undoubtedly, you already use demand and supply analysis in your daily life. Just as we don't need to have learned applied physics or geometry (force, angles) in order to play pool, we don't need a course in economics to tell us that if war breaks out in the Middle East, then we should expect a price hike in a gallon of gasoline or that if worker benefits increase in this country, then illegal immigration and outsourcing are likely to increase.

Examples of using demand and
supply analysis informally

Suppose there is a late freeze in Florida that destroys much of the orange crop. What will happen to the price of orange juice? It will increase (because the supply of a key ingredient has been reduced). What if news reveals that apples have been sprayed with an insecticide that causes cancer? We'll buy fewer apples and the price will fall (because demand has decreased). If the government imposes a carbon tax on gasoline-fueled cars, predict what will happen to the demand for electric cars. They'll become more popular! And, as they become more popular, will we expect more (or fewer) electric cars to be marketed? More! If Burger King raises the prices of its menu items, will you start going to McDonald's more or less frequently (assuming you go at all!)?

So we are already quite familiar with thinking about markets and, in practice, using demand and supply analysis. All of these situations can be investigated using demand and supply analysis.

In this chapter we develop a model of how individuals interact within markets. A market is an environment, physical or otherwise, where buyers and sellers interact.

Demand

We can define **demand** as the willingness and ability to purchase a quantity of a good or service at a range of prices during some time period. To be part of the demand for a good we must be both willing and able to buy. Many of us would be willing to buy a sleek Ferrari sports car but few of us are able to: only the few who are able and willing are demanders at the high price that Ferrari sets. Note that written into our definition of demand is the notion that there is a time frame. It makes no sense to talk about "the demand for bananas," but it does make sense to refer to "the demand for bananas per week," "the demand for gasoline per month," or "the demand for motel rooms at the beach per summer season."

As the price of orange juice increases we become less willing to buy ("It's too expensive!") and we look for alternatives such as grapefruit juice, and we become less able to buy ("I can't afford that!"). When the price of a good rises we buy less: when the price falls we buy more. This behavior is summarized in the Law of Demand.

Law of Demand

Simply, the Law of Demand states that there is a negative relationship between two variables, the "price" of a good and "the quantity demanded per time period." "Quantity demanded" is how much the buyer is willing and able to purchase at a single price during some time period. (From now on, for convenience, we'll make the "per time period" phrase implicit.) As "price" changes, "quantity demanded" changes.

This negative relationship can be shown as a demand schedule or as a demand curve. This relationship is true whether we are looking at the behavior of an individual buyer or all buyers together. At the level of the market, demand is merely the sum at each price of the demand of individual buyers. By convention, we label our demand curve "D," as in Figure 2-1.

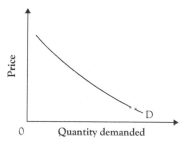

Figure 2-1. A general demand curve relationship.

A demand schedule is a table showing the "quantity demanded" at each of a number of prices. The following demand schedule shows plausible values for the quantity of apples demanded at a Saturday morning farmer's market at a range of prices.

Table 2-1 shows that, as the price of apples increases, fewer apples are demanded.

Table 2-1. A Demand Schedule for Apples

Price of an apple	Quantity demanded of apples
60¢	300
50¢	450
40¢	550
30¢	650
20¢	800
10¢	1000

The Law of Demand, which states that the two variables ("price" and "quantity demanded") exhibit a negative relationship, can be depicted by a downward-sloping demand curve on a diagram with "price" on the vertical axis and "quantity demanded" on the horizontal axis. The demand curve for apples is plotted in Figure 2-2 as an example.

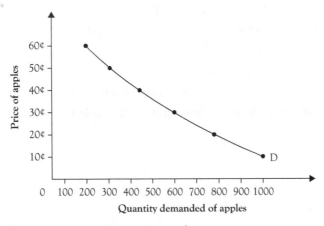

Figure 2-2. The demand curve for apples.

When the price of apples changes from 20¢ to 50¢, it causes a "change in quantity demanded" from 800 apples to 450 apples, and that this "change in quantity demanded" is shown as a movement along the demand curve as shown in Figure 2-3.

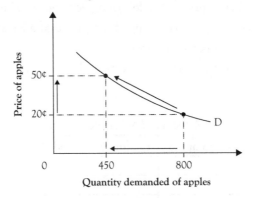

Figure 2-3. A change in quantity demanded.

A **change in quantity demanded** is a movement along the demand curve and it is caused by a change in the price of the good. The ONLY thing that can cause a change in quantity demanded is a change in the price of the good.

Comment: "But," you object, "surely there are factors other than the price of apples that affect how many apples are demanded!" You are correct. We'll resolve this apparent paradox soon; however, now is a convenient point at which to introduce and discuss modeling.

Modeling and the *ceteris paribus* assumption: We wish to construct a model of how buyers and sellers operate within markets and, within such an environment, many things could be happening at the same time. Such a buzz of activity may make it difficult to isolate a particular factor that we'd like to study—imagine trying to isolate the playing of the third violin in a large orchestra. Models are formal statements of relationships between variables of interest that simplify and abstract from reality. They can be in the form of graphs, words, or equations. Scientists try to simplify by imposing order by factoring out distracting real-world details—chemists, for example, assume the experiments are conducted at a standard temperature and pressure. Physicists may assume that a body in motion is frictionless even when it isn't. When testing a model (for example, the relationship between the price of a good and quantity demanded of that good), it is convenient to assume that all other variables have been held constant. This is the *ceteris paribus* assumption, sometimes expressed as "all else remaining equal."

Supply

We can define **supply** as the willingness and ability to produce (and make available for sale) a quantity of a good or service at a range of prices during some time period. To be part of the supply of a good we must be both willing and able to bring the good to market. A producer who keeps his or her output in a warehouse is not counted as part of supply. As with demand, we have written a time frame into our definition. When we talk about "the supply for Honda Civics" or "the supply of oil" we should have some time period in mind.

As the price of orange juice increases we become more willing to produce (higher rewards increase motivation to redirect resources from alternative uses) and we become more able to produce (higher revenues allow us to hire more resources). When the price of a good rises we increase the quantity supplied: When the price falls we reduce the quantity supplied. This behavior is summarized in the Law of Supply.

THINK IT THROUGH: If the price of apples rises and we devote more resources to apple production, then we must be switching those scarce resources from some other use. In its deepest sense, the cost of the extra apples produced is the value we place on the other goods given up—in other words, opportunity cost.

Law of Supply

Simply, the Law of Supply states that there is a positive relationship between two variables, the "price" of a good and "the quantity supplied per time period." "Quantity supplied" is how much the seller is willing and able to produce and make available at a single price during some time period. (Again, for convenience, we'll make the "per time period" phrase implicit.) As "price" changes, "quantity supplied" changes.

This positive relationship can be shown as a supply schedule or as a supply curve, as shown in Figure 2-4. This relationship is true whether we are looking at the behavior of an individual firm or all firms together. At the level of the market, supply is merely the sum at each price of the supply of individual producers. By convention, we label our supply curve "S."

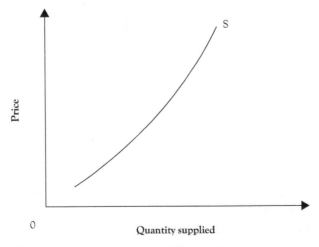

Figure 2-4. A general supply curve relationship.

A supply schedule is a table, such as Table 2-2, showing the "quantity supplied" at each of a number of prices. The following supply schedule shows plausible values for the quantity of apples supplied at a Saturday morning farmer's market at a range of prices.

Table 2-2. A Supply Schedule for Apples

Price of an apple	Quantity supplied of apples
60¢	700
50¢	650
40¢	550
30¢	450
20¢	300
10¢	200

The table shows that, as the price of apples increases, more apples are made available for sale.

The Law of Supply states that the two variables ("price" and "quantity supplied") exhibit a positive relationship. This relationship can be depicted by an upward-sloping supply curve on a diagram with "price" on the vertical axis and "quantity supplied" on the horizontal axis. As an example, the supply curve for apples is plotted in Figure 2-5.

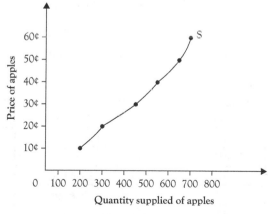

Figure 2-5. The supply curve for apples.

When the price of apples changes from 20¢ to 50¢, there is a "change in quantity supplied" from 300 to 650 apples, and that this "change in quantity supplied" is shown as a movement along the supply curve as shown in Figure 2-6.

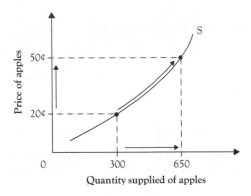

Figure 2-6. A change in quantity supplied.

A **change in quantity supplied** is a movement along the supply curve, and it is caused by a change in the price of the good. The ONLY thing that can cause a change in quantity supplied is a change in the price of the good.

Comment: As with the earlier assertion that a "change in quantity demanded" can only be caused by a change in the price of the good, you may object that other factors may affect how many apples farmers will market. This is correct. Again, we must wait to resolve this apparent paradox.

Modeling the Market

We can now examine how participants interact in a market. Table 2-3 and Figure 2-7 combine the previous demand and supply schedules.

Table 2-3. Adjustment to Equilibrium

Price	Quantity demanded	Quantity supplied	Result	Price Pressure
60¢	300	700	Surplus	Downward
50¢	450	650	Surplus	Downward
40¢	550	550	Equilibrium	None
30¢	650	450	Shortage	Upward
20¢	800	300	Shortage	Upward
10¢	1000	200	Shortage	Upward

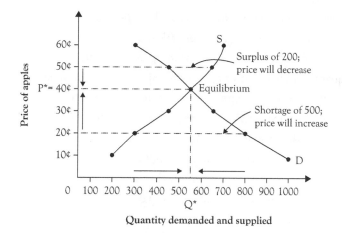

Figure 2-7. Adjustment to equilibrium.

When the price is 60¢ per apple, quantity supplied exceeds quantity demanded and there is a **surplus** of 400 apples (700–300). A surplus occurs when quantity demanded is less than quantity supplied. When there is a surplus, there is a downward pressure on price. In an effort to sell the unwanted apples, sellers will reduce the price. If the price decreases to 50¢, the same result occurs—a surplus and a downward pressure on price. Note that, as the price decreases, quantity demanded increases from 300 to 450. This is shown on the diagram as a movement along the demand curve. Similarly, as the price decreases, some producers will withdraw apples from sale, causing the quantity of apples supplied to decrease from 700 to 650. This is shown as a movement along the supply curve.

A **shortage** occurs when quantity demanded exceeds quantity supplied. When there is a shortage there is an upward pressure on price as buyers scramble to meet their needs. Suppose the price tumbles to 10¢ per apples. Quantity demanded (1,000 apples) exceeds quantity supplied (200 apples), and there will be a shortage of 800 apples. Buyers, some of whom are willing to pay 60¢ or more and are desperate to secure apples, will bid up the price. As price rises, quantity demanded will decrease and quantity supplied will increase until the shortage is competed away until equilibrium will be established. **Equilibrium** occurs at the price level where quantity demanded equals quantity supplied. The equilibrium price (P*) is 40¢ and the equilibrium quantity (Q*) is 550 apples. When the market is in equilibrium there is no pressure for the price to change and, at this price, all buyers and sellers in the market are receiving an acceptable outcome.

Prices are a signaling and rationing mechanism in markets. When the quantity demanded of apples exceeds quantity supplied and there is a shortage, we would expect the price of apples to increase. The rise in the price of apples signals to apple growers that more resources should be allocated to the production of apples. At the same time, the rise in price encourages some potential buyers of apples to look elsewhere for alternatives (such as pears) and the apples that are available are channeled to those who are most willing and able to pay for them.

Caution: The assumption being made at this point is that those who buy the apples value them more highly than those who are priced out of the market. You might wish to consider whether this is always true!

What's So Great About Equilibrium?

To this point, we have developed a model of how a market reflects the wishes of buyers and sellers and establish equilibrium. Markets achieve equilibrium where quantity demanded equals quantity supplied. With this result, all of the market participants receive an outcome with which they are satisfied. In fact, society's overall satisfaction is maximized. This happy result is due to the activities of each individual participant pursuing his or her own self-interest within a free market. Adam Smith referred to this process as the "invisible hand" that directs market-driven economies to the allocatively efficient mix of goods and services.

Sometimes, governments feel the need to regulate markets. Two such forms of regulation are price ceilings and price floors.

A **price ceiling** is a maximum price limit imposed on a market. A price ceiling may be established at any price level, but an effective price ceiling is set *below* the equilibrium price and it causes a shortage in the market. The classic example of a price ceiling is the rent controls in New York and other cities.

Price ceilings are not imposed malevolently—indeed usually they are well intentioned—but they have unintended adverse consequences.

Let us suppose that a crisis in the Middle East has led to a disruption of oil supplies, reducing supply and driving up the price of gasoline. The market price of a gallon of gasoline is $7.00. However, a price of $7.00

per gallon will certainly cause severe hardship to many citizens, particularly the working poor who must travel to work and who will find it difficult to curtail their gasoline consumption.

The president intervenes and imposes a maximum price of $4.00 per gallon. (Here is the good intention!) The immediate effect of the price control is that there will be a gas shortage. In the absence of prices, some other method of rationing must emerge. The simplest method is "first come, first served," which will create lines at the gas pumps.

Unintended effects of a price ceiling: The shortage will impose additional nonmarket costs on consumers. With a "first come, first served" rationing method, there will be additional search time to find sellers with gas to sell, queuing (and possible violence), and the risk of being stranded on the highway. Unscrupulous sellers may attempt to take advantage of the situation by requiring additional purchases before gas is pumped—a car wash, for example. Black markets may develop or the quality of gasoline (or the service provided) may be degraded, perhaps by the addition of cheaper additives. This is, after all, a seller's market.

A **price floor** is a minimum price limit imposed on a market. A price floor may be established at any price level but an effective price floor is set *above* the equilibrium price and it causes a surplus. Although there have been price supports in agriculture, trucking, and the airline industry, the classic example of a price floor is the minimum wage.

Consider Figure 2-8. The demand curve is the demand for labor by employers and the supply curve is the supply of labor by workers seeking jobs. The equilibrium market wage (W^*) is $6.00.

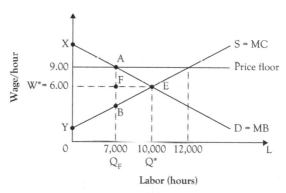

Figure 2-8. A price floor in the labor market.

Politicians believe that a reasonable "living wage" is not less than $9.00 per hour and impose a minimum wage (W_f) at that rate. At a wage rate of $9.00, the quantity of labor supplied (by workers) is 12,000 hours and the quantity demanded (by employers) is 7,000 hours—the immediate effect of the wage control is that there will be a labor surplus where previously none existed.

As with a price ceiling, some groups may gain but, on balance, society loses because of the minimum wage. Note that, whereas at equilibrium, there was a job for all interested workers, the imposition of the wage floor creates unemployment, partly through an increase in workers seeking jobs and partly through a reduction in job opportunities.

The bottom line is that even well-intentioned efforts to prevent markets from reaching equilibrium threaten the efficiency of the economic system. Unless there is a very strong reason otherwise, our goal ought to be to foster competitive equilibrium in all markets.

Factors That Can Shift the Position of the Demand Curve Causing a "Change in Demand"

Although price is an important element in determining willingness and ability to purchase it is certainly not the only factor. In terms of the diagram, consumers of apples may decide that, at any price, they want more apples than they did before. In Figure 2-9, this greater demand for apples would be shown as a rightward shift of the demand curve from D_1 to D_2

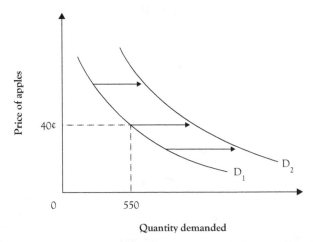

Figure 2-9. An increase in demand.

and would be termed an **increase in demand**. If demand decreases, then the curve would shift over to the left.

Numerous factors may shift the position of a demand curve for a good but to keep our model manageable we will restrict ourselves to a short list of the major factors, including changes in tastes and preferences, after-tax income or wealth, expectations about price, income or wealth, the prices of related products, and the number or composition of buyers.

Tastes and Preferences

As goods come into style or fall out of fashion, demand shifts. If apples become more popular, perhaps because of new advertising claims emphasizing health benefits of an "apple a day," then, even at the same price, more apples would be demanded and the demand curve would shift to the right. The demand for ice cream will increase on a hot summer day; the demand for leaf blowers is lower in the spring than in the fall; the demand for wrapping paper increases in December.

THINK IT THROUGH: Come up with at least one real-world example of both an increase in demand and a decrease in demand in response to a change in tastes and preferences.

After-Tax Income or Wealth

As our spending power increases, we buy more. Research has shown that a 10% increase in disposable income will cause a 24% increase in the demand for automobiles, a 14% increase in the demand for restaurant meals, and a 5% increase in the demand for oil and gasoline products. This is the response that we see for a **normal good**—higher income, higher demand; lower income, lower demand.

Conceptually, wealth differs from income (a wealthy person may have no income this year but may still remain wealthy), but the relationship with demand is similar. As wealth increases, the demand for normal goods increases. The burgeoning consumer spending during the 1990s was due, in part, to the steep rise in the values of stock market portfolios while much of the clampdown in consumer spending at the start of the Great Recession was, similarly, due to the slashing reductions in the value of consumers' financial and property assets.

Most, but not all, goods, though, react this way. Some goods are **inferior goods**. The demand for "inferior" goods decreases as consumers become better off and increases when the household's fortunes turn downwards. Ramen noodles, beans and rice, and bologna are examples. Can you think of examples of goods that you would demand more if you lost your job? During the Great Recession there was a boom in the demand for bankruptcy lawyers, condoms, and community college courses.

THINK IT THROUGH: Come up with at least one real-world example of both a normal good and an inferior good.

Expectations About Price, Income, or Wealth

If we expect the price of a good to increase, we'll tend to buy more today. If, though, we hear news that a good's price will fall soon, then we may try to postpone purchase until after the decrease in price. Note that the price has not yet changed—only the expectation that the price may change.

Similarly, demand can be affected by expectations about income or wealth. If credible rumors circulate through your firm that there soon will be layoffs, or if you expect adverse effects on your retirement plan, then this new information will affect your purchasing behavior—demand for normal goods will decrease but demand for inferior goods will increase. A threatened layoff may lead you to shelve plans for that European vacation (a normal good) and choose to stay home and plant a vegetable garden (an inferior good) instead.

If income or wealth is expected to increase, then the demand for normal goods will increase and the demand for inferior goods will decrease. College students tend to spend more freely and incur debt (student loans and credit cards) because, although they are poor now, they expect to be prosperous after graduation. Expectations make students a prime target for lenders.

THINK IT THROUGH: Find at least one real-world example of a good (a normal good) whose demand would increase if you expected your income or wealth to increase and one real-world example of a good (an inferior good) whose demand would increase if you expected your income or wealth to decrease.

Prices of Related Products

Substitutes are goods that are alternatives for each other—Exxon gasoline or BP. Many goods are substitutes for each other—some are close substitutes (Coca-Cola and Pepsi), some are more distant (Coca-Cola and Snapple).

Other goods may be complements for each other. **Complements** are goods are those that tend to be used together. Tennis balls and tennis racquets, CD players and batteries, cat food and kitty litter are all examples of complementary pairs of goods. Driving your car involves a mass of goods that are consumed at the same time—gasoline, oil, tires, insurance, and so on.

Note that substitutes or complements need not be purchased at the same time or at the same rate, merely that the demand for one affects the demand for the other.

THINK IT THROUGH: Find at least one real-world example of two goods that are substitutes and two goods that are complements.

Note: For convenience, from now on we will abbreviate "Price" to "P" and "Quantity" to "Q" in our diagrams.

Given two substitutes (Coke and Pepsi, for example), if the price of Coke increases P_1 to P_2 then this will cause a decrease in the quantity demanded of Coke (a movement along the demand curve for Coke from Q_1 to Q_2). We look around for alternatives such as Pepsi. More shoppers than before will demand Pepsi, even although the price of Pepsi (P) has not changed. The demand curve for Pepsi will shift to the right from D_1 to D_2 because of the increase in the price of Coke. See Figure 2-10.

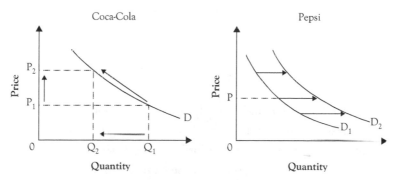

Figure 2-10. The relationship between substitutes.

THINK IT THROUGH: Verify this result that the demand for Good B will increase if the price of substitute Good A increases, using your own example of two substitute goods. Can you also construct the argument if the price of Good A decreases instead?

Given two complements (peanut butter and jelly, for example), if the price of peanut butter increases from P_1 to P_2 then this will cause a decrease in the quantity demanded of peanut butter (a movement along the demand curve for peanut butter from Q_1 to Q_2 as we would expect from the Law of Demand). Because we use peanut butter and jelly together and we're buying less peanut butter, then we'll buy less jelly too, even although the price of jelly (P) has not changed. The demand curve for jelly will shift to the left from D_1 to D_2 because of the increase in the price of peanut butter. See Figure 2-11.

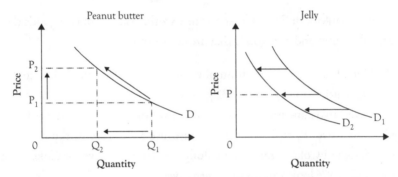

Figure 2-11. The relationship between complements.

THINK IT THROUGH: Verify this result that the demand for Good B will decrease if the price of complementary Good A increases, using your own example of two complements. Can you also construct the argument if the price of Good A decreases instead?

Number or Composition of Buyers

If more buyers enter a market, we'd expect the demand for a product to increase. For instance, on the other hand, if the legal drinking age were increased to 30, then the demand for beer would decrease; on the other hand, as the population grows older, the demand for artificial hip joints increases. Prohibition reduced the demand for alcohol. The demand for eBay and other online goods would increase with greater Internet access.

On the other hand, the demand for antiwrinkle creams, gyms, and Rogaine will increase as the population ages; on the other hand, a young (child-bearing) population will experience increased demand for diapers, bassinets, toys, and car seats for children.

THINK IT THROUGH: Again, devise your own intuitive examples of situations where changes in the number and composition of buyers would influence demand.

Factors That Can Shift the Position of the Supply Curve Causing a "Change in Supply"

Price is an important factor in determining willingness, and the ability to produce other factors are important too. In terms of Figure 2-12, apple growers may decide that, at any price, they wish to produce more apples than they did previously. In Figure 2-12, the greater supply of apples would be shown as a rightward shift of the supply curve from S_1 to S_2 and would be called as an "increase in supply." If supply decreases, then the curve would shift over to the left.

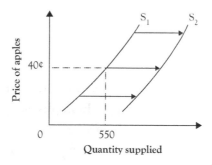

Figure 2-12. An increase in supply.

Caution: As noted earlier, although we say "demand has gone up" and "supply has gone down," demand and supply curves should be thought of as moving *left* and *right* on the diagram, not vertically up and down.

Numerous factors may shift the position of a supply curve for a good but, as with demand, to keep our model manageable we will restrict ourselves to a short list of the major factors, including changes in technology, productivity, the price of inputs, after-tax revenues, the prices of related products in production, and the number of sellers.

Learning Tip: Be aware that most students find supply more diffi-cult to grasp than demand—we're more used to thinking of ourselves as consumers. When thinking about how the supply curve shifts, keep in mind the phrase "Follow the profit!" If something happens (other than a change in price), will it directly affect profit? If profit increases as a conse-quence of the change then supply will increase (shift to the right); if profit decreases then supply will decrease (shift to the left).

Price of Inputs

If the price of inputs (for example, workers' wages, the price of fuel, and the salaries of executives) increases, then profitability will decrease and supply will be reduced. A decrease in input prices will have the opposite effect.

THINK IT THROUGH: Verify the effect that an increase in the minimum wage will have on production in an industry that depends on minimum-wage workers. Recall the *ceteris paribus* assumption—there is no expecta-tion that workers will "work harder" just because their wages have been increased.

Technology

An improvement in technology will decrease costs of production, increase profit, and cause an increase in supply. Examples include a more effective floor plan for the factory or a cheaper storage/distribution system. It's hard to imagine a situation where a technology would be adopted that would knowingly cause a decrease in profit but, if this happened, then the supply curve would shift to the left. An example of choosing inferior technology might be antipollution regulations forcing the adoption of a "greener" but less cost-effective method of production.

Caution: Just because there is a technological improvement in the method of production of a good should not be taken to mean that the product itself has been improved. That is quite a different issue. As con-sumers, we don't know or care much about the methods used to produce the goods we buy.

THINK IT THROUGH: Find an example of a technological improvement (perhaps from your own experience) and demonstrate that, at the same price as before, because costs are reduced and profits are increased, producers will be more able and willing to increase output.

Productivity

If workers become more productive, then the unit costs of production will be decreased, profitability will increase, and producers will be able to expand output. Note that we are assuming that the increase in productivity is not caused by an increase in wages nor, in turn, does it cause an increase in wages. A decrease in productivity (perhaps a new law mandating longer breaks for workers or more frequent inspections of machines) would decrease productivity and drive the supply curve to the left.

THINK IT THROUGH: Again, devise your own intuitive example of a situation where productivity has increased and determine the effect on supply.

After-Tax Revenues

An increase in taxes on producers will reduce revenues and reduce supply. An excise tax levied on gasoline, for example, will increase the price of gasoline because supply has been reduced. A reduction in such a tax will have the opposite effect. A subsidy is almost like a "negative" tax—a tax takes money away while a subsidy bestows money. A new subsidy (or an increase in an existing one) will increase profitability and prompt a greater supply.

THINK IT THROUGH: Separate from the government's need to collect revenues, "sin" taxes are imposed on cigarettes, wine, and spirits, and gasoline in order to discourage production and consumption of such "bad" goods. For many years, a honey subsidy was part of the Agriculture Bill because pollination by bees was felt to be beneficial for agriculture in general. The subsidy increased the supply of honey and the pollinating services of the bees.

THINK IT THROUGH: Apart from the examples given, can you think of other examples of "sin" taxes? Also, what would happen to supply of, for example, beer if the government increased corporate income taxes?

Prices of Related Products in Production

We included the price of related goods (substitutes and complements) among the factors that could shift the position of a demand curve. The same is true for supply—but we must be careful! Just because two goods are, for instance, complements for consumers, it does not guarantee that they will also be complements for producers. For the Smith family, a wooden table and four wooden chairs are complements—the family will buy the table and chairs to use them together. However, for the furniture producer, the table takes up resources that could be used to produce chairs—tables and chairs are substitutes in production. As we can see from this example, it is unwise to assume that, because Good A and Good B are substitutes (or complements) for consumers, they must therefore have any particular relationship from the standpoint of producers.

To make this issue a little clearer, let's adopt the practice of referring to two goods that are substitutes on the supply side as **substitutes in production** and to two goods that are complements on the supply side as **complements in production**. We reserve the simple terms *substitutes* and *complements* exclusively for demand-side relationships.

Consider a farmer who can produce soybeans or corn. If the price of corn increases from P_1 to P_2, then the Law of Supply tells us that the farmer will devote more of her resources to the production of corn and, therefore, less of her resources will be devoted to the production of soybeans. Soybean production will decrease from S_1 to S_2 at every price level. Corn and soybeans are substitutes in production and when the price of one of the goods increases, then the supply of the other good will decrease. See Figure 2-13.

Although goods are most likely to be substitutes in production because they are in competition for the firm's resources, it is possible that two goods may be complements in production. This case occurs when two goods are produced together, usually with one being

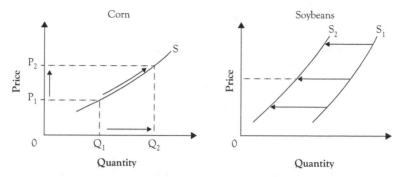

Figure 2-13. The relationship between substitutes in production.

a by-product of the other. Beef and hides are the standard textbook examples. Other examples include natural gas and helium; mutton and wool; doughnuts and doughnut holes; and ethanol and high-protein corn mash for cattle.

The production of milk requires pregnant cows. If the price of milk increases from P_1 to P_2, then there will be an increase in the quantity of milk supplied (from Q_1 to Q_2) due to an increase in bovine pregnancies and deliveries. There will, in short, be more calves born. About half of these calves will be non-milk-producing males, so, because of the increase in the price of milk, there will be an increase in the supply of veal from S_1 to S_2. See Figure 2-14. Milk and veal are complements in production.

THINK IT THROUGH: Find at least one real-world example of two goods that are substitutes in production and two goods that are complements in production.

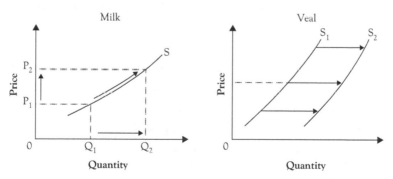

Figure 2-14. The relationship between complements in production.

Number of Sellers

We assume that as more firms enter an industry, then there will be greater supply. With more restaurants in town, the supply of restaurant meals will increase. If, however, the number of plumbers in town is halved (perhaps because of a new regulation requiring certification), then the supply of plumbing services will be reduced.

Applying Demand and Supply Analysis

Single-Shift Cases: We can now apply the tool we have developed by considering the beer industry. Suppose we are given four snippets of information about circumstances in the beer industry and asked to predict their consequences. The four pieces of information are:

> Case 1. Beer has been proved conclusively to increase male sexual performance.
> Case 2. Wine has become much less expensive than before.
> Case 3. There has been a very large harvest of hops. (Hops are an ingredient in the production of beer.)
> Case 4. Beer workers have negotiated a ten percent increase in their wages.

We will treat each of these situations separately. First, think about each situation. Jot down in the following table what you think will happen, as a consequence of this shock to the market, to the price of beer (increase or decrease) and to the size of the beer market (increase or decrease). We'll check your predictions later.

	Effect on Price	Effect on Quantity
Case 1	_____	_____
Case 2	_____	_____
Case 3	_____	_____
Case 4	_____	_____

As in many areas of life, it is useful to have a style of approach when dealing with demand and supply analysis. First, make it a habit to sketch a demand and supply diagram as shown in Figure 2-15, with "price" (P) on the vertical axis and "quantity" (Q) on the horizontal axis. Draw in a downward-sloping demand curve and label it D_1, then an upward-sloping supply curve and label it S_1. We know that equilibrium occurs where the two lines cross, so we can draw in the equilibrium price level (P*) and the equilibrium quantity (Q*). We now have a representation of the beer market as it stands at the beginning of the analysis.

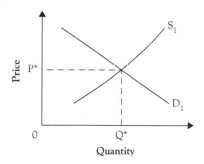

Figure 2-15. The initial equilibrium diagram.

Learning Tip: Once you've identified that you're dealing with a demand and supply problem, always sketch your initial diagram like this before you continue. It's easier to identify the initial equilibrium price and quantity before you start shifting lines back and forth.

Case 1: Beer has been proved conclusively to
        increase male sexual performance.

The first question to answer is "Will this market shock affect the demand for beer or the supply of beer?" The instinctive but almost certainly incorrect answer is "Both!" We have a list of factors that can shift the position of the demand curve and another list of factors that can shift the position of the supply curve. Which factor on which list best fits this situation?

Certainly there will be a change in demand (tastes and preferences) following this information—isn't that what advertising is all about? In each case, you should be able to identify the category of factor that is causing the change in demand (or supply).

The second question to address is "Will demand—because now we've determined it is a demand change—increase or decrease?" It's a safe bet in this situation of promised enhanced sexual performance that the demand for beer will increase. The demand curve will shift to the right.

Draw the demand curve in its new position (D_2). We know that equilibrium occurs where the demand curve and the supply curve cross. Draw in the new equilibrium price level (P**) and the new equilibrium quantity (Q**) on your diagram. Price has increased and quantity has increased. See Figure 2-16.

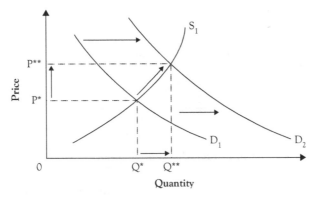

Figure 2-16. An increase in demand.

A successful advertising campaign or the discovery of a new use for an existing product will cause an increase in its price and an increase in the size of the market. Is this the result you predicted?

"Not so fast!" you exclaim. "Won't supply increase too? Why is 'both' an incorrect response?" Typically, the predominant effect will fall on only one side of the market, so, although it sometimes may be true that a market shock will affect the positions of both curves, the "both" response is usually the result of misthinking. Removing the "both" response forces a considered choice.

False logic: It is also true that more beer will be supplied, but this is not because of an increase in supply. It's an "increase in quantity supplied" in response to the initial change in demand. The cause-and-effect sequence goes like this: The increase in demand causes a shortage at the initial equilibrium price (P*) and the shortage pressures the price to increase. As the price of beer increases, the "quantity supplied of beer" increases—this is a movement along the existing supply curve, not a shift in the position of the curve—and decreases the "quantity demanded of beer" along the new demand curve (D_2).

In summary, this market shock makes only the demand curve shift.

A useful rule to remember is: "One factor shifts one curve and it shifts it only one time."

A note on the difference between a "change in demand" and a change in quantity demanded": The one major source of confusion in a Principles of Economics course is the distinction between a "change in quantity demanded" and a "change in demand." Beware! These two terms have very precise meanings in economics.

A "change in quantity demanded" refers to a movement along a demand curve, from one point to another. The only thing that can cause a change in quantity demanded is a change in the price of the good. The only thing! A "change in demand" refers to a shift (left or right) in the position of the demand curve. If income, the price of a substitute, tastes and preferences (and so on) change, then the demand curve must be redrawn—a change in demand. Although this might sound easy enough, it causes endless confusion even for the most diligent student.

Remember: A change in price causes a "change in quantity demanded," which is a movement along the curve. A change in some other factor causes a "change in demand," which is a movement of the entire demand curve.

Case 2. Wine has become much less expensive than before.

As in Case 1, we must answer two questions: "Will this market shock affect the demand for beer or the supply of beer?" and "Will it be an increase or a decrease?" For most beer drinkers, wine is an acceptable substitute, so cheaper wine will have an impact on the demand for beer. In fact, if the price of wine has decreased, the demand for beer will decrease. The demand curve will shift to the left.

Draw the demand curve in its new position (D_2). Equilibrium price decreases from P* to P** and equilibrium quantity decreases from Q* to Q**. See Figure 2-17.

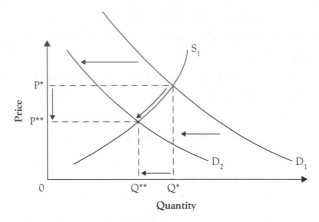

Figure 2-17. A decrease in demand.

THINK IT THROUGH: Verify that this result makes sense to you. Does it square with your prediction? If not, why not?

Case 3. There has been a very large harvest of hops.
        (Hops are an ingredient in the production of beer.)

Will this market shock affect the demand for beer or the supply of beer? Unless the quality of the hops has changed, affecting the taste of the beer, beer drinkers are unlikely to care about hop yields. This is a production side issue and supply will increase. There's a brief explanation for this—more ingredients, more beer! We can be more subtle than that. With a large harvest of hops, the price of hops will decrease so the price of an input has decreased. Follow the profit! With lower costs, profitability will increase, leading to an increase in supply. The supply curve will shift to the right.

Draw the supply curve in its new position (S_2). Equilibrium price decreases from P^* to P^{**} and equilibrium quantity increases from Q^* to Q^{**}. See Figure 2-18.

THINK IT THROUGH: Does this result—that a large hop harvest is great news for beer drinkers—make sense to you? Does it match your prediction? If not, why not?

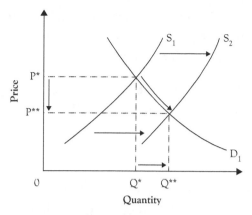

Figure 2-18. An increase in supply.

Case 4. Beer workers have negotiated a 10% increase in their wages.

Will the wage increase affect the demand for beer or the supply of beer? Beer workers may be beer drinkers, but the predominant effect is on the costs of producing beer. Following our "one factor shifts one curve" rule, it's the supply curve that will be affected. Follow the profit! With higher costs, profitability will be reduced, leading to a cutback in supply. The supply curve will shift to the left.

Draw the supply curve in its new position (S_2). Equilibrium price increases from P* to P** and equilibrium quantity decreases from Q* to Q**. See Figure 2-19.

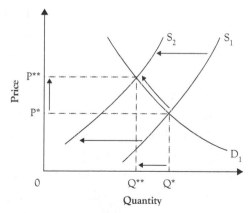

Figure 2-19. A decrease in supply.

THINK IT THROUGH: Does this result make sense to you? Higher wage payments should drive up prices and cause layoffs in the beer industry. Does it match your prediction? If not, why not?

Review: There are four single-shift cases. Either demand increases or decreases, or supply increases or decreases. The following table summarizes the results we have found and should agree with the predictions you made earlier.

	Effect on Price	Effect on Quantity
Demand Increase	increase	increase
Demand Decrease	decrease	decrease
Supply Increase	decrease	increase
Supply Decrease	increase	decrease

Multiple-Shift Cases: It is possible that two shocks could hit a market at the same time. Suppose we are given two pieces of information about circumstances in the market for domestically produced wine and asked to predict their consequences. The two pieces of information are that import taxes on foreign wine have been reduced and that improved fermenting techniques have reduced the costs of wine production.

Initially, we deal with this as two "single-shift" cases.

If import taxes on foreign wine have been reduced then this reduces the demand for domestically produced wine because the price of the substitute has decreased. Adopting improved fermentation processes techniques should reduce production costs and increase the supply of domestically produced wine. Because we have a decrease in demand (which will decrease price) and an increase in supply (which also will decrease price) we would predict unambiguously that the price of domestically produced wine will decrease. However, we can't be so sure about the effect of the two shocks on quantity. We have a decrease in demand (which will decrease quantity) and an increase in supply (which will increase quantity) therefore the overall effect on quantity is indeterminate unless we know something more specific about the magnitude of the shifts in demand and supply.

THINK IT THROUGH: Try drawing this example. As always, begin with the initial equilibrium diagram (Figure 2-15), including the initial equilibrium price (P*) and quantity (Q*). Verify that the effect on equilibrium quantity depends on the magnitudes of the two conflicting shifts.

THINK ABOUT IT: Come up with an example where two shocks cause an ambiguous result, not for equilibrium quantity, but for equilibrium price.

Application: Foreign Exchange and the International Market for Dollars

Most of us, if asked the price of a dollar, would respond "One dollar," puzzled that the question was even asked. However, there is an active market for dollars and the price of the dollar is constantly adjusting according to the demand and supply. Certainly, domestically, there is a demand for dollars in order to finance our transactions, to store our wealth, and so on, but there is an additional demand for dollars from overseas and there is a flow of dollars into this market. It is to this market that we now turn our attention.

We can examine the price of foreign exchange (such as the yen) in terms of "so many dollars per yen" but, as currencies (except the British pound sterling) are ordinarily valued in the form "so many yen per dollar," it is easier to examine the international currency market from the viewpoint of the demand for and supply of dollars.

The demand for the dollar is said to be a **derived demand**, in that demanders seek dollars, not for their intrinsic value, but because of what they can buy. If the foreign demand for American-produced goods increases, then there will be an increase in the demand for dollars with which to buy those goods, because, usually, American companies do not accept foreign currencies as payment for their goods or services.

THINK IT THROUGH: If a German tourist wishes to buy a hotel room in Boston, the hotelier will expect to receive payment in dollars. Even if the tourist pays with a credit card issued by a German bank, ultimately the payment must be made in dollars.

Comment: Americans travelling abroad are rather spoiled in this respect, because some traders *will* accept dollars in *lieu* of their domestic currency. In the case of other currencies, however, this is quite unusual.

Let us begin by considering the demand and supply of dollars for the purposes of buying and selling goods internationally. To simplify, we have two countries, the United States and Japan. The American currency is the dollar, the Japanese the yen. Let us establish an exchange rate—Exchange Rate 1. At Exchange Rate 1, $1 trades for 100 yen. If the exchange rate changes to Exchange Rate 2, then the dollar trades for 200 yen.

An exchange rate movement from Exchange Rate 1 to Exchange Rate 2 represents an increase in the strength of the dollar (and a corresponding decrease in the strength of the yen). This exchange rate movement is said to be an **appreciation** in the value of the dollar and a **depreciation** in the value of the yen.

Let us now suppose that the United States exports only one good—rice. Domestically, a sack of rice sells for $40. Japan exports only one good—television sets. Domestically (in Japan, that is), a television set sells for 20,000 yen.

A Japanese wished to buy a sack of American rice would have to pay $40 to the rice producer. At Exchange Rate 1, $40 represents a price tag of 4,000 yen (as shown in Table 2-4).

Table 2-4. Relative Prices with Changing Exchange Rates

	United states (Rice)		Japan (Television sets)	
	Domestic price	Foreign price	Domestic price	Foreign price
Exchange Rate 1	40 dollars	4,000 yen	20,000 yen	200 dollars
Exchange Rate 2	40 dollars	8,000 yen	20,000 yen	100 dollars

At Exchange Rate 2, the same sack of rice would still cost $40 to American buyers but, to the Japanese, the price tag would have risen to 8,000 yen. A depreciation in the value of a country's currency (the yen, in this case) leads to an increase in the price of its imports. Put differently, if the dollar appreciates in value, U.S. exporters will find it more difficult to attract foreign customers because the price of their exports is rising overseas.

The television set, bought in Japan, would cost an American purchaser 20,000 yen. At Exchange Rate 1, this translates into a price of $200. At Exchange Rate 1, each dollar is worth 100 yen, so 200 dollars are the equivalent of 20,000 yen. At Exchange Rate 2, the television set will cost the American purchaser $100. See Table 2-4.

THINK IT THROUGH: If you have traveled abroad, or have conducted transactions in foreign currency, you may have caught yourself complaining, "What's that in real money?" For the American purchaser, the 20,000 yen price tag is irrelevant—he wishes to know how much it will cost him *in dollars*.

An appreciation in the value of the dollar leads to a decrease in the price of American imports, such as television sets. If the dollar appreciates in value, then domestic producers of import-substitutes will find it harder to retain domestic buyers because the goods of their foreign competitors are decreasing in price.

The demand for dollars: Figure 2-20 graphs the demand curve for dollars (D$) on the international currency exchange market.

The international demand for dollars comes from foreigners who need dollars in order to purchase American goods. At Exchange Rate 1 ($1 trades for 100 yen), American goods, as typified by the sack of rice, are relatively cheap—only 4,000 yen for the rice—so the demand by Japanese for American rice will be fairly high and, therefore, the quantity of dollars demanded to buy the rice will be fairly high.

At Exchange Rate 2, however, American-produced rice is expensive for Japanese purchasers. They may choose to buy from domestic (Japanese) producers or, perhaps, look to other suppliers, such as China or India. We should expect less American rice to be demanded by Japanese purchasers and, therefore, that the quantity of dollars needed to buy American rice will decrease.

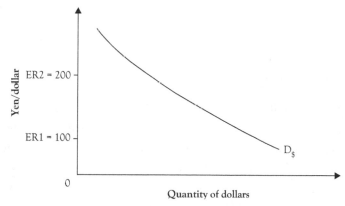

Figure 2-20. The international demand for dollars.

As the "price" of the dollar appreciates and American goods become less attractive to foreign buyers, the quantity demanded of dollars decreases.

THINK IT THROUGH: A movement up the vertical axis represents an appreciation in the value of the dollar (and a depreciation in the value of the yen) whereas a downward movement signifies a depreciation in the value of the dollar (and an appreciation in the value of the yen).

The supply of dollars: Figure 2-21 graphs the supply curve of dollars (S\$) on the international currency exchange market.

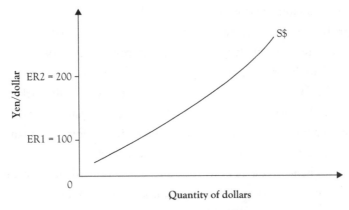

Figure 2-21. The international supply of dollars.

The international supply of dollars comes from Americans who wish to purchase foreign goods—to buy foreign goods one requires foreign currency and one must supply dollars to get that foreign currency.

THINK IT THROUGH: The easiest way to envision this transaction is to consider an American tourist at an airport *bureau de change* exchanging dollars to yen in preparation for a flight to Japan. Yen are being demanded and dollars are being supplied.

At Exchange Rate 1 ($1 trades for 100 yen), Japanese goods are quite expensive—$200 for the television set—so the demand by Americans for Japanese television sets will be comparatively low and, therefore, the quantity of yen demanded to buy those television sets also will be comparatively low.

At Exchange Rate 2, Japanese television sets are cheaply priced for American purchasers and more will be demanded. There will be an increased quantity of yen demanded in order to buy the goods and, therefore, an increased quantity of dollars supplied to buy those yen.

As the dollar appreciates in value and foreign goods become more attractive to American buyers, the quantity supplied of dollars increases.

Equilibrium: If currency rates are free to adjust, the equilibrium exchange rate will be established where quantity demanded equals quantity supplied. As shown in Figure 2-22, the equilibrium exchange rate is $1 equals 150 yen. If the price of a dollar is 100 yen, then there is a shortage of dollars (the quantity of dollars demanded exceeds the quantity available) and the price (the exchange rate) will increase. If, by contrast, the price of a dollar is 200 yen, then there is a surplus of dollars and the exchange rate will decrease.

Comment: Across the globe, some exchange rates are not "free to adjust" (float) but are pegged (fixed) in value to other currencies, but the prevailing system for the world's major currencies is that market forces largely drive their values. A gold standard is one type of fixed exchange rate regime.

We shall use the abbreviations EX for exports and IM for imports. To help us remember that the demand for dollars is closely linked to the volume of American exports, we shall add the "EX" tag to the dollar demand curve, $D_{\$(EX)}$, and, similarly, the "IM" tag to the dollar supply curve, $S_{\$(IM)}$.

If the dollar is valued above the equilibrium exchange rate, at Exchange Rate 2, for example, then this would indicate that United States is running a *deficit on its balance of trade*, (with the value of imports exceeding the value of exports). If, conversely, the dollar's value is below the

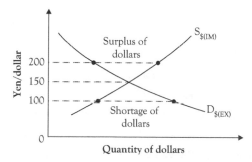

Figure 2-22. Equilibrium in the international market for dollars.

equilibrium exchange rate, at Exchange Rate 1, for example, then the United States is running a *surplus on its balance of trade* (the value of exports exceeds the value of imports).

THINK IT THROUGH (A trade conundrum): According to the model we have developed, a nation with a floating exchange rate, such as the United States, should expect the quantity of dollars demanded and supplied to be more or less equal over time. If the demand and supply of dollars mirrors the U.S. exports and imports then these too ought to be equal over time. But, clearly, this is untrue—the United States has run a chronic trade deficit since the mid-1970s! We will find an answer to this puzzle in Chapter 8.

Shifts in demand and supply: The demand for dollars is related to the foreign demand for American exports—the greater the demand for exports, the greater the demand for dollars. If the Japanese economy becomes more prosperous and its citizens increase their demand for American rice, then the demand curve for dollars will shift to the right. The dollar will appreciate in value.

The supply of dollars is affected by the American demand for imports—the greater the demand for imports, the greater the supply for dollars. If the American economy slips into a recession, then the American demand for (normal) foreign goods will decrease as will the supply of dollars. The dollar will appreciate in value.

Which is better—a strong dollar or a weak dollar? The knee-jerk response to this question is "Strong, of course!" but the well-considered answer is more complex. Some Americans gain and some lose when the dollar appreciates.

Gainers: If the exchange rate appreciates from Exchange Rate 1 to Exchange Rate 2, then foreign goods will be cheaper for American consumers and American tourists will find their dollars stretching further. Similarly, importers of foreign resources (such as oil) will experience a decrease in production costs.

Losers: If the exchange rate appreciates from Exchange Rate 1 to Exchange Rate 2, then we have already established that American rice producers will lose foreign customers. Workers in the rice industry may lose their jobs. Also producers of import-substitutes will find it harder to retain customers.

An appreciation in the value of the dollar should be seen as a mixed blessing.

A New Way to Look at Demand and Supply:
Marginal Benefit and Marginal Cost

Before leaving this chapter, let us consider a different way to look at demand and supply analysis. Usually when we look at a demand curve, we read it from the vertical axis (price) to the horizontal axis (quantity demanded), but we could read from quantity to price. The same holds true for a supply curve.

Marginal Benefit

Suppose we ask Adam how much an apple is worth to him—perhaps in an auction context—and we are told 90¢. It is worth this much to him because he is willing to pay 90¢ to get it. Probably, the second apple would be worth less to Adam—perhaps only 80¢. And so on. Each apple's extra value, or marginal benefit, can be recorded as shown on the diagram and a marginal benefit curve plotted as shown in Figure 2-23.

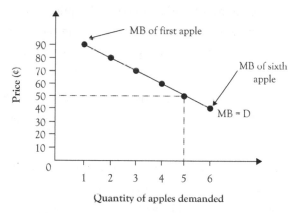

Figure 2-23. *Adam's marginal benefit curve for apples.*

But surely this is Adam's demand curve for apples! A demand curve plots the relationship between price and quantity demanded and we can see that, if the price of apples is 50¢, then Adam will wish to buy five apples. The demand curve and the marginal benefit curve are identical.

Consumer Surplus

Figure 2-23 contains other information of interest. **Consumer surplus** (or net consumer benefit) is the difference between the price that the buyer is willing to pay and the price he or she does pay. If the price of apples is 50¢, then Adam will buy the first apple (which he values at 90¢) for 50¢ and receives a consumer surplus of 40¢ on that apple. The second apple will yield a consumer surplus of 30¢, and so on. Overall, Adam's consumer surplus from the five apples he buys is $1.00 (40¢ + 30¢ + 20¢ + 10¢ + 0¢). When he decides whether or not to buy each successive apple, Adam compares the marginal benefit received versus the price paid. He will buy if the marginal benefit exceeds the price. He will not buy the sixth apple because he would be giving up 50¢ in order to receive something worth only 40¢.

Graphically, the consumer surplus for each apple is the vertical distance between the marginal benefit curve and the price. It is the triangular area below the demand curve and above the price. Given demand, a price reduction increases consumer surplus while a price increase reduces it.

THINK IT THROUGH: When you enter a car dealership you start an economic game. The salesperson tries to discover how high a price you are willing to pay—and you try not to tell her. The lower you can move the price, the greater your consumer surplus. The higher she can raise the price, without losing the sale, the more of your consumer surplus she can extract from you.

If the apple vendor could determine Adam's marginal benefit for each apple and then charge that price for each apple separately, then she could appropriate all of Adam's consumer surplus.

THINK IT THROUGH: The demand curve depicts marginal benefit. Review the factors that can shift the demand curve. Can you "translate" them into factors that can affect marginal benefit?

To maximize his consumer surplus, Adam should buy apples until the marginal benefit of the last apple bought (MB_A) equals the price (P_A). Thus

$$MB_A = P_A$$

To maximize consumer surplus, the buyer should purchase each good in amounts such that the marginal benefit per dollar is equal for all goods.

Do we always follow this rule? No—this is a counsel of perfection and our real-world decisions are imperfect—but we should get as close to it as possible.

All maximizing consumers of apples should follow this rule, so, summing the benefits, we get the rule for maximizing total consumer surplus (total net consumer benefit):

$$\Sigma MB_A = P_A$$

where Σ means "the sum of." All this rule says is that to get the best possible deal from a given demand curve, we should let the price determine the quantity demanded.

Marginal Cost

In the previous section we discovered that marginal benefit is identical to demand and that consumer surplus is the difference between the maximum price a consumer is willing to pay and the market price. In this section we will reach quite parallel conclusions on the supply side of the market.

We first came across marginal cost (MC) in Chapter 1 where we defined it as "the additional cost incurred when an additional unit of a good is produced." Fundamentally, marginal cost is opportunity cost, and it is also related to the supply curve.

A supply curve shows the relationship between price and quantity supplied. As we did with demand, let us read it from the horizontal axis (quantity supplied) to the vertical axis (price). Consider Eve's marginal cost curve for apples as shown in Figure 2-24.

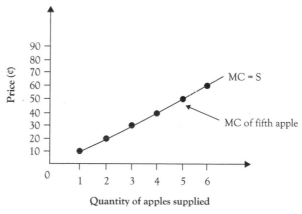

Figure 2-24. Eve's marginal cost curve for apples.

We ask Eve what is the lowest price she will accept for the first apple she supplies and we are told 10¢. As this is the lowest price she will accept and still be willing to produce, this price must equal the cost of producing the apple—in other words, 10¢ is the marginal cost of the first apple.

Recall that in Chapter 1 we saw that production is subject to the law of increasing costs. Given this, we would expect that the second apple would cost more for Eve to produce—perhaps 20¢. And so on. Each apple's marginal cost can be recorded as shown on the diagram and a marginal cost curve plotted. It is the same as the supply curve! A supply curve plots the relationship between price and quantity supplied and we can see that, if the price of apples is 50¢, then Eve will wish to sell five apples. The supply curve and the marginal cost curve are one and the same.

Producer Surplus

As with demand, our supply-side analysis has more to tell. **Producer surplus** (net producer benefit) is the difference between the lowest price that the seller is willing to accept for an item and the price he or she does receive. If the price of apples is 50¢, then Eve will sell the first apple—her producer surplus is 40¢. The second apple produced will yield Eve a producer surplus of 30¢, and so on. Eve's total producer surplus from the five apples she sells is $1.00 (40¢ + 30¢ + 20¢ + 10¢ + 0¢). When she makes the decision whether or not to produce each successive apple, Eve compares the revenue received and the marginal cost incurred. If the price exceeds the marginal cost then she will produce. She will not produce the sixth apple because the price would not cover the marginal cost of production.

To maximize her producer surplus, Eve should produce until the marginal cost of her product (MC_A) equals its price (P_A). Thus

$$MC_A = P_A$$

All maximizing producers of apples should follow this rule so, summing the costs, we get the rule for maximizing total producer surplus (total net producer benefit):

$$\Sigma MC_A = P_A$$

Graphically, the producer surplus for each apple is the vertical distance between the marginal cost curve and the price. It is the triangular area above the supply curve and below the price. If price increases, then producer surplus increases too.

Maximizing Society's Total Economic Surplus

Consider Figure 2-25, which shows the market for apples. The market demand curve represents the sum of the marginal benefits received all buyers (ΣMB) and the market supply curve represents the sum of the marginal costs incurred by all sellers (ΣMC).

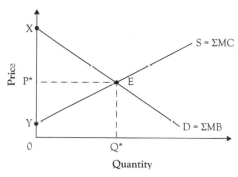

Figure 2-25. The market and efficiency.

Diagrams depicting consumer and producer surplus conventionally have the demand and supply curves begin at the vertical axis. Point X represents the maximum value that anyone would be willing to pay for an item whereas Point Y represents the lowest price at which any output will be offered for sale. P* and Q* are the equilibrium price and quantity, respectively. The area PXE represents the consumer surplus or total net benefit received by apple buyers whereas the area PYE depicts the producer surplus or total net benefit received by apple sellers.

The area XYE represents the **total economic surplus**, or **total net benefit**, received by all market participants. This area—the overall net gain to members of society from the exchange of apples—is maximized when the market is at its equilibrium price and quantity. The area 0XEQ* represents the total benefit received by the recipients of Q* units while the area 0YEQ* represents to costs incurred in producing Q* units—the difference is the net gain.

If output is established at any level other than Q* then the total net benefit will be reduced. Consider Figure 2-26.

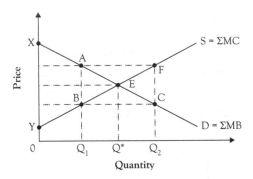

Figure 2-26. The Market and an inefficient situation.

If producers limit output to Q_1 units then, for the last item exchanged, the marginal benefit exceeds the marginal cost. Any unit where the marginal benefit exceeds the marginal cost should be produced because there is a gain to society. All units up to Q* should be produced. By restricting output to Q_1, the market is forfeiting those additional gains and causing a **deadweight loss**. The benefit of the additional units is the area Q_1AEQ^* while the cost of the additional units is the area Q_1BEQ^*. The deadweight loss—the surplus given up—is the area BAE.

If, conversely, producers expand output beyond Q* there is also a deadweight loss. At Q_2, for example, for the last item exchanged, the marginal benefit is less than the marginal cost. Such a unit should not be produced because there is a loss to society. Only units up to Q* should be produced. By expanding output to Q_2, the market is reducing its total economic surplus. The benefit of the additional units beyond Q* is the area Q^*ECQ_2 but the additional cost is the area Q^*EFQ_2. The deadweight loss in this case is the area CFE.

This point is quite subtle and deserves additional comment. Recall that marginal cost is opportunity cost and that opportunity cost, in turn, is "the value of the next most preferred alternative given up" when a choice is made. If we choose to produce an apple and use resources to produce it, then the opportunity cost of that apple is the value we place on the items we otherwise would have produced with those resources. We make an allocatively efficient choice if the value gained by producing the apple exceeds the value given up, but, if the value gained is less than the value given up, then the choice is allocatively inefficient and shouldn't take place.

To maximize consumer surplus, buyers should buy until marginal benefit (MB) equals price (P) whereas, to maximize producer surplus, producers should produce until marginal cost (MC) equals price. Thus

$$MB = P = MC$$

To maximize total economic surplus and achieve allocative efficiency, the market should produce the quantity at which marginal benefit equals marginal cost. If MB exceeds MC, then production should increase; if MB is less than MC, then production should decrease.

Left to its own devices, a free market does move to the situation where "demand equals supply" or, the same thing, "marginal benefit equals marginal cost." Markets, then, are a powerful engine for maximizing allocative efficiency. We shall return to this conclusion in Chapter 8 when we look more closely at the benefits springing from international trade.

Review: This has been a long, arduous chapter dealing, as it does, with the primary analytical tool of economists—demand and supply. The single best piece of advice is "practice, practice, practice" and, with respect to diagrams, "draw, draw, draw." The slippery distinction between a "change in quantity demanded" (caused by a change in price and shown as a movement along an existing demand curve) and a "change in demand" (caused by other factors and shown as a shift in the position of the demand curve) is controlled if a diagram is drawn. Like any tool, demand and supply analysis requires repeated practice before there is any sense of perfection but it is worth the effort because the tool is so generally applicable in the real world.

CHAPTER 3

Measuring the Macroeconomy

By the end of this chapter you will be able to:

1. Define gross domestic product (GDP) and its components and use the expenditure approach to calculate GDP.
2. List those transactions that are excluded from GDP calculations and explain the reason for the exclusion.
3. Describe the circular flow diagram and explain its implication for national income accounting.
4. Outline the process through which investment and saving are made equal.
5. Distinguish the various national income accounts.
6. Outline the limitations of GDP as a measure of social well-being.
7. Distinguish between real GDP and nominal GDP and explain why real GDP is the preferred measure of production.
8. Describe the behavior of the business cycle and distinguish its four phases.

Every day, the government publishes a great many economic statistics. Most of these are highly technical and of interest only to professional economists and other financial analysts and to policymakers. A few numbers, however, are widely reported, closely analyzed, and hotly debated by pundits in the media. The unemployment rate and the inflation rate, for example, may be of profound political significance, and unexpected or unwelcome changes in these values can trigger substantial changes in the stock market that may affect our 401ks or other financial assets. The economic growth rate is chief among these highly significant numbers published by the government. To determine how rapidly economic production is growing, the government must first determine the level of economic production. It does this through national income accounting—the topic of our current chapter.

Chapter Preview: This chapter deals with **national income accounting**, the method used by economists to calculate the total value of production within the macroeconomy. We will encounter many definitions. Our main measure of production and the primary focus of this chapter is **Gross Domestic Product** (GDP), but other useful measures are introduced. As with any measure, though, GDP is imperfect and its limitations must be kept in mind when interpreting it. In addition, we shall encounter a useful device of segmenting the economy—the **circular flow diagram**—and conclude by examining the series of economic fluctuations in GDP known as the **business cycle**.

National Income Accounting: Gross Domestic Product

Definition of Gross Domestic Product and Exclusions from the Definition

Our current framework of national income accounting began in the 1930s when the need was pressing to monitor the effectiveness of New Deal policy actions. The primary measure used nowadays is Gross Domestic Product (GDP). GDP is defined as the *total market value of all final goods and services produced within an economy's boundaries in a given period of time*.

Note the definition's emphasis on production. This year's GDP measures the value of what is produced this year, not how much is bought and sold this year. For this reason, we are not interested in resold goods or second-hand sales. Our focus is *production*—these goods have only been produced once and, therefore, must only be counted once.

THINK IT THROUGH: There are complications. The services of a recycling firm should be counted as part of this year's GDP—the services provided are new and, therefore, require inclusion. Similarly, restoration services on a 1955 Cadillac that is then sold on eBay must be included—a productive service has been rendered.

Note, too, the word *"final."* Many goods and services are classified as *intermediate* items in national income accounting, because they contribute to the value of the final good produced. It is assumed that the market value of the final good takes into account the values of all the intermediate goods and services used in its production—the salary of a car worker, the value of the steel, glass, and tires, the commission of the salesman in the showroom are all included in the price of the shiny new car we buy. If we counted the value of the intermediate goods and services, such as the value of the steel produced, as a separate item, then we would be guilty of *double counting*.

Furthermore, we must exclude paper transactions, such as the sale of stocks and bonds, from the calculations. Again, we wish to measure production—the shuffling of small pieces of paper from one person to another is not, in itself, a productive activity. However, if a stockbroker is involved in the transaction, then her fees must be included—a service has been rendered—and her commission represents the market's valuation of that service.

THINK IT THROUGH: If you buy stock and then resell it at a profit, then should that profit be included in GDP calculations? Has any production taken place? Because nothing has been produced, the capital gain is not counted in GDP.

THINK IT THROUGH (MORE): Changing stock market prices reflect changing expectations about the future profitability of firms or, possibly, speculation and, as such, the gains (or losses) are far removed from a measure of current production. This is very clear if stock prices fall—certainly, negative production is unlikely to have occurred!

Transfer payments are excluded. A **transfer payment** is a payment, in cash or kind, for which no good or service is required in return—a gift, in other words. Transfers may be private, such as a worker sending cash back home to her retired parents, or a student receiving a "care package" from home, or public, such as Food Stamps. Again, the key point is that we are interested in measuring production, not income or sales and, by its very nature, a transfer such as Food Stamps is given precisely *because* the recipient is not producing anything.

THINK IT THROUGH: When the contents of the care package are bought by the donor, or when the Food Stamps are spent by the recipient at the grocery store, it is these transactions that record the market value of goods that have been produced. It is at this point that production is measured.

Finally, our GDP definition refers to production "within an economy's boundaries." The output of an American citizen working in France is not part of America's GDP. Similarly, profits earned abroad by American companies do not count—they do not reflect production within this country's boundaries. However, a French national working in New York is contributing to American GDP and the profits earned here by a foreign-owned company such as Honda are counted as part of the GDP of this country.

Gross National Product (GNP) is another, older, measure of production. It is defined as the *total market value of all final goods and services produced by the resources owned by a country's citizens, regardless of the location of production, in a given period of time.*

For most countries, the difference between GDP and GNP—*net factor payments to the rest of the world*—is slight. For the United States, net factor payments consistently amount a negligible fraction of the value of GDP, although, for some countries, such as those with a large population of migrant workers, the differences can be extreme.

THINK IT THROUGH: Lesotho—a tiny landlocked nation with a poor domestic economy—is entirely surrounded by wealthy South Africa. Many Lesothans cross the border to work in South Africa's mines, farms, and factories. Which is larger, Lesotho's GDP or its GNP?

The income earned in South Africa by Lesotho's workers is not included in Lesotho's GDP, because the production that the income represents occurs outside Lesotho, but it is included in Lesotho's GNP. Lesotho's net factor payments *to* the rest of the world is a large negative number (that is, its net factor payments *from* the rest of the world is a large positive number). In 2011, Lesotho's GNP was about 30 percent higher than its GDP. Similarly, over 30 percent of Tajikistan's GDP comes from remittances sent home by workers living in Russia.

There is an apparent exception to the exclusions—investment in capital stock. A worker hired at a car plant, the steel and glass used for the car, the seats installed inside the car are all intermediate goods, but, if the car company buys a car-assembly robot, then that purchase is not counted as an intermediate good but as a purchase by the final user because the services it provides extend over several years. We look more closely at the meaning and significance of investment later in this chapter.

Consider Figure 3-1, which is for the fictitious nation of Pippin, an economy that produces only apples. For simplicity, we assume that Pippin has neither a government sector nor does it engage in foreign trade.

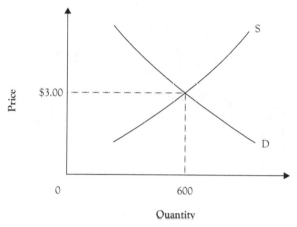

Figure 3-1. Apple production in Pippin.

The price of a bag of apples is $3.00 and 600 bags of apples are exchanged. If we wished to calculate Pippin's GDP then we would have two approaches open to us. We could ask apple buyers how much they spent on apples or we could ask apple producers how much income they received. The former approach—the **Expenditure Approach**—and the latter approach—the **Income Approach**—will each yield an answer of $1,800.

The expenditure approach and the income approach should yield the same answer—after all, a dollar spent is also a dollar received as income. The two approaches capture the two sides of the same transaction. In actual fact, expenditures (E) must equal income (Y), and both must equal the market value of production.

In actual fact,

Expenditures (E) = Income (Y) = Production

or,

$$E = Y$$

We can establish this equality using the circular flow diagram.

The Circular Flow Diagram:
Will it go Round in Circles?

We have two sectors in our economy—households and firms. We have assumed that there is no government sector and no foreign trade sector in our economy. The circular flow diagram given in Figure 3-2 shows all the transactions in Pippin, including sales of resources and sales of final goods.

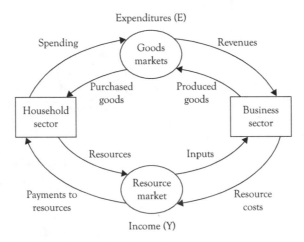

Figure 3-2. A simple circular flow diagram.

Resources—human resources, capital, natural resources, and enterprise— flow from households to firms, and households are rewarded for the use of the resources with income (Y). The income received as payment for the use of the resources must equal the value of what is produced by them.

Similarly, the expenditures of households (and received as revenue by firms) must also equal the value of production. A dollar spent is also a dollar received as income.

A Complication: What if households choose not to spend all of their income but instead decide to save some of it? In that case, some of the nation's output would not be sold and would be held by firms in inventory. This change in inventory is counted as part of investment and, therefore, is still included in GDP. Remember, we're measuring the value of production, not the value of sales—although goods placed in inventory have not been sold, they have been produced.

Some Definitions

Consumption (C), or *personal consumption expenditures*, is the market value of purchases of goods and services by persons and nonprofit institutions and the value of food, clothing, housing, and financial services received by them as income in kind.

Consumption spending is divided between *consumer durable goods* (cars, refrigerators, jewelry), *consumer nondurable goods* (candy, gasoline), and *consumer services* (car mechanic, dentist). As a rule of thumb, a good is considered "durable" if it lasts 3 or more years.

THINK IT THROUGH: Is your house or apartment a consumer durable good? It would seem so but, no, housing is not classed as consumption of any kind. Instead, it is considered as part of the economy's capital stock. As is explained later, the construction of a new condo or apartment complex is investment.

Saving (S), or *personal saving*, is the income of households that is not spent. An unspent dollar, even if it is not deposited in a bank, still counts as saving. Bury it in the back yard, keep it in your wallet—if you don't spend it, it's saved.

Note, too, that there is a profound distinction between the two terms, *saving* and *savings*. Saving is the portion of this period's income that has not been spent—if Jason receives $100 and spends $90 then he has saved $10. Savings, however, is the accumulation of saved income over several periods. Jason may not save during the current period but he may still have savings. Put differently, saving is a flow or process, whereas savings is a stock or product.

Investment (I), or *gross private domestic investment*, is the total of private expenditures on new capital. Recall from Chapter 1 that *capital* resources are goods that are produced to make other goods. Financial capital and financial investment have no place in our consideration.

Investment spending is divided between nonresidential investment in plant and equipment, residential investment, and changes in the level of business inventories. Each of these components deserves some elaboration.

Nonresidential investment in plant and equipment. This is the type of investment that most people think of when they hear the term "investment" in the nation's capital stock. It includes purchases of plant, tools, and equipment by firms for productive use.

Residential investment includes expenditures by firms *and households* on new houses and apartments. Clearly, the construction of an apartment complex can be seen as "investment," but even the building of an extension onto the back of one's home ought to be included.

THINK IT THROUGH: It's fairly obvious that a firm constructing a warehouse or a new factory building is involved in creating "goods that are produced to make other goods," but home construction is less so. Should not a house be considered a consumer durable good? Two justifications can be offered.

Most consumer durables have a fairly limited life span—a fridge, a TV set, a computer, even a car, will be fortunate to survive for more than 10 years. That can't be said about a house—houses last for decades, perhaps centuries. So, if a house was to be treated as a consumer durable, then it would be a most unusual one. However, there is a more compelling reason to group residential construction as investment rather than consumption. Our homes help us to be productive. We rest, we eat, we sleep and, next day, we set out, ready to go to work. Just like our factory buildings and offices, our housing stock is part of capital—those "goods that are produced to make other goods."

THINK IT THROUGH (MORE): Sometimes the decision regarding whether a purchase represents consumption or investment seems fairly arbitrary. If I buy a car to drive my family around town, then it's a consumption purchase. But if I buy that same car for use in my job as a sales rep, then it's investment. Same car, same purchaser, but different classificationt.

Further, a computer bought by a firm is counted as investment, but the toner bought at the same time is not investment. Typically, items that last less than 1 year are considered to be intermediate goods.

Changes in the level of business inventories. Inventory is unsold production. An increase in inventory indicates that some items that have been produced have not been sold. If, though, we count only those items that are sold, then we will be undercounting the number of items that have been produced. If inventories decrease, this shows that sales have outstripped production. Remember, GDP is a measure of production so, by counting the change in inventories, we prevent this miscalculation.

The change in business inventory is included in investment (expenditures on new capital) because their future sale will create future revenue. For bookkeeping purposes, it is assumed that the firm purchases its own unsold inventories and then resells them in the future.

Earlier, we established that, in actual fact, expenditures (E) must equal income (Y).

Expenditures (E) = Income (Y) = Production

or,

$$E = Y$$

Expenditures in our simple economy, lacking both government and foreign sectors, are comprised of consumption (C) and investment (I) whereas income is divided between consumption and saving (S). Therefore,

$$C + I = C + S$$

Because consumption is the same value on each side of the equation, then it must therefore be true that investment and saving are equal, in actual fact.

$$I = S$$

You may have noticed the emphasis on the phrase, "in actual fact." The reason for this will now become clear. A little reflection should be sufficient to convince yourself that it is extremely implausible that the individual investment decisions of millions of firms and the individual saving decisions of millions of households will come out to be exactly equal. Firms and households are different entities with differing perspectives and goals—there is no requirement that their intentions will coincide—yet our model asserts that, in actual fact, investment and saving *must* be equal. How so?

To answer this question, let us return to the apple-producing nation of Pippin as shown in Figure 3-3.

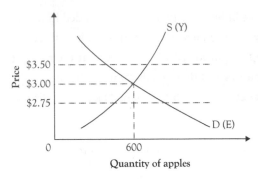

Figure 3-3. Apple production in Pippin.

We can think of the demand curve (D) as being synonymous with expenditures (consumption plus investment), whereas the supply curve (S) can be thought of as representing the income of productive resources (consumption plus saving), or production.

Let us consider, though, what the demand curve and the supply curve convey. A demand curve shows how much consumers are willing and able to buy. It indicates intended, or planned, demand rather than the actual number of units that will be purchased—intention, not actuality. Similarly, a supply curve depicts what producers are willing and able to make available for sale—it shows a *willingness* to sell, not actual sales.

In this market, the equilibrium price is $3.00 and the equilibrium quantity traded is 600 bags of apples. At this price, quantity demanded equals quantity supplied. Planned (intended) expenditures equal planned production. Together, planned consumption and planned investment equal planned consumption and planned saving and, therefore, planned investment equals planned saving.

If the price is $3.50, however, then there is a surplus of apples. Quantity demanded is less than quantity supplied. Planned (intended) expenditures fall short of planned (intended) production. Planned consumption and planned investment are less than planned consumption and planned saving and, therefore, planned investment is less than planned saving.

However, in actual fact, investment and saving must be equal! How can this be? The answer to this puzzle lies in unplanned inventory change. The actual level of investment is the sum of planned investment and unplanned (forced) investment.

If, at a price of $3.50, apple growers produce 800 apples but only 500 are demanded, then 300 remain unsold and will be added to inventory.

This inventory change is unintended because an intended change in inventory would have been part of planned investment expenditures and, as such, part of demand. The difference between planned investment and planned saving is filled by unplanned inventory change, causing actual investment to equal actual saving.

THINK IT THROUGH: In equilibrium, when demand-side intentions exactly match supply-side intentions, there is no forced change in inventory, so actual investment equals planned investment. This is surely a good definition of equilibrium—having a result that exactly meets your plans.

If the price is $2.75, then there is a shortage of apples. Quantity demanded exceeds quantity supplied. Planned expenditures are greater than planned production. Planned investment is less than planned saving. To satisfy demand, producers will draw down their inventory of apples. This is an unintended decrease in inventory. Once more, the difference between planned investment and planned saving is filled by unplanned inventory change, causing actual investment to equal actual saving.

At this price, unplanned inventory decumulation acts as a signaling mechanism for producers. If inventories are accumulating, then it is a sign of overproduction and production should be cut and price reduced. If, conversely, inventories are declining, then this indicates relatively high demand, and it signals a need to expand output and to increase price. Only at the equilibrium price of $3.00 is there no signal to producers through unplanned inventory change that they should adjust their price and output level.

Review: The factor that causes expenditures and income (production) to be equal, in actual fact, is unplanned inventory change. The economy is only at equilibrium when unplanned inventory change is zero. When this is the case, planned investment and actual investment are equal and, because businesses are fully achieving their objectives, there is no incentive to adjust that output level.

The Expenditure Approach to Calculating Gross Domestic Product

Of the two approaches used to calculate GDP, the expenditure approach, is the method relied on by the federal government and, as it is also the more useful for us, we will focus mainly on it. This approach adds up all the expenditures on final goods and services during the relevant time period. Expenditures are categorized as those we have already met, personal consumption expenditures (C) and gross private domestic investment (I), and two others—*government consumption and gross investment* and *net exports*.

Government spending (G), or *government consumption and gross investment*, includes expenditures by federal, state, and local governments on final goods and services. Expenditures on teachers' salaries or fighter jets are classified as government consumption whereas expenditures on the construction of new schools or bridges are classified as government investment in social capital. Government transfer payments, such as Food Stamps, are not included because transfer payments are not made in exchange for produced goods and services.

Net exports (EX – IM) is the difference between the value of American exports (EX) and the value of foreign goods imported into the country (IM). Because we wish to account for all sources of expenditure on American-produced goods, we must include the value of exported goods purchased by foreigners. The value of imports is subtracted to correct for the fact that consumption, investment, government spending, and exports, which include expenditures on goods regardless of where they were produced, therefore overstate the value of domestic production. Subtracting imports corrects this overstatement.

In equation form, the expenditure approach is as follows:

$$E = C + I + G + (EX - IM)$$

To get an idea of the relative magnitudes of the different components that comprise GDP, in the second quarter of 2012 consumption was 71.0 percent of total expenditures, investment 13.3 percent, government spending 19.5 percent, exports 14.0 percent, and imports 17.9 percent. Current figures are available from the Bureau of Economic Analysis at www.bea.gov.

The Income Approach to Calculating Gross Domestic Product

Briefly, the income approach sums the income of the economy's productive resources—compensation of employees, rental income, interest payments, proprietor's income, and corporate profits—and adjusts the total to account for the effects of government taxes and subsidies. Because we are interested in the market value of production, the role of sales taxes, excise taxes, and subsidies must be included.

A Family of Accounts

Beyond GDP lies a family of national income accounts. Of these, GNP (gross national product) has been referred to earlier.

Net National Product (NNP) is derived by subtracting *depreciation* from GNP. Depreciation, also known as capital consumption allowance—the allowance made for the consumption, or using up, of capital during the production process—is as much a cost of production as compensation of employees and, although it is not received by anyone as a payment, it adds to the final market value of goods and services.

National Income (NI) is the income received by the economy's productive resources—compensation of employees, rental income, interest payments, proprietors' income, and corporate profits. Additionally, indirect taxes minus subsidies, the surplus of government enterprises, and net business transfer payments are included. Unless there is a statistical discrepancy, National Income and Net National Product are equivalent measures.

Disposable Personal Income (after-tax income) is the income received by households after the payment of taxes and the deduction, by firms, of retained earnings. At the theoretical level, disposable personal income will be highly significant in subsequent chapters.

Table 3-1 gives the family of national income accounts, showing the relationships between them and assuming no statistical discrepancies in the calculations.

Table 3-1. A Summary of National Income Accounts

Gross Domestic Product	C + I + G + (EX – IM) OR National income + depreciation + net factor payments to the rest of the world
Gross National Product	GDP – net factor payments to the rest of the world
Net National Product	GNP – depreciation
National Income	Compensation of employees + rental income + interest payments + proprietors' income + corporate profits + three other minor items
Disposable Personal Income	National income – (personal income taxes + amount of national income not going to households)

Figure 3-4 presents the family of national income accounts graphically.

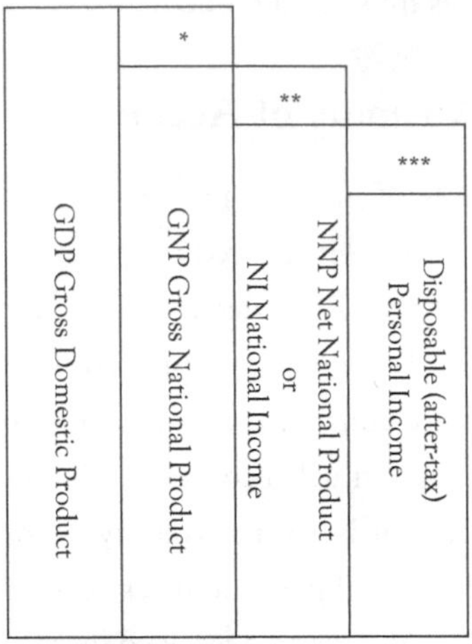

Figure 3-4. A depiction of the national income accounts.
* Net Factor Payments to the Rest of the World.
** Depreciation (Capital Consumption Allowance).
*** Personal income taxes + amount of national income not going to households + three other minor items.

Limitations of The GDP Concept:
An Incomplete Picture

We have already seen that the calculation of GDP requires art as well as science—whether a car is classified as consumption or investment requires some judgment. GDP has other limitations.

Market transactions: GDP is the "market value" of production—but some goods and services are never recorded in a market. There is no market for soldiers or police officers, for instance.

Household production is another potentially large area that is not counted—home preparation of meals is a valuable service but is not accounted for. As an economy develops, or with the increasing participation of women in the labor force, families become less reliant on homegrown food, home-cooked meals, and domestic production of items such as child care, clothing, toys, and home and yard maintenance. As a consequence, GDP will grow simply because activities will be recorded that previously were not. The actual level of production may not have changed—merely our measure of it.

The "underground economy" (also known as the informal sector) may be a significant area of economic activity that is not counted. In particular, in countries with high tax rates, there is a strong incentive to do work "off the books." In India, plagued with corruption, the underground economy is estimated to be worth perhaps 40 percent of the value of recorded GDP. In the United States, the underground economy may represent a more modest 10 percent of reported GDP. The services of a ticket scalper are unlikely to be included in GDP, nor is criminal activity, such as drug dealing or prostitution.

The housing sector is another troublesome area. The rent paid for the use of an apartment this year captures a service that has been provided and, accordingly, should be included in this year's GDP. But what of nonrental homes? Although a house may have been built many years ago, it continues to provide housing services just as much as does a rental apartment, but there is no "market" transaction. In this case, the Bureau of Economic Analysis imputes (makes up) a value for the services provided by the house.

Leisure and the quality of life: It is tempting to equate a rising GDP, or a rising per capita GDP (GDP per person), with greater well-being, but the limitations of the measure should dissuade us from accepting this conclusion too readily. GDP ignores the quality of our leisure time— our time with family and friends or in solitude may be unproductive in a material sense, although, to us, it may be highly prized. In fact, an increase in leisure time may indicate an improved quality of life but may cause a decline in GDP. GDP is an imperfect measure of social well-being.

Furthermore, increased production may cause "bads" such as pollution and ecological concerns that detract from our contentment. The increased stress and alienation, and the breakdown of family relationships, caused by a more rapid pace of activity ought to be set against the improvements wrought in our material well-being.

THINK IT THROUGH: In 1972, the Himalayan kingdom of Bhutan proposed a Gross National Happiness index, arguing that there's more to life than the accumulation of "stuff." More recently, a team headed by Nobel Laureate economist Joseph Stiglitz assessed GDP and, finding it to be a poor measure of well-being, proposed incorporating measures of factors that contribute to happiness, such as social relationships, political voice, education, and leisure.

Nominal GDP versus Real GDP: Nominal GDP is GDP measured in current-dollar terms whereas **real GDP** is GDP measured in constant-dollar terms—in other words, after having corrected for changes in the price level.

When we considered apple production in Pippin, using Figure 3-1, we concluded that the equilibrium market value of GDP was $1,800. This value resulted from multiplying the price of a bag of apples by the quantity traded, or price times quantity. If the price of apples remained constant, then any change in GDP would be due to changes in the level of production—nominal GDP and real GDP would be identical. Prices change, however. In an extreme case, if the price level increased enough, a decrease in apple production (and it's apple production that we wish to measure!) might be entirely masked by the price increase, causing nominal GDP to increase despite apple production having decreased. Our measure of production would be misleading.

Indexation: To control for the misleading effects of changing price levels, economists reduce nominal GDP values that are inflated by rising prices by applying a *GDP price deflator*. This is a highly technical issue but, briefly, the GDP price deflator measures how much the overall price level has changed and corrects the nominal GDP value by that amount in order to derive a real GDP figure, measured in constant-dollar terms, corrected for inflation. If, for example, the overall price level has risen by 10 percent since last year, then 10 percent should be knocked off the value of this year's nominal GDP in order to make the figures comparable.

THINK IT THROUGH: We have all heard seniors reminiscing about the times when "a dollar was worth a dollar," forgetting that a dollar was also more difficult to come by in those distant days. The need to be alert to the distinction between nominal and real values is significant in economics and we shall address the issue later in this book.

The Terminology of The Business Cycle: The Ups and Downs of the Economy

A primary reason for collecting GDP information is to permit comparisons—comparisons of the performance of the United States' economy over time, comparisons with the performance of other economies, and comparisons between performance before and after a policy initiative. The national income accounts were developed as a response to the Great Depression because there was an urgent need to assess economic circumstances and monitor the effectiveness of policy actions. That need endures today. One goal of government economic policy has been to smooth out business fluctuations and to have the economy stay on a more even keel.

Over the past century, the United States has experienced an underlying long-term expansion in aggregate production, measured in constant dollars, but there have been short-term fluctuations around that trend. These fluctuations show some regularity and are known as **business cycles**. Each business cycle, of which the Great Depression of the 1930s was the most profound, consists of four phases—a peak, a recession or slump, a trough, and an expansion or boom.

A stylized business cycle is shown in Figure 3-5. The peak and the trough are the two turning points, with the *peak* being the cycle at its maximum value (point A) and the *trough* at its minimum (point B).

Business cycles are not as regular as an unguarded glance at Figure 3-4 might suggest. They last varying spans of time and have turning points that are likely to be past before they are recognized. The duration of a business cycle is the period between peaks.

An *expansion* (between points B and A) occurs when real GDP grows. The upswing that began in mid-1991 and continued until early 2001 was the longest sustained period of growth recorded for the American economy.

As a general rule, an economy is considered to be in a *recession* (between points A and B) if real GDP shrinks for two successive

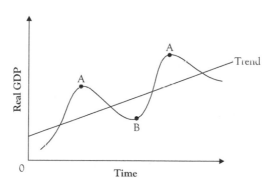

Figure 3-5. A stylized business cycle.

quarters—a mere slowdown in growth is not sufficient and, further, a growing economy *cannot* be in a recession. The Great Recession of 2008–2009 reached its turning point in the summer of 2009 when the economy began to expand. Despite high and unresponsive unemployment rates, an ailing housing market, a troubled financial sector, and widespread gloom among citizens that persisted for several more years, the Great Recession had ended.

Review: In Chapter 2, we developed the demand and supply model to allow us to examine the operation of individual markets. In Chapter 5, we expand that framework to include aggregate demand and aggregate supply, encompassing all the goods and services produced in the macroeconomy. In this chapter, we used the demand and supply model as a stepping stone from individual markets to the aggregate perspective, learning some of the vocabulary of macroeconomics on the way.

CHAPTER 4

The Twin Evils of Macroeconomics

By the end of this chapter you will be able to:

1. Define the labor force and give the official definition of employment.
2. Provide the official definition of the unemployment rate.
3. Describe the limitations of the unemployment rate statistic and outline the impact of the "discouraged worker effect" on official unemployment statistics.
4. Distinguish among the three types of unemployment—frictional, structural, and cyclical—and give examples of each.
5. Define the natural rate of unemployment and relate it to the concepts of full employment and the full-employment output level.
6. Describe the economic and social costs of unemployment.
7. Define inflation and the inflation rate.
8. Give the rationale behind demand-pull inflation and cost-push inflation.
9. Distinguish between anticipated and unanticipated inflation and indicate how their impacts on the economy differ.
10. Define hyperinflation and state its effects.
11. Define deflation and state its effects.
12. Outline the Quantity Theory and explain the view that inflation is a "monetary phenomenon."

A bank robber from the 1930s, Willie Sutton, allegedly was once asked why he robbed banks and was reported to have answered, "Because that's where the money is!" The story, sadly, is apocryphal but the lawlessness of Bonnie and Clyde, John Dillinger, and other gangsters was real. The Great Depression has left us enduring images of hardship—breadlines and soup kitchens, Hoovervilles and marches on Washington.

In Toledo, Ohio, at the depths of the Great Depression, the unemployment rate reached 80 percent. The bitter experiences of the Great Depression shaped the behavior of a generation.

Some years earlier, in the streets of Berlin in the aftermath of the Great War, children used thick wads of money as building blocks, because the German currency, the mark, was virtually worthless, as the economy suffered through a hyperinflation that saw prices doubling every 4 days. From this financial chaos, a small political party was spawned in 1923. Its leader was Adolf Hitler.

Unemployment and inflation are known as the "twin evils" of macroeconomics because they can threaten the very structure of society, if not controlled.

Chapter Preview: This chapter, the second of the largely definitional chapters, focuses on the twin evils of macroeconomics, namely unemployment and inflation. A working knowledge of these concepts is essential when we study policy formulation in subsequent chapters because they are of primary importance for policymakers when they seek to construct short-run stabilization measures. We learn about the causes and effects of unemployment, the limitations of the main measure that is reported, and consider the idea that the economy has a "natural rate" of unemployment. We then turn our attention to the causes and consequences of inflation, a consideration of hyperinflation and deflation, and round things off by introducing the Quantity Theory of Money—one of the most venerable of economic theories.

Unemployment: Its Measurement and Its Causes and Consequences

In a speech in 1967, Dr. Martin Luther King, Jr. poignantly described unemployment as a form of psychological murder, depriving, as it does, the worker of life, liberty, and the pursuit of happiness—even the right to exist. Certainly, many of us define ourselves by our jobs and by the function we fulfill in society and, therefore, it is a great shock to lose that function, to say nothing of the associated paycheck. Our study of unemployment is the study of an issue important to all citizens.

The Unemployment Rate

The **unemployment rate** is the percentage of the labor force that is unemployed. Not all members of the population are part of the labor force, however. In the United States, the **labor force** includes those persons of working age (16 years of age or older) who either have a job or have been actively seeking a job during the previous 4 weeks. Those who are not actively looking for a job or cannot accept a job are excluded. Those such as retirees, students, stay-at-home parents, or institutionalized inmates are not counted as participating workers and are considered to be *not in the labor force*. Workers, discouraged by their inability to find employment, who have given up the job search are also excluded from the labor force and these *discouraged workers* are classified as *not in the labor force*.

The *employed* include any person 16 years of age or older who works 1 hour or more per week for pay, or works 15 or more hours a week without pay in a family enterprise, or has a job but is temporarily absent from work, with or without pay (such as on furlough or through illness).

The **labor-force participation rate** is the percentage of the population aged 16 or older that is in the labor force. In the United States, the overall participation rate has risen slightly (from 59 percent to 64 percent) since the end of the Second World War. This statistic, however, masks profound changes in the labor market. The male participation rate has shown a steady decline since the 1940s. It was about 86 percent in 1950 and has fallen by approximately 3 percent each decade since until in 2010 it stood at 72 percent. The female participation rate tells a quite different story, starting in 1950 at nearly one-third of the female population, reaching one-half by 1978, and rising to a peak of 60 percent by the end of the century. During the Great Recession and its aftermath, both male and female participation rates have sagged as workers have returned to college or otherwise left the labor force.

THINK IT THROUGH: The population of Pippin is 300,000, of which 180,000 are aged 16 or older. Of this 180,000, there are 140,000 who have jobs and 40,000 who do not; 13,000 are unemployed but actively seeking jobs, and there are 27,000 who have given up the job search in frustration. What is the labor-force participation rate? The unemployment rate?

The labor-force participation rate is 85 percent. Of the 300,000 citizens, only 180,000 are of an age that qualifies them to be in the labor force. Of the 180,000, 140,000 are employed, and an additional 13,000 are unemployed (without jobs, seeking work). There are, then, 153,000 workers in the labor force—the remaining 27,000 discouraged workers have dropped out of the labor force.

The unemployment rate is 8.49 percent—there are 13,000 workers out of a labor force of 153,000.

There are gender, racial, and age differences in unemployment rates, with women having lower unemployment rates than men (a recent reversal of the previous pattern), whites having higher rates than Asian Americans, but lower rates than Latinos or African Americans, and teenagers typically experiencing the most severe difficulty in securing employment. There are regional differences too, with heavily industrialized states faring poorly due to increasing foreign competition. It should be no surprise to find that, during the Great Recession, unemployment rose sharply in states that were heavily dependent on the production of consumer durable goods such as cars and furniture because, during hard times, the purchase of such goods can easily be postponed.

THINK IT THROUGH: Go to the website of the Bureau of Labor Statistics (http://www.bls.gov). What is the most recent national unemployment rate? What is the unemployment rate for the demographic group that you feel best fits you (based, for example, on age, sex, and ethnicity)? Why is it lower (or higher) than the national average?

THINK IT THROUGH: Can you suggest any reasons why female workers have lower unemployment rates than comparable male workers? In earlier times, this relationship was reversed, with lower unemployment rates for bread-winning males and higher unemployment rates for marginalized females.

Discouraged workers: To the extent that unemployed workers become discouraged in their job search and stop looking, the reported unemployment rate is an underestimate. In some sense, this would not be a significant issue if the size of the *discouraged worker effect* remained stable over the business cycle, but this is unlikely to be the case. Workers are more likely to become discouraged, cease seeking a job, and, consequently, drop out of the official unemployment numbers during a recession or slowdown in the economy, when jobs are hard to come by. During an optimistic, expanding economy, with many job openings, the job seeker is likely to persevere for longer. Accordingly, the magnitude of the underestimate in the unemployment rate should be greater during a recession than during an expansion.

Workers who are employed part-time but who wish to be employed full-time are, in some sense, unemployed (or, at least, underemployed) but are counted as employed. The presence of underemployed workers, it has been argued, ought to be recognized in the unemployment statistics and, currently, the Bureau of Labor Statistics reports additional measures of unemployment.

The official and widely reported unemployment rate is known as U-3. U-4 incorporates an estimate of discouraged workers, while U-6 expands the definition of unemployment to include the underemployed and those workers who would like a job and can work, but who haven't recently been seeking employment.

In September 2004, the unemployment rate (U-3) was 5.4 percent but, had discouraged workers been included, it would have been 9.4 percent. This difference represented 4.5 million discouraged or underemployed workers. As the economy emerged from the Great Recession in October 2009, the unemployment rate (U-3) was 9.9 percent, but the broadest measure (U-6) stood at 17.5 percent.

Types of Unemployment

Economists have identified three types of unemployment, based on the primary cause of the unemployment—frictional, structural, and cyclical unemployment.

Frictional unemployment, which is usually thought to involve perhaps 2 or 3 percent of the labor force at any time, is caused by movement—movement between jobs or between regions, transition from college to a position. The frictionally unemployed worker has desirable job skills but, as yet, no job. A college student, with a desirable degree in hand, and interviewing for or considering job offers, is frictionally unemployed. In a normal labor market, frictional unemployment is very short-lived—such qualified applicants will be snapped up quickly by enthusiastic employers.

Structural unemployment is also thought to involve 2 or 3 percent of the labor force at any time. It is caused by changes that result in the decline in particular industries and, therefore, a decline in the demand for the skills used in those industries. The changes could be due to technological innovation, shifts in tastes, increased foreign competition or, perhaps, legal changes. The decline in the tobacco industry through changes in tastes, the decline in the textiles and furniture industries through foreign competition, and the decline in the demand for telemarketers because of legal restrictions are examples of structural unemployment.

Structural unemployment differs from frictional unemployment in that structurally unemployed workers have few marketable skills and require retraining. Because of this, these workers are likely to be unemployed for a longer period of time. During economic hard times, such as the Great Recession, structurally unemployed workers may comprise a large part of those who suffer long-term unemployment (more than 26 weeks). In such circumstances, there is a great danger that these workers may be unemployed so long that they become untrainable.

Perhaps surprisingly, economists argue that frictional and structural unemployment are "good" forms of unemployment, in that they are a consequence of a dynamic, changing labor market. To be sure, we wish the duration of unemployment to be minimized—through effective dissemination of information about job openings for the frictionally unemployed (so that worker and job can be matched up quickly), and through retraining or relocation for the structurally unemployed—but some such unemployment is unavoidable in a healthy economy.

The rate of unemployment that is present when the economy is operating at its "healthy" level is known as the **natural rate of unemployment**. The natural rate of unemployment is the sum of the frictional rate and the structural rate of unemployment. Given the estimates for the frictional and structural rates, it is reasonable to estimate the natural rate as lying between 4 percent and 6 percent. Note that the actual unemployment rate may lie above or below the natural rate of unemployment. In the early 2000s, the national unemployment rate dipped below 4 percent and, as a consequence, labor markets were extremely constrained.

Cyclical unemployment is due to job loss caused by a general slowdown in the overall economy—the downturn in the business cycle. This is the "bad" unemployment that macroeconomic stabilization policy seeks to prevent or control. Any unemployment rate greater than the natural rate of unemployment is due to cyclical unemployment.

THINK IT THROUGH: The natural rate of unemployment is an important, if imprecise, concept. A normally functioning economy has some excess capacity and some rate of unemployment. It is unreasonable to expect the unemployment rate to be zero. However, the natural rate of unemployment has increased gradually in the decades following the Second World War. Can you suggest why?

Factors causing a rise in the natural rate of unemployment include increasing female participation in the labor force, reducing the urgent need for an unemployed "bread winner" to find another job, a growing rate of technological change, more fickle consumer preferences, and greater overseas competition.

THINK IT THROUGH (MORE): In the mid-1990s, economists predicted that the natural rate of unemployment would continue to rise into the new century. On the contrary, it began to decrease. Can you suggest why?

The major reason for the decline in the natural rate of unemployment has been demographic—the aging baby boomers. As this bulge in the labor force grew older and closer to retirement, frictional unemployment among the boomers decreased—as senior-level employees, comparatively few would seek to change careers, location, or move into the labor force. With age, ambition is trumped by security.

Full Employment and the Full-Employment Output Level

The 1946 Employment Act accepted government responsibility for promoting maximum employment, or **full employment**. In the early 1960s, President Kennedy pledged to achieve a target of 4 percent unemployment, this being the unemployment rate at which the economy was felt to be at its maximum sustainable level of production, or **full-employment output level**. At the full-employment output level, 96 percent of the labor force would be employed.

The Kennedy Administration's target proved to be overoptimistic and was abandoned in the 1970s, although no new numerical target was offered. Because full employment is really the reverse of the natural rate of unemployment, currently it lies between 94 and 96 percent employment. The full-employment output level is also known as *potential GDP*.

The Consequences of Unemployment

Lost output: Each day a worker does not work, society bears a cost—the lost production that worker could have created. **Okun's Law** (in truth, a rule of thumb, not a precise relationship) states that, for each percentage point increase in the unemployment rate over the natural rate of unemployment, there is approximately a two percent decrease in GDP.

In August 2012, with full-employment GDP estimated at $14.2 trillion, the national unemployment rate was at 8.3 percent, and assuming the natural rate to be about 5.0 percent, unemployment would be 3.3 percent above the natural rate. According to Okun's Law, the value of lost production due to avoidable (cyclical) unemployment would be $937.2 billion per year.

Stress and Psychological Costs: Long-term unemployment has been likened to the death of a spouse in terms of stress. Certainly, recessions are linked to psychological problems, substance abuse, broken homes, higher rates of suicide, stress-related illnesses, and violent crime.

In addition, there is a decline in job skills and a loss of the work ethic with prolonged periods of unemployment—one loses one's edge.

Social Divisiveness: The burden of unemployment is distributed unequally, falling more heavily on the shoulders of the young, the poorly educated, and low-skilled workers. Ethnic minorities, such as Latinos and African Americans, suffer a greater impact than whites, and this is true in good times or in bad. For example, in 2004, when the national unemployment rate was only 5.5 percent (extremely close to the natural rate), it was 2.7 percent for college graduates but 8.5 percent for high-school dropouts, 3.1 percent for married men but 31.7 percent for African American male teenagers.

Inflation: Its Causes and Consequences

In 1974, in a speech to a joint session of Congress, President Gerald Ford described inflation as "Public Enemy number one," and went on to assert that, unless whipped, inflation would destroy the United States, and the liberties, property, and national pride of its citizens. From this, we can infer that inflation was seen then as the 1970s equivalent of terrorism. Like unemployment, inflation threatens to unravel the fabric of the economy but, unlike unemployment, whose burden is borne by a particular group, namely the unemployed and their families, inflation's effects range more widely across the economy.

Comment: The word "whipped" springs out of the previous paragraph. President Ford's speech was initiating a program—*Whip Inflation Now*, or WIN—to combat inflation, which was running at 11 percent that year.

The economy is like a well-tuned and intricate machine, with our money supply acting like the oil that facilitates the movement and articulation of the many parts. Money fulfills several key functions: as the medium of exchange (we are able to conduct transactions because money is universally acceptable), as a store of value (we are willing to accept money because we expect it to retain its value until we, in turn, wish to spend it), as a unit of account (the dollar is our yardstick in gauging value), and as a means of deferred payment (we borrow and lend based on the assurance that funds repaid will be equivalent in value to funds loaned). Inflation, which upsets all these expectations, is like a handful of grit thrown into the economy's lubricating system.

Inflation, by eroding the purchasing power of the dollar, undermines all of the functions that money fulfills, making us less willing to accept currency in exchange for tangible goods and services; less willing to store dollars and, instead, more keen to spend and to dispose of them rapidly; less able to assess the value of items; and more reluctant to enter into loan agreements.

Because, over the past two decades, inflation has been tamed, running at a seemingly innocuous 2 to 3 percent each year, it may be difficult to understand why inflation is one of the "twin evils." However, consider, for a moment, gas prices, and the uncertainty caused by their daily fluctuations. It is challenging to determine when one should buy and, when filling the tank, to wonder whether it would have been worthwhile to have shopped around some more. There is a sense that there might have been a better price at the next gas station. Take that sense of unease and multiply it by all the goods and services that can be bought and some idea of the corrosive effects of inflation may be gained.

The Inflation Rate

Inflation is a sustained increase in the overall, or aggregate, price level whereas **deflation** is a sustained decrease in the aggregate price level. The **inflation rate** (symbolized in economics by the Greek letter, π) is the percentage rate of growth in the aggregate price level from one period to the next. The Consumer Price Index (CPI) is the most popular measure used to assess the aggregate price level (although other indices—such as the *GDP price deflator* referred to in Chapter 3, or the *Producer Price Index*—are also used).

If, for example, the CPI was 110.0 last year and 115.5 this year, then the inflation rate over the period would be 5 percent, calculated:

$$\text{Inflation rate } (\pi) = [(115.5 - 110.0)/110.0] \times 100\% = 5 \text{ percent}$$

Disinflation refers to a situation where the aggregate price level is rising, but the rate of inflation is decreasing. If, for example, next year's inflation rate was only 2 percent, then the economy would be experiencing disinflation.

The Causes of Inflation

Initially, we shall consider the short-run causes of inflation, postponing until the end of this chapter an examination of the long-term cause of sustained increases in the aggregate price level. To understand the two broad *short-run* causes of inflation, let us think back to the apple-producing nation of Pippin that we met in Chapter 3, as shown in Figure 4-1.

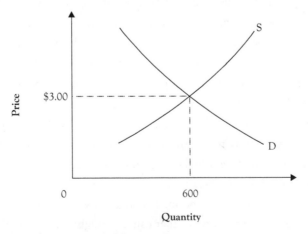

Figure 4-1. The economy of Pippin.

In terms of this diagram, Pippin's aggregate price level will increase if either the demand for apples increases or if the supply of apples decreases. Inflation caused by rising demand is termed **demand-pull inflation** whereas inflation caused by a decrease in supply is termed **cost-push inflation.**

Demand-pull inflation: The early Keynesian economists, focusing primarily on the demand-side of the economy, referred to inflation as a situation where there was "too much money chasing too few goods."

If an economy's inflation is caused mainly by rising demand, then we would also expect to see rising production and a decreasing unemployment rate. Statistical evidence in support of the presence of demand-pull inflation was published in the late 1950s, when the **Phillips Curve** showed an apparently durable negative relationship between the inflation rate and the unemployment rate. A representative Phillips Curve is shown in Figure 4-2.

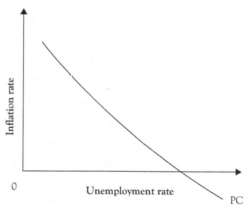

Figure 4-2. A representative Phillips Curve.

The Phillips Curve and Okun's Law, which also posited reliable relationships within the economy, were used by the Kennedy Administration to help construct policy options. Unfortunately, almost as soon as it was discovered, the Phillips Curve relationship between the inflation rate and the unemployment rate began to fail. As we shall see in future chapters, it is, at best, a short-run relationship and is dependent on a stable production sector. In the face of supply-side shocks, such as the OPEC oil price hike of the mid-1970s, the relationship disintegrated.

Cost-push inflation: If supply is reduced, perhaps because powerful monopoly elements in the economy, such as OPEC or a strong union sector, have forced up resource costs then, even without changes in the demand side of the economy, the aggregate price level can increase. This is cost-push inflation.

If resource costs increase and supply is reduced, then, by considering Figure 4-1, we can see that the aggregate price level will increase and, simultaneously, production will decrease. With declining production, we would expect rising unemployment. This combination of a slowing or stagnating economy, a faltering labor market with increasing unemployment, and inflation is known as **stagflation**.

Comment: The underlying causes of inflation, and its cure, are one of the central issues in macroeconomics, and one that we shall return to in subsequent chapters.

The Consequences of Inflation

To understand the effects of inflation we must first distinguish between unanticipated inflation and inflation that is fully anticipated.

Unanticipated inflation: One major problem with inflation is that it is unpredictable—it takes us by surprise. At the moment, even as a student of macroeconomics and an informed participant in our economy, it is highly unlikely that you know what the current inflation rate is. No one does. But, every time you trade currency for goods at the grocery store or sign a contract for future delivery, you are gambling on the future value of the dollar. If your expectations are incorrect, then you may gain or lose as a consequence.

Redistributional effects
Certain groups within the economy gain and others lose when the actual inflation rate is higher than the expected rate, causing a redistribution of spending power.

Let us assume that inflation unexpectedly differs from the predicted rate. Those on fixed incomes or pensions tend to lose because those incomes were established with an underestimate of inflation in mind. Indeed, any signatory to a contract—wage, rental lease—risks a loss due to unanticipated inflation. To correct for this inflation penalty, economies have introduced devices such as index-linking of benefits and cost-of-living adjustments (COLAs).

Lenders lose and borrowers gain during unexpectedly high inflation. When a loan contract is negotiated, the lender must determine how much of an interest payment she will require to fully compensate her for the inconvenience and risk involved in giving up control of her funds. This reward that is sufficient compensation for the inconvenience and risk she bears is the **real interest rate** (r). The inflation that occurs during the period of the loan is an additional cost in the sense that it erodes the value of the repaid currency. The lender must predict the rate of inflation during the period of the loan and add that inflation premium onto the interest rate that she charges—π^e is the expected inflation rate. The interest rate charged is the **market** or **nominal interest rate** (i) and it includes the real interest rate and the markup based on the expected inflation rate:

$$i = r + \pi^e$$

If the real interest rate (r) is 5 percent and inflation is expected to run at 3 percent, then the nominal interest should be 8 percent. If, however, the inflation prediction falls short, and the actual inflation rate is, say, 6 percent during the loan period, then the lender's real reward is reduced to 2 percent. Unexpectedly high inflation hurts lenders and, by the same token, savers, who lend deposits to banks but, because they are paying a lower-than-expected real interest rate, borrowers benefit.

THINK IT THROUGH: Inflation reached 13.5 percent in 1980. During the double-digit and unpredictable inflation of the period, both borrowers and lenders naturally were reluctant to enter into long-term contracts, such as 30-year fixed-rate mortgages—the risks of costly miscalculations were just too high. Savings and loan associations struggled to attract customers. As a consequence, the Garn-St. Germain Depository Institutions Act (1982) permitted the development of adjustable-rate mortgages (ARMs). Can you think of other examples where markets have adjusted their procedures to soften the effects of unanticipated inflation?

Output effects: Because unanticipated inflation creates winners and losers, it also can create hostility. A worker who may be willing to do "a fair day's work for a fair day's pay" may feel that he is not receiving a fair day's pay (although he might be). This sense of injustice may lead to more tardiness or absenteeism, pilfering, shirking, or, if more pronounced, vandalism, strikes, and industrial action. In any of these cases, output suffers.

In addition, when the rate of inflation is variable and unpredictable, because of the risk of making "bad" deals, negotiators may try to compensate by overestimating wage claims and price increases. Adding this safety margin fuels the fires of inflation.

Shoeleather costs: Rising prices reduce the value of funds held in wallets—the effect is sometimes called an inflation tax. To reduce the size of the effect, depositors may choose to hold less cash and keep more funds in interest-bearing bank accounts that, to some degree, offset the loss on purchasing power caused by inflation.

THINK IT THROUGH: You need $400 in cash to see you through the month. Instead of visiting a bank to withdraw $400 at the start of the month, it may be more appealing to visit each week, withdrawing $100 each time, to "top up" your wallet. This keeps a larger portion of your funds as interest-bearing assets.

Although appealing, this tactic imposes additional "shoeleather" costs—it requires more planning and time spent going to the bank and, unless there is a fairly predictable flow of transactions, some additional risk and inconvenience in purchasing.

Fully anticipated inflation: Suppose everyone in the economy knew for certain that the inflation rate would be maintained at 10 percent this year and for all foreseeable years into the future. Would such fully anticipated inflation impose any costs on society? In fact, it would, because of the presence of menu costs. *Menu costs* are the administrative costs of keeping pace with inflation—reissuing catalogs, changing store price tags and raising magazine subscriptions, reprinting menus, and so on.

THINK IT THROUGH: Menu costs are somewhat akin to our practice of moving the clocks backward and forwards—"spring forward, fall back"— a bit of a nuisance, especially when not totally synchronized.

Allowing for some menu costs, a low rate of fully anticipated inflation is not much of a problem, particularly if the economy has incorporated indexation practices. Despite some inconvenience and confusion, rational economic behavior can continue.

Hyperinflation

If you owned the entire value of Hungary's GDP in 1944 then, by July 1946, the monetary value of those funds would have been able to buy you two shirts. Hungary's postwar hyperinflation was the worst ever recorded, with prices doubling every 15 hours! Hyperinflation occurs when the aggregate price level is rising very rapidly. There is no neat dividing line between a condition of inflation and one of hyperinflation, but an economy experiencing a triple-digit inflation rate is certainly in the grips of hyperinflation. In addition to the costs associated with inflation, hyperinflation imposes additional stresses. The effects of extreme inflation are, themselves, extreme.

Loss of confidence in the currency: With galloping prices, and because financial authorities may make sudden changes in the status of existing currency, there is little advantage to holding currency. *Barter* (trading goods for goods), which in stable times is usually considered to be inefficient, becomes the preferred method of transaction. The advantages gained from having a financial system are swept away.

Cost of currency replacement: During the Bolivian hyperinflation of the mid-1980s, it was necessary to replace and increase the stock of currency, which was printed in Germany. New currency became Bolivia's third largest import.

Speculation and hoarding: During hyperinflation, an item bought today will sell for a higher price tomorrow. *Speculation*—buying now in the expectation of selling at a profit in the future—becomes an attractive option. An asset that is increasing in value is substituted for currency, which is declining in value.

Hoarding is another aspect of the same phenomenon. It is a rational response to rapidly rising prices to hoard real goods and shun currency. As a result, the demand for goods is increased and their availability is reduced, adding further inflationary pressures.

Deflation

When there is a sustained decline in the aggregate price level, that is, when the inflation rate is negative, the economy is said to be experiencing

deflation. It might seem that, if inflation is a macroeconomic "evil," then deflation must be beneficial but, in fact, deflation poses threats of its own to the economy. Certainly, menu costs and the output and redistributional effects of inflation are still present, but with winners and losers reversed.

If there are decreases in the prices of assets such as housing and stocks, then consumers, feeling less well-off than before, may cut back in spending, causing an economic slowdown, unemployment, and lost production. Further, with substantial decreases in the prices of assets used as collateral for loans, financial institutions may see their liabilities exceed their assets and, therefore, become insolvent.

Inflation—Always and Everywhere a Monetary Phenomenon?

Nobel Laureate Milton Friedman asserted, "Inflation is always and everywhere a monetary phenomenon." By this, he meant that the root cause of sustained increases in the aggregate price level is expansion in the supply of money. There is much evidence to support Friedman's view that, without enabling increases in the money supply, inflation could still occur, but would be short-run in nature. To be sure, surges in consumer confidence or a bad harvest may trigger demand-pull inflation or cost-push inflation, but an ongoing increase in the aggregate price level seems inextricably linked to money expansion.

The role of the government: Roman emperors were fond of clipping coins and other forms of currency debasement. Almost every one of a hoard of 14,000 silver Roman coins found in 1992 at Hoxne, England had been clipped. By clipping coins, or reducing their size or silver content, emperors could stretch the same amount of precious metal to issue more coins. With more coins to buy the same amount of goods, prices rose.

This is a familiar pattern. Especially following expensive wars, governments have a habit of overusing their printing presses. As an example, after the Great War, the Weimar Republic printed increasingly large quantities of German marks in order to buy the foreign currency necessary to meet its reparation obligations. Hyperinflation ensued.

The Quantity Theory of Money: The Quantity Theory, which we explore in more detail in later chapters, is based on the Equation of

Exchange, an equation stating that the *quantity of money* (M) times the *velocity* at which that money circulates (V) is equal to the *aggregate price level* (P) times the *quantity of real goods* (y).

$$M \times V = P \times y$$

The value (P × y) is nominal GDP and y is real GDP. Put simply, the Equation of Exchange states that the money supply will circulate enough times to purchase the market value of production, that is, nominal GDP. If the economy of Pippin has $200, the aggregate price level is $3, and real output is 600 bags of apples (nominal GDP is $1,800), then each dollar will, on average, be used nine times.

$$M \times V = P \times y$$
$$\$200 \times 9 = \$3 \times 600$$

The Equation of Exchange becomes an economic theory—the Quantity Theory—when behavioral assumptions are imposed upon it. In its "strong" form (which is our focus at this point), the proponents of the Quantity Theory postulate that the velocity of circulation is a constant. Further, if we assume that the economy tends to be close to full employment and that our production decisions are influenced by real, rather than purely monetary, factors, then the level of real GDP is not easily adjusted. If the money supply increases from $200 to $400, then nominal GDP will increase to $3,600 because, although real GDP (y) does not change, the aggregate price level doubles.

$$\$400 \times 9 = \$6 \times 600$$

The additional money flowing through the economy is the reason the aggregate price level rises and, therefore, is the cause of the inflation. Is inflation "always and everywhere" a monetary phenomenon? No, but, in country after country, the long-run relationship between rates of growth in money supply and rates of growth in the aggregate price level is sufficiently close to permit almost all economists to agree that *sustained* inflation is a purely monetary phenomenon.

This conclusion seems to rest on the dubious assertion that the velocity of circulation is constant but, in fact, the Classical economists made the more reasonable claim that velocity does change but changes slowly. Even with a slowly evolving velocity of circulation, the general insight of the Quantity Theory—that sustained inflation is due to excessive expansion in the money supply—is sound.

There is a useful *proportional form* of the Quantity Theory that, instead of looking at the levels of variables, considers percentage rates of change in variables. It can be expressed as

$$\text{percentage change in M} + \text{percentage change in V}$$
$$= \text{percentage change in P} + \text{percentage change in y}$$

If we believe that real GDP typically increases at a rate of 3 percent each year and that velocity increases (perhaps because of a more efficient financial system) at 1 percent per year then, given a desired target for the inflation rate (for example, 2 percent), the policymakers' optimal rate of growth in the money supply is specified—4 percent. Given those historical "facts" and the inflation target, the controls of monetary policy should be set to achieve a stable rate of change in the money supply and, following that, not be tampered with.

Review: In this chapter we have defined and examined the causes and consequences of the two major macroeconomic policy concerns—unemployment and inflation. With respect to unemployment, we have seen that the presence of discouraged workers renders the standard measure less accurate. Turning to inflation, we have discovered that, although other factors may wield a short-term influence, excessive money supply growth is the predominant cause of a sustained rise in the aggregate price level.

You may have noticed that there seems to be an important distinction between long-run and short-run effects. This is an important debate in macroeconomics and we will see more of it in Chapter 5.

CHAPTER 5

Aggregate Demand and Aggregate Supply

By the end of this chapter you will be able to:

1. Define aggregate demand and explain why the aggregate demand curve has a negative slope.
2. Identify seven factors that can shift the position of the aggregate demand curve.
3. Describe how aggregate demand is affected by fiscal and monetary policy actions.
4. Distinguish between the short run and the long run.
5. Explain the slope and location of the long-run aggregate supply curve.
6. Explain the slope of the short-run aggregate supply curve and its relationship to the long-run aggregate supply curve.
7. Identify the factors that shift the long-run and short-run aggregate supply curves.
8. Explain how the economy achieves short-run equilibrium.
9. Outline the operation of the self-correcting mechanism and its relevance to the achievement of long-run equilibrium.
10. Distinguish the beliefs of the Classical economists from those of the Keynesians.
11. Describe the role of the expenditure multiplier in the macroeconomy.

In this chapter you may gain some insight into yourself and your own beliefs. Do you favor dealing with short-run problems as they arise because "in the long run we're all dead," or do you subscribe to the view that we should "stay the course," not be distracted by short-term troubles, and let long-term objectives dominate our actions? Each is a valid preference—there is no one-size-fits-all answer.

The great majority of car drivers believe that they are better drivers than the great majority of car drivers! Each of us believes that we are above average because each of us tends to overvalue those skills in which we are most proficient and to discount those skills in which we are least proficient. Fast drivers believe that the ability to drive fast reveals mastery, whereas slow drivers believe that prudence and consideration for other road users are the true mark of the "good" driver. We each have biases that influence our perception of the world. So with economics.

Chapter Preview: In Chapter 1 we discovered the benefits of exchange and, in Chapter 2, elaborated that analysis by developing the demand and supply model. Chapters 3 and 4 have given us some of the measures used to monitor economic performance. In this chapter we turn our attention to our main tool of macroeconomic analysis—aggregate demand and aggregate supply, or the ADAS model.

Aggregate Demand

In this section we define aggregate demand, outline the appearance of the aggregate demand (AD) curve and the reasons for that appearance, and consider the factors that can shift the position of the curve.

Definition of Aggregate Demand and the Aggregate Demand Curve

Aggregate demand is the total amount of intended spending on a nation's final goods and services by its households, firms, the government sector, and foreigners. The **aggregate demand curve** depicts the negative relationship between the quantity of aggregate output (real GDP) demanded and the aggregate price level (P) as shown in Figure 5-1.

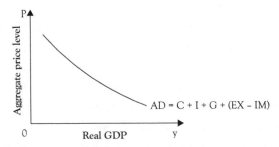

Figure 5-1. The aggregate demand curve.

We discussed real GDP (y) in Chapter 3, and the aggregate price level (P) in Chapter 4, but let us review. Real GDP is our measure of aggregate output, measured in constant dollars. The aggregate price level is our measure of the overall average price of goods and services, as measured by the Consumer Price Index or the GDP price deflator.

Composition of Aggregate Demand: From Chapter 3 and the Expenditure Approach to calculating GDP, recall that the demand for goods and services is composed of expenditures by households (consumption, C), businesses (investment, I), government (government purchases, G), and foreigners (net exports, EX – IM). Aggregate demand, then, is composed of these elements:

$$AD = C + I + G + (EX - IM)$$

What the AD curve *isn't*: Although the AD curve looks very similar to the demand curves we have seen in previous chapters it is different in significant ways—it's not just a "big" demand curve.

Note that, on the vertical axis, "price" is the aggregate price level (P). In the "demand for oranges" diagram, the price of one good (oranges) is on the price axis—here, it's the price of *all* goods and services in the macroeconomy. The distinction is important. In Chapter 2, when we considered the behavior of quantity demanded in a single market such as the market for oranges, we assumed that, if the price of oranges were to rise, then all other factors would be held constant—the *ceteris paribus* assumption. A change in the price of oranges would occur in isolation, without changes in income, wealth, prices of other goods, and so on. As the price of oranges rises, consumers become less willing and less able to buy oranges and a negative relationship between price and quantity demanded is revealed.

Comment: In a microeconomics course, two effects—the substitution effect and the income effect—are identified as influencing the behavior of consumers, and, since the AD curve *looks* like the demand curves we have seen before, it is tempting to apply the same logic when wishing to explain demand behavior. In this case, however, it is incorrect to extend the logic applicable in one market to overall macro demand.

The *ceteris paribus* assumption does not apply at the macroeconomic level because, as the aggregate price level rises, not all prices change in the same direction or at the same rate and also because changing prices reflect changing income. If, as appears to be the case from Figure 5-1, the AD curve has a negative slope, then different reasons will have to be found to explain it.

The Slope of the Aggregate Demand Curve

We can identify three reasons for the aggregate demand curve's negative slope. In each case, we examine the effect on quantity demanded of an increase in the aggregate price level. For practice, consider a decrease in the aggregate price level and see if you can reverse the argument.

The Wealth Effect (Real Balance Effect): An increase in the overall price level causes a decrease in household wealth. Certainly, with higher prices, there is a decline in the real value of the money balances of consumers (the dollars in one's wallet and one's other assets that are fixed in money terms, such as the savings in a bank account)—those dollars are worth less as the price level increases. In addition, other assets—such as the funds in one's 401k or the value of one's house—may fail to keep pace with the overall rise in prices. If so, households become less well off and, with less real wealth, consumption spending will decrease. An increase in the aggregate price level reduces consumption spending.

The Real Interest Rate Effect: An increase in the overall price level means that there is a greater demand for cash with which to finance transactions. An increase in the demand for a product, such as oranges, causes an increase in the price of that good. In a similar way, an increase in the demand for money increases the "price" of money. The interest rate is the "price" of money. Accordingly, an increase in the aggregate price level would cause the interest rate (the real cost of borrowing) to increase. Because higher interest rates discourage borrowing by firms for investment projects and by households for consumption expenditures, we would expect to see less consumption and investment spending as the aggregate price level increases.

Comment: An alternative way to interpret this effect, with respect to households, is to realize that the interest rate is the "reward" for saving.

The incentive to save increases with the interest rate and, as we know, saving and consumption are two aspects of the same decision—as we save more of our income, we spend less of it.

THINK IT THROUGH: Figure 5-2 shows two aggregate demand curves, AD_1 and AD_2.

One of the curves is that of a country (Country A) whose citizens follow the adage "never a borrower nor a lender be," and who avoid credit transactions whereas the other AD curve is that of a country (Country B) whose citizens indulge in a great many credit transactions. Suppose the

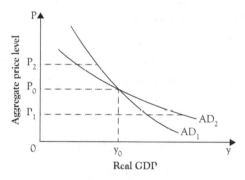

Figure 5-2. The slope of the AD curve.

economy's aggregate price level is initially P_0 and that it decreases to P_1. Focusing purely on the real interest rate effect, can you reason out which curve goes with which country?

The AD curve, AD_1, is associated with Country A. The real interest rate effect tells us that, as the aggregate price level decreases, the real interest rate will decrease. In Country A (where little borrowing occurs), this will have little impact on households or firms and quantity demanded will increase only modestly. In Country B, however, the same decrease in interest rate will prompt greater increases in borrowing, consumption, and investment, and quantity demanded will increase more aggressively. The stronger the real interest rate effect, the flatter the AD curve.

The Foreign Trade Effect: An increase in the aggregate price level for American goods encourages domestic purchasers to buy foreign goods whose prices have now become relatively cheaper. Imports will increase, reducing the quantity of American goods demanded. Simultaneously, exports will decrease as foreigners are put off by the comparatively higher prices of American goods. An increase in the aggregate price level reduces net exports.

THINK IT THROUGH: Consider Figure 5-2 once more. Let us suppose that one of the two curves is that of a country that is very "open" to foreign trade (the Netherlands), whereas the other AD curve is that of a country that is comparatively self-contained and experiences very little foreign trade (Nepal). Suppose the economy's aggregate price level is initially P_0 and that it increases to P_2. Focusing only on the foreign trade effect, can you reason out which curve goes with which country?

The steeper AD curve, AD_1, is associated with Nepal and the flatter AD curve, AD_2, is associated with the Netherlands. The foreign trade effect states that, as the aggregate price level increases, net exports will decrease. In Nepal, the effect on aggregate demand will be slight but, in the Netherlands, a substantial contraction in aggregate demand will take place. The stronger the foreign trade effect, the flatter the AD curve.

Factors That Can Shift the Aggregate Demand Curve

The three effects just described explain why the aggregate demand curve is negatively sloped. What, though, may cause the AD curve to shift position? Except for a change in the aggregate price level or real GDP, anything that causes intended consumption, investment, government spending, or net exports to change will cause the AD curve to shift position—to the right for an increase in demand, as shown in Figure 5-3, and to the left for a decrease. We identify seven major factors.

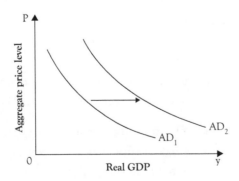

Figure 5-3. An increase in aggregate demand.

Government Policy: Fiscal and monetary policies are the two broad branches of government economic policy. Fiscal policy is intended to manipulate the economy through changes in government spending and net taxes, and monetary policy operates through changes in the financial sector. An *expansionary* policy is intended to make the economy grow by shifting the AD curve to the right whereas a *contractionary* policy's intent is to dampen down economic activity by shifting the AD curve to the left.

Fiscal Policy: Government spending (G) *is* one of the components of aggregate demand—an increase in government spending will shift the aggregate demand to the right. **Net taxes** (T), or *taxes minus transfers*, are taxes paid to the government by firms and households less transfer payments received by households. A decrease in net taxes (either a decrease in taxes or an increase in transfer payments) would boost disposable income and encourage increased consumption, shifting the AD curve to the right. Further, the introduction of a policy such as an investment-tax credit, or reduced taxes on corporate income, would stimulate additional investment spending. Decreasing government spending or increasing net taxes will shift the AD curve to the left. In Chapter 6, we consider fiscal policy actions in more detail.

Monetary Policy: An increase in the supply of money should decrease the "price" of money (the real interest rate) and lower the cost of borrowing. A lower interest rate will encourage additional borrowing by firms for investment purposes and by households for consumption. An increase in the money supply is an expansionary policy and will shift the AD curve to the right. In Chapter 7, we look more closely at how monetary policy is conducted.

Wealth: We know that household wealth can be influenced, via the wealth effect, by changes in the aggregate price level. However, wealth may change without changes in the overall price level if, for example, there is a stock market boom. With greater wealth, consumption spending will increase and the AD curve will shift to the right.

Expectations: The current spending plans of consumers and business owners are affected by optimism and pessimism about future conditions including wealth, profits, income, and job security. John Maynard Keynes referred to "animal spirits" (bullishness and bearishness) as a force shaping particularly the behavior of firms—after all, the act of business investment is a vote of confidence in the future health of the economy. If the public is convinced that better times are ahead, then current consumption spending and investment will increase. If we are convinced that the incoming Administration will cut benefits and raise taxes then we will moderate our spending today in anticipation of hard times ahead.

THINK IT THROUGH: The dot com boom of the 1990s swelled stock portfolios and fueled expectations of further prosperity and, consequently, consumers purchased more enthusiastically than would otherwise have been the case—financing their behavior by running up consumer credit.

THINK IT THROUGH: In the depths of the Great Depression, Franklin D. Roosevelt stated, "we have nothing to fear but fear itself." Anxiety about unemployment induced consumers to trim back on spending, leading to the decreases in the aggregate demand that resulted in the unemployment they feared. President Reagan's "Morning in America" advertising campaign emphasized future prosperity and President Obama's keynote phrase, "hope and change," were coined to instill optimism in the midst of economic gloom.

Foreign Economic Conditions: Foreigners demand American goods. If there is an economic downturn in a trading partner such as Japan, then American exports to Japan will suffer. Also, adjustments in the trade environment, such as the imposition of *tariffs* (taxes on imported goods) or *quotas* (limitations on the number of items that can be imported), can cause the level of net exports to change.

THINK IT THROUGH: During times of economic hardship, there is a tendency toward increased "protectionism," clamping down of imports through tariffs or quotas or, perhaps, appeals to patriotism.

Exchange Rates: The international price of the dollar can be affected by factors such as expectations about the performance of trading partners, expectations about future interest rates, or speculation. A decline in confidence in the euro, for example, would provoke an increased demand for the dollar, causing the dollar to appreciate in value. As we saw in Chapter 2, when the dollar becomes stronger, American consumers are able to buy more imports but American firms find it more difficult to sell exports—net exports decrease, causing the aggregate demand curve to shift to the left.

Income Distribution: Those with lower incomes typically spend a greater proportion of their income than do those who are more prosperous. Similarly, wage earners usually spend more of their income than do those who earn profits. Given the overall income level, an increase in the distribution of income toward wage earners and the comparatively poor and away from the wealthy and those who earn profits, through taxes and transfers, will lead to increased spending.

THINK IT THROUGH: The assumption is that those who save do not convert their funds into investment spending. If they do, however, then the income redistribution would lead to a change in the composition of spending rather than a change in its level.

Demographics: As the demographic structure of the population evolves, the types of goods and services households wish to buy change too. A youthful population will seek starter homes, college degrees, and cars whereas an aging population will desire cataract surgery and hip replacements. The *life cycle hypothesis of consumption* suggests that individuals seek to maintain a fairly steady standard of living throughout life and, therefore, for retirees, consumption spending is high relative to their current income (as they live off their savings). Similarly, the young borrow and spend at a comparatively high rate, based on expected future earnings whereas middle-aged income earners tend to spend less and save more for their golden years. If there is a demographic bulge, such as the baby-boomers, then it will influence the composition and the level of consumption over time.

Review: We have developed a model for the overall demand for goods and services in the macroeconomy by the private sector, the public sector, and the foreign sector. As the aggregate price level increases, the amount of goods and services demanded is reduced—the AD curve is negatively sloped. We have identified a number of factors that can shift the position of the AD curve.

Aggregate Supply: The Long Run and the Short Run

In this section we define aggregate supply and distinguish between the long run and the short run. We then consider the appearance of the long-run aggregate supply (LRAS) curve and the short-run aggregate supply (SRAS) curve, the relationship between the two and the factors that cause the curves to shift.

Definition of Aggregate Supply and the Long-Run and Short-Run Time Periods

Aggregate supply is the total output of final goods and services (real GDP) produced by the economy and an **aggregate supply curve** shows the relationship between the quantity of aggregate output that producers are willing and able to supply and the aggregate price level (P). Whereas there is only one aggregate demand curve, the aggregate supply curve's behavior depends intimately on the particular time period being considered. We define two time periods—the *long run* and the *short run*—and, therefore, we have *two* aggregate supply curves—the *long-run aggregate supply* curve and the *short-run aggregate supply* curve.

The **long run** is a period of time that is sufficiently long to permit resource markets to adjust fully to a change in the aggregate price level whereas, in the **short run**, resource markets do not have sufficient time to adjust fully to a change in the aggregate price level.

THINK IT THROUGH: The distinction between the long run and the short run can be confusing. Focus on the long run first. In the long run, temporary discrepancies (between rates of increase in prices and wages, for example, or between workers' expectations and actual outcomes) disappear. As we shall see, price changes have no effect on long-run employment or output decisions. In the short run, by contrast, we can make errors, with firms and workers in particular failing to read price signals correctly. In the long run, having learned from and made adjustments for our temporary mistakes, their influence disappears.

An obvious question to ask at this point is, "How long does it take for markets to respond completely to a change on the aggregate price level?" Unfortunately, there is little consensus among economists on this point and we will discuss the significance of this lack of agreement later. Given that, today, the *average* length of a labor contract is 3 years, we might feel confident in assuming, as a rule of thumb, that it is unlikely that the economy will achieve the long run much sooner than 5 years after a significant price shock.

The Long-Run Aggregate Supply Curve

The Slope of the Long-Run Aggregate Supply Curve: Let us first consider the long-run relationship between aggregate output and the aggregate price level. To do this, we shall revisit the labor market diagram that we first saw in Chapter 2 and let this be a proxy for all resource markets.

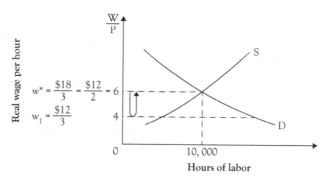

Figure 5-4. The labor market.

In Figure 5-4, the demand (D) curve is the demand for workers by employers—at higher wages, fewer workers will be demanded as firms seek to trim labor costs. The supply (S) curve is the supply of labor by workers seeking jobs—at higher wages, workers will be willing to work for a greater number of hours. The vertical axis measures *real wage per hour*. When we work, we do not work for the number of dollars we receive—the nominal wage—we work for the goods those dollars will buy—the real wage. The real wage (w) is the nominal wage (W) divided by the aggregate price level (P).

THINK IT THROUGH: To determine whether a job offer is attractive or not, we need to know the nominal wage and the price of the goods we wish to buy with that wage, in other words, the real wage. A job offer of $12 per hour is meaningless—it can be evaluated only if we know how much those dollars are worth. If the price of a unit of consumption (a loaf of bread, perhaps) is $3, then the employer's offer of $12 is worth four loaves of bread. If the price of bread rises to $4, then the employer's offer of $12 is worth only three loaves of bread.

Let us suppose that, initially, the labor market is in equilibrium. The equilibrium real wage (w*) is 6 units of consumption per hour. If the aggregate price level is $2, then the nominal wage must be $12 per hour. The equilibrium quantity of labor is 10,000 hours and this will generate some particular amount of production—say, 900 units of output.

THINK IT THROUGH: In equilibrium, the quantity of labor demanded equals the quantity of labor supplied—there is a job for every worker participating in the labor market. The economy is at full employment, with only some unavoidable frictional and structural unemployment present. The full-employment output level, therefore, is 900 units.

We have a point on the long-run aggregate supply curve! When the aggregate price level is $2, real GDP is 900 units of output, as shown in Figure 5-5 at point A.

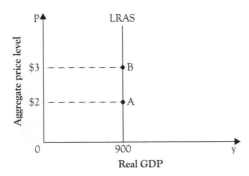

Figure 5-5. The long-run aggregate supply curve.

If the aggregate price level increases to $3, but the nominal wage remains at $12 per hour, then the real wage shrinks to 4 units of consumption (w_1) and there is a shortage in the labor market. Because of the labor shortage, workers can bid up the nominal wage they receive until the equilibrium real wage is restored. Given the aggregate price level, equilibrium will be restored only when the nominal wage increases to $18 per hour. The negotiating process that bids up the nominal wage may take some time and, during that period of transition, the economy is operating in the short run. It is only when the real wage is restored to its equilibrium level of 6 units of consumption and the market is clearing that the long run has been reached.

After equilibrium has been restored, 10,000 hours of labor are being hired and, with those hours, 900 units of output are being produced. In the long run, when the aggregate price level is $3, real GDP is 900 units of output, as shown at point B. We can conclude that the long-run aggregate supply (LRAS) curve is vertical. Real GDP is unaffected by price level changes in the long run.

There is one further point—the LRAS curve is located at the full-employment output level (y_{FE}). The implication is profound—in long-run equilibrium, the economy achieves full employment. In other words, there is a natural long-run pressure for the economy to operate at full employment. Harking back to Chapter 1, the economy will be operating at a point on its production possibility frontier in the long run—the assumptions behind the Law of Comparative Advantage are justified.

Factors That Can Shift the Long-Run Aggregate Supply Curve

There is a strong conceptual link between the LRAS curve and the production possibility frontier and the factors that can shift the LRAS curve are the same ones that can shift the production possibility frontier—improvements in the quantity or quality of resources and improved technology.

Improvements in the Quantity of Resources: By reference to Figure 5-4, if the supply of labor increases, through higher participation rates or immigration, then the supply of labor curve will shift to the right, increasing the equilibrium number of hours worked and, therefore, increasing full-employment real GDP from y_{FE_0} to y_{FE_1}. The LRAS curve will shift to the right as shown in Figure 5-6.

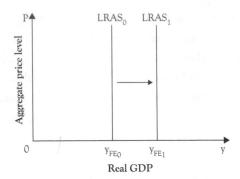

Figure 5-6. An increase in long-run aggregate supply.

Improvements in the Quality of Resources or Technology: The demand for labor is determined by the amount of output that workers can produce—if workers achieve greater productivity then there is a greater demand for their services. Given the same quantity of labor, an improvement in the quality of labor (or an increase in the resources it has available to it) or an improvement in technology will increase the demand for labor and, subsequently, an increase in the equilibrium quantity of labor hired. Full-employment real GDP will increase and the LRAS curve will shift to the right.

The Short-Run Aggregate Supply Curve

The Slope of the Short-Run Aggregate Supply Curve: In general, there is a positive short-run relationship between aggregate output and the aggregate price level. Higher prices induce greater production. There are several explanations for this relationship in the economics literature but the common theme is that, when the aggregate price level changes, individuals are slow to adjust fully and, therefore, the expected price level is at variance with the actual price level. Basically, people miscalculate. Following are three explanations for the upward-sloping short-run aggregate supply (SRAS) curve.

The Sticky-Wage Theory: Firms are in business to earn profits. Given an increase in aggregate demand, the demand for the typical firm's specific product will increase and, if its resource costs do not respond as rapidly to rising prices—if its resource costs are "sticky," in other words—then the firm can increase its profits by raising its price and increasing production. If higher wage claims lag behind the firm's ability to raise its prices, then it is in the firm's best interests to increase production.

This is a short-run situation. In the long run, by definition, wages and other resource costs will adjust fully to the increasing prices.

THINK IT THROUGH: Can you work through how this process leads to a decline in output when the aggregate price level decreases?

The Producer Misperceptions Theory: This explanation for the positive SRAS curve relationship begins from the assumption that producers derive information about changes in the overall price level through what happens in their own market. Each individual market is buffeted by changing conditions, some being general in nature, but many being exclusive to itself. For any given price change, the entrepreneur assumes that it has market-specific causes. A genuine increase in the aggregate price level, therefore, is interpreted as an increase in price only in their particular market and other markets are assumed not to have experienced a similar price change. Accordingly, producers believe that the price of their product has increased relative to prices of other goods. This is the misperception—the relative prices have not changed.

An increased relative price is taken as a market signal to increase production. Across all industries, firms increase production in the mistaken belief that the reward for producing their particular product has risen.

The Worker Misperception Theory: This theory argues that workers are slower than are employers to realize that the overall price level has increased. Initially, the market is in equilibrium at a real wage of 6, with the nominal wage having a value of $12 per hour and the aggregate price level at $2. Following an increase in the aggregate price level to $3, employers generously raise the nominal wage to $18 per hour to keep pace with rising prices. Workers, however, are unaware that the aggregate price level has risen and, believing it to be $2, think that their real wage has increased to 9. This is the misperception and, because a rising real wage encourages an increase in the quantity of labor supplied, more resources flow toward production and output increases. As time passes, workers realize their mistake and the long-run equilibrium is restored.

The Slope of the Short-Run Aggregate Supply Curve Refined: The SRAS curve is generally upward-sloping but, as shown in Figure 5-7, it becomes horizontal at low levels of production and vertical at high levels of production.

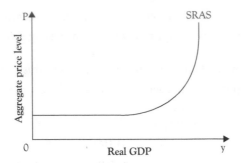

Figure 5-7. The short-run aggregate supply curve.

At very low levels of economic activity, such as during the Great Depression, firms will have much excess capacity—including underemployed workers—and, outside the factory gates, stand many unemployed workers desperate for a job. In such an environment, an increase in the demand for output may be met without much (or any) increase in average cost of production and, therefore, with minimal upward pressure on price.

At the other extreme, the SRAS curve must become vertical—regardless of the aggregate price level, there must be some maximum level of output that cannot be surpassed. Having attained that output level, any additional increase in the aggregate price level will have any impact on real GDP.

The Relationship Between the Long-Run and the Short-Run Aggregate Supply Curves: Comparing Figures 5-5 and 5-7, we know that the LRAS curve is vertical and the SRAS curve becomes vertical. It is tempting to conclude that the SRAS curve converges with the LRAS curve. This is wrong, however. The correct relationship between the two curves is displayed in Figure 5-8.

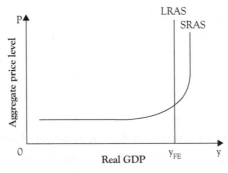

Figure 5-8. The relationship between the LRAS curve and the SRAS curve.

The LRAS curve is located at the output level at which the economy has full employment. The SRAS curve protrudes beyond the LRAS curve because it is possible, at least in the short run, to achieve rates of resource usage greater than what can be sustained in the long run—we can sprint at a faster rate for a brief interval than we can maintain over the long haul.

A Simplified Diagram: From now on, we will draw the SRAS curve as a simple upward-sloping line, as shown in Figure 5-9.

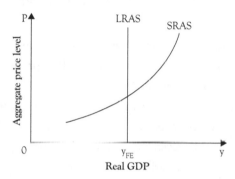

Figure 5-9. The simplified relationship between the LRAS curve and the SRAS curve.

Factors That Can Shift the Short-Run Aggregate Supply Curve

In addition to the factors that can shift aggregate supply in the long run—changes in technology and in the quantity and quality of resources—numerous other factors can influence the economy's short-run ability to produce. Changes in factors such as resource costs, taxes and the amount of regulation imposed on producers, temporary changes in productivity, and expectations about inflation will all have only a short-run influence on aggregate supply, as will temporary supply-side shocks such as strikes, weather conditions, terrorist attacks, and trade embargos.

Looking at the list of factors, increases in resource costs such as wages or the price of imported oil due to a depreciation in the value of the domestic currency, additional excise, sales, or payroll taxes, or more stringent regulation will all conspire to increase the per-unit cost of production, causing the SRAS curve to shift to the left. Productivity improvements will have the opposite effect, reducing per-unit costs, and driving the SRAS curve to the right as shown in Figure 5-10.

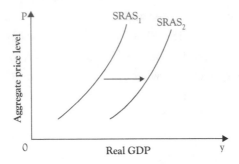

Figure 5-10. An increase in short-run aggregate supply.

THINK IT THROUGH: "Wait," you may object, "this list considers factors that have only a short-run influence but, surely, a productivity improvement affects the LRAS curve too!"

Quite correct! Healthier, better-educated workers, with more efficient machines, are permanently more productive—and the LRAS curve shifts to the right. However, in some circumstances, productivity may increase or decrease temporarily. Evidence shows strongly that productivity increases during recessions, for example, as workers, concerned about their jobs, put in a bit more effort. This is a temporary phenomenon—once normality returns, workers ease off once more.

Expectations about Inflation: We have concluded that changes in resource costs affect the position of the SRAS curve. But, one step back, expectations about inflation influence resource costs. If workers expect the inflation rate to be zero, then they ought to be content with their current wage settlement. However, if they believe the inflation rate will rise to 7 percent, then (even although this belief is mistaken!) they will feel justified in asking for a wage hike of 7 percent that will increase per-unit costs, decrease profits, and push the SRAS curve to the left.

Macroeconomic Equilibrium: Balance in the Short Run

Reaching Short-Run Equilibrium

In this section, we examine how the macroeconomy achieves short-run equilibrium. Considering Figure 5-11, we have done enough economics to realize that equilibrium occurs where the two curves, AD_1 and $SRAS_1$, intersect, at an aggregate price level of P^* and an output level of y^*. However, it is worthwhile to trace through the process by which the economy achieves that equilibrium.

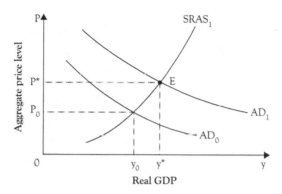

Figure 5-11. Short-run equilibrium.

To analyze the equilibrating process, let us suppose that the AD curve initially is at AD_0, and that the equilibrium price and output are P_0 and y_0, respectively. Now aggregate demand increases from AD_0 to AD_1. Can you think of a reason for such a shift? If not, refer back to the section on aggregate demand.

At the initial aggregate price level, P_0, the quantity of goods and services demanded exceeds the quantity supplied. Inventories are falling below firms' desired levels. This is a signal for firms to increase their prices and to hire more workers and increase production. As the aggregate price level rises and wages and other resource costs lag behind, the economy's output level increases. At the same time, as the price level increases, the wealth, real interest rate, and foreign trade effects are felt by consumers and firms, and there is a decline in the quantity of aggregate output demanded.

As long as there is a mismatch between quantity demanded and quantity supplied in the economy, there will be an ongoing process to achieve equilibrium. That (short-run) equilibrium is reached at point E.

THINK IT THROUGH: Note that the short-run equilibrium output level, y^*, need not be the full-employment output level (y_{FE}). In our example, we have *two* short-run equilibria, at y_0 and y^*. Clearly, even if one of these were the output level at which full employment occurs, then the other equilibrium could not be, so, in general, we cannot assume that, in the short run, the economy will achieve full employment.

The Self-Correcting Mechanism: Harmony in the Long Run

At this point, you may feel that there is an inconsistency in economics. On the one hand, we have just concluded that there is no guarantee that the economy will be at the full-employment output level in the short run but, on the other hand, we asserted earlier that the economy will operate on the long-run aggregate supply curve, which is located precisely at that output level. In this section, we resolve this puzzle.

The economy has inherent forces that inexorably move it toward the output level at which full employment is achieved—there is a **self-correcting mechanism** within the economy.

The Long-Run Behavior of the Short-Run Aggregate Supply Curve

As a starting point, let us reconsider the "simplified" relationship between the LRAS curve and the SRAS curve as shown in Figure 5-12.

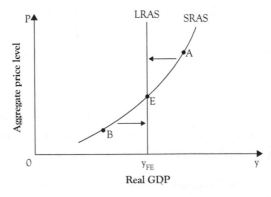

Figure 5-12. **The interaction between the SRAS curve and the LRAS curve.**

The LRAS curve is positioned at the output level at which the economy has full employment (y_{FE}). At this output level, some frictional and structural unemployment is present as a normal condition of a well-tuned economy, but no cyclical unemployment exists.

Compared with the LRAS curve, the SRAS curve has three regions— where output exceeds y_{FE}, as typified by point A; where output falls short of y_{FE}, as typified by point B; and point E, where the SRAS curve intersects the LRAS curve and output equals y_{FE}. Let us discuss the economic conditions prevailing in each of these circumstances and their implications for the SRAS curve.

At point A, current output is greater than the level that can be sustained in the long run. The unemployment rate has been pushed lower than the natural rate of unemployment. Inventory levels are minimal, labor markets are tight, fresh resources are hard to find, and breakdowns and bottlenecks in production and distribution are disrupting the ability of firms to coordinate their activities effectively. If you will, the economic machine is overheating.

As a consequence, production costs will rise. Bottlenecks and delays reduce productivity. Firms, wishing to hire workers, but with unemployed workers thin on the ground, must headhunt employees from other firms by offering them more attractive wages and benefits. Increasing resource costs and declining productivity are among the factors that shift the SRAS curve to the left; therefore, as time passes, we would expect to see the SRAS curve shift to the left.

Conclusion: Any time the economy is in a situation like point A, we would expect the underlying economic pressures to shift the SRAS curve to the left over time.

At point B, the opposite environment exists. Production level is low and the unemployment rate exceeds the natural rate of unemployment. Unsold production is piling up in warehouses. Cyclically unemployed workers, desperate for a job, may be willing to accept lower wages and reduced benefits. Other resources, sitting idle or underused, may become cheaper to acquire. In such a situation, productivity tends to increase, as workers who still have a job strive to avoid layoffs. Declining resource costs and increasing productivity will push the SRAS curve to the right.

Conclusion: If the economy is in a situation similar to point B, then we would expect the underlying economic pressures to shift the SRAS curve to the right over time.

At point E, the economy is neither overstressed nor underutilized. Labor and other resource markets are operating efficiently and sustainably, and firms have achieved their optimal inventory levels. There is no compelling pressure for change—the economy is at long-run equilibrium.

The Self-Correcting Mechanism

Let us suppose that the economy is initially at point E_0 as shown in Figure 5-13.

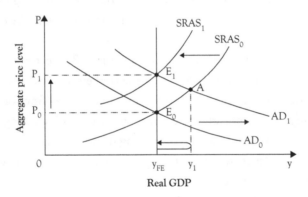

Figure 5-13. The self-correcting mechanism.

The aggregate demand curve is AD_0, the short-run aggregate supply curve is $SRAS_0$, and the long-run aggregate supply curve is LRAS. The economy is in short-run and long-run equilibrium at point E_0.

Now, perhaps because of increasing consumer and business confidence, aggregate demand shifts to AD_1. At the initial price level, P_0, there will be disequilibrium between aggregate demand and short-run aggregate supply, with declining inventories and swelling waiting lists for orders. The aggregate price level will start to increase. Following the short-run equilibrating process described in the previous section, the economy will achieve a new short-run equilibrium at point A. At this point, the economy is producing at an output level, y_1, that exceeds the sustainable full-employment output level, y_{FE}, and, based on our earlier conclusions, we would expect to see the SRAS curve start to move to the left because of the economic pressures imposed. This move must continue until the unsustainable stresses are alleviated—this will only take place when the economy once more reaches full employment (at point E_1). Here, with AD_1 and with the SRAS curve pushed by economic forces to its new location at $SRAS_1$, the economy simultaneously is in short-run and long-run equilibrium. Short-run and long-run equilibrium can only be achieved at the full-employment output level.

THINK IT THROUGH: Confirm that the SRAS curve must keep moving left until it reaches $SRAS_1$ because, until that position is reached, a "point A" situation still obtains.

We have established that, in the long run, the economy will "self-correct" back to the full-employment output level if, in the short run, it is pushed beyond that level.

Although we assumed that an increase in aggregate demand has initiated the process, it could just as readily been triggered by a short-run increase in supply, perhaps caused by an exceptionally good harvest or reduced business taxes. How, then, would the economy restore long-run equilibrium? By exactly the same process! The self-correcting mechanism always and only operates through a counterbalancing shift in the short-run aggregate supply curve.

THINK IT THROUGH: It is tempting to believe that, if an increase in aggregate demand is "balanced" by a decrease in short-run aggregate supply, then an increase in aggregate supply ought to be "balanced" by a decrease in aggregate demand. Tempting, but false! Again, the self-correcting mechanism *always and only* operates through a counterbalancing shift in the short-run aggregate supply curve.

Let us now suppose that the economy is again initially at point E_0, as shown in Figure 5-14.

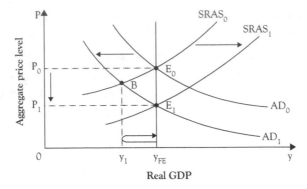

Figure 5-14. The self-correcting mechanism again.

Once more, the aggregate demand curve is AD_0, the short-run aggregate supply curve is $SRAS_0$, and the long-run aggregate supply curve is LRAS. The economy is in short-run and long-run equilibrium at point E_0. In this example, aggregate demand decreases to AD_1, perhaps due to a recession in Europe that has caused a decrease in our exports or an increase in interest rates that has deterred investment and consumption. Short-run equilibrium will occur at point B. Output will be at y_1, an output level at which many workers are unemployed.

Our earlier analysis of a "point B" situation indicates that the SRAS curve will shift to the right, as anxious employees increase productivity and unemployed workers bargain down labor costs. Long-run equilibrium will be restored, at point E_1, only when the SRAS curve has moved to $SRAS_1$.

A similar situation would occur if the initial "shock" affected the SRAS curve, shifting it to the left. The OPEC oil-price hike of the 1970s shifted the SRAS curve dramatically to the left, causing **stagflation** between 1973 and 1975. In 1979, a second oil-price shock had a similar effect, spawning double-digit inflation rates. In both episodes, draconian measures were implemented to combat the inflation—the Nixon Administration imposed wage and price controls and the Reagan Administration engineered a credit crunch and high unemployment (over 10 percent) to squeeze the inflationary pressures out of the economy. The self-correcting mechanism indicates that, left to its own means, the economy would have restored long-run balance without such policies, by pushing the SRAS curve back to the right.

It is worth reiterating: The self-correcting mechanism *always and only* operates through a counterbalancing shift in the short-run aggregate supply curve.

An Asymmetrical Process: On paper, the self-correcting mechanism looks deceptively simple and even-handed—like a large inflatable Bobo doll, it seems that, if pushed in one direction, it will automatically rock back in the other direction until balance is reestablished.

Although there is significant consensus among economists about the *existence* of the self-correcting mechanism, there is much debate regarding the speed and symmetry of its operation. We may be quite willing to raise wages and prices in response to a booming economy and burgeoning demand, but a process that relies on workers to increase productivity or to accept wage cuts to alleviate widespread unemployment may take a long time to be effective. In the former case, the mechanism may be relatively strong and rapid but, in the latter circumstance, it is likely to be weak and slow—in theory, the two sides of the adjustment mechanism may look equivalent, but in practice, not so.

Further, the closer the economy approaches full employment, the weaker the forces propelling it become. Cyclical unemployment may linger, impacting millions of households, for months or years, as the economy drifts toward long-run equilibrium.

There are two responses to this conclusion—either adopt practices that strengthen the self-correcting process or initiate corrective stabilization policies to compensate for its inadequacies. In particular, if the process of pulling out of a recession is weak, then there may be scope for government intervention.

Differing Perspectives: The Long Run versus the Short Run

The proof of the pudding, they say, is in the eating. Similarly, our economic model's implications are subject to differing interpretations and evaluation.

For instance, if we believe that markets, left to themselves, adjust swiftly and effectively to imbalances, then we ought to support the view that the self-correcting mechanism will rapidly propel the economy to full-employment equilibrium—the long run arrives quickly. If, on inspection, we discover that the self-correcting mechanism is nonetheless weak, then we must find reasons for this—perhaps government rules that restrict market forces and competition, or well-intentioned government meddling that distorts the competitive price signaling system.

On the one hand, given our belief in well-tempered and responsive privately run markets and a smooth transition from one long-run equilibrium to the next, the need for government intervention must seem unnecessary and even counterproductive. We would lean heavily toward smaller governments and less intrusive policies.

On the other hand, if we believe that markets, left to themselves, are sluggish and that they respond lethargically to imbalances, and that the self-correcting mechanism is virtually impotent, then we ought to support the view that the economy could, for example, wallow in a recession for months or years unless an outside force, such as the government, intervenes to fix things. The existence of the self-correcting mechanism is not in dispute, merely its efficacy.

There is an ongoing tension in macroeconomics between those who favor focusing on long-run objectives and those who believe that short-run concerns must be addressed. There is no simple solution. Clearly, there would seem to be a political dimension to this issue but analysis on that point is left to the reader.

"In the Long Run We Are All Dead": This famous statement by John Maynard Keynes, admitting the existence of the long run but denying its relevance, exposes the contrast between "Keynesian" economists, who favor short-run demand-side interventionist policies to stabilize the economy and "Classical" economists, who favor the long-run view and policies that support and enhance supply-side efficiency. In the following section, we explore the foundations of the two views.

The Demand-Side (Keynesian) versus Supply-Side (Classical) Debate

Let us consider the underlying beliefs of the two camps about the nature of the economy and their views on the causes and cures of the twin evils of macroeconomics—unemployment and inflation.

Classical Economics: Basic Principles and Conclusions

Classical economics has deep roots, stretching back at least as far as Adam Smith's *Wealth of Nations* (1776) and David Hume's essay *On Interest* (1748). Indeed, to talk of "the" Classical model is misleading because, over time, variants, and outgrowths have occurred, sometimes sufficiently distinctive to warrant a new tag—Austrian, neoclassical, monetarist, and so on. However, the similarities in ideas are more enduring and significant than any differences and it is to these common themes that we turn now.

The long run is the focus of attention: For the Classical economists, the long run is of prime importance. Of course, given their belief that the short run is a brief, transitory period, this is understandable. Their confidence in the power of the economy to achieve virtually automatic full employment colors their other conclusions.

Wages and prices are flexible: Market clear, and do so quickly. This includes the labor market, so involuntary unemployment ought to be short-lived. To the extent that it is not true that markets clear quickly, the impediments to flexibility—long-term contracts, powerful negotiating blocs, poor information—can be alleviated by adding competitive elements. If the labor market fails to clear because of the presence of a minimum wage, it is not the market that has failed, but the restrictive regulation imposed on it. In a sense, this Classical postulate is true—in the long run, as we have seen, markets do clear.

"Supply creates its own demand": This is a brief statement of **Say's Law of Markets**. Note the preeminence of the supply side! French economist Jean-Baptiste Say argued that the act of producing goods and services generates enough income for households (within which the productive resources reside) to be able to purchase all of that output. In other words, the production process creates exactly the spending power needed to buy the nation's output. If, for some reason, this is not so, then prices will adjust. If there is an overabundance of goods (a very good harvest), then prices will decrease to ensure that all goods are bought. According to Say's Law, aggregate supply and aggregate demand will be equal and, given full employment in the labor market, that equality will be at the full-employment output level.

THINK IT THROUGH: "But what if, instead of spending their income, households choose to save some of their money?" Again, the Classical perspective is long run—short-run fluctuations in consumption and saving are irrelevant. In addition, if saving flows into the *loanable funds market*, then it will be channeled to borrowers who will spend with no loss of spending power. We consider the loanable funds market later in this section.

The economy is self-correcting: This is directly contradictory to Keynes' view that the economy could become stuck in a situation like the Great Depression. Today, this previously discredited view can be found repeated in introductory texts—the economy does have a self-correcting mechanism that eliminates cyclical unemployment through the application of market forces. As referred to earlier, the remaining bone of contention is how rapidly the process operates.

"Money is a veil": In Chapter 4, we discussed the Quantity Theory of Money ($M \times V = P \times y$), which states that the money supply (M) will circulate at a velocity (V) sufficient to purchase nominal GDP ($P \times y$). Changes in the money supply will have no impact on real wages, real GDP, the level of employment, or any other real variable in the economy and, in that sense, money is said to be *neutral*. However, "money matters" with respect to inflation because, if the money supply were to be doubled then, after the dust had settled (in the long run!) there would be a doubling in the aggregate price level. For the Classicals, a tight grip on the government's ability to print money is the key to controlling inflation.

Policy Views: With unemployment a temporary, self-correcting problem and price stability under the control of the financial authorities, there is no place in the Classical world for demand-side policies. Prosperity springs from the economy's self-interested supply-side ability to develop new resources and to find better ways of using existing ones. Short-run fiscal and monetary policies, at best, are futile; at worst, are disruptive.

THINK IT THROUGH: The long-run aggregate supply curve is the centerpiece of Classical economics. With a vertical supply curve, no change in demand can have a permanent impact on output or employment.

If a monetary policy action boosts aggregate demand, then the consequence will be an increase in the aggregate price level but there will be no permanent benefit in terms of production or employment. Further, by jolting financial markets, such policies may reduce the effectiveness of private sector investment decisions and stunt future growth. Accordingly, the Classical opinion of monetary policy is that the money supply should grow at a steady pace that would ensure stable prices, that policy changes for short-run advantage should be avoided, and that policies should be clearly announced in order to facilitate private sector choices.

The effects of fiscal policy are more complex and require us to consider the loanable funds market and the crowding-out effect in some detail.

The Loanable Funds Market and the Crowding-Out Effect: There is a market for "loanable funds." In the final analysis, the supply of loanable funds flows from household saving and because, as the real interest rate increases the reward for saving increases, the supply of loanable funds curve (S) is upward-sloping, as shown in Figure 5-15.

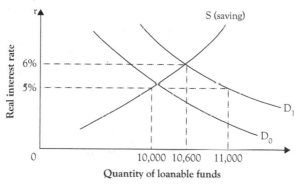

Figure 5-15. The loanable funds market.

Businesses demand loanable funds for investment purposes. The government, to the extent that it must borrow to finance a deficit, is also part of the demand for loanable funds but let us suppose that, initially, the government has balanced its budget and, therefore, the demand for loanable funds derives purely from the private business sector. The higher the interest rate, the more expensive it is to borrow, and the fewer profitable investment opportunities there will be—the demand for loanable funds curve (D) is negatively sloped.

Market forces establish a market-clearing interest rate (5 percent) and a quantity of funds ($10,000) is exchanged. The "leakage" of spending power represented by saving has been compensated for by the "injection" of spending power represented by investment, supporting the conclusions of Say's Law.

Let us now suppose that there is an increase in government spending of $1,000, intended to boost aggregate demand and to stimulate the economy. Whereas previously the government had balanced its budget, it now has a deficit of $1,000. If the spending is financed by printing money, then it will be inflationary. If, however, borrowing finances it, then the demand for loanable funds will increase by $1,000 from D_0 to D_1, causing the interest rate to increase to 6 percent and the quantity of funds exchanged to increase to $10,600.

Because the government is borrowing $1,000, borrowing for private investment purposes has fallen by $400 to $9,600—government spending has crowded out investment. This is not the end of the story because the interest rate increase encourages saving to increase, from $10,000 to $10,600. Given income, if households are saving $600 more, then they must be consuming $600 less—government spending has crowded out consumption. Because one component of aggregate demand has increased by $1,000, but two other elements (investment and consumption) have decreased by $1,000, the policy has no effect on the level of aggregate demand. An expansionary fiscal policy, financed by borrowing, will increase the size of the government sector, swell the deficit, increase interest rates, shrink the size of the private sector, and, because of the reduction in investment spending, jeopardize future growth.

The Classical view is that fiscal policy is impotent and, therefore, that government intervention should be limited, with the goal of achieving a balanced budget.

Keynesian Economics: Basic Principles and Conclusions

In the introduction to his *General Theory*, Keynes stated that "the postulates of the Classical theory are applicable to a special case only" and that those characteristics were not applicable to modern economic society. The following statements present the Keynesian position. Keep in mind that, for the Keynesians, the LRAS curve is a far-distant and continually receding rainbow's end, never to be reached.

The short run is the focus of attention: For Keynes and his followers, the Classical theory's "long run" is an abstraction and its "wait and see" prescription untenable, having little to do with practical policy concerns. Certainly, the misery witnessed during the Great Depression seemed to brook no delay. Harry Hopkins, Franklin D. Roosevelt's welfare chief, remarked that "People don't eat in the long run—they eat every day."

THINK IT THROUGH: Keynes, writing during the depths of the Great Depression, was reacting to an economic theory that claimed that protracted involuntary unemployment was not possible and that the economy would quickly self-correct. Keynes could see no evidence to support such beliefs and branded Classical economists "a gang of incompetent bunglers."

Wages and prices are sticky: The Keynesians argue that long-term labor contracts, powerful negotiating blocs (unions and powerful industrialists), lack of information and regulations conspire to make wages and prices "sticky" and, because of this stickiness, resource markets fail to clear as predicted by the Classical model. Certainly, even during the Great Depression, there was a strong institutional reluctance to accept wage cuts, changes in wage differentials, or redefinition of job responsibilities.

"Demand creates its own supply": We might think of this statement as "Keynes' Law" to draw the contrast with Say's Law. In opposition to the view of the Classical school, the Keynesians believe that the economy is demand driven. The act of spending income and demanding goods and services will stimulate production and employment—will stimulate supply.

The economy can get stuck in a recession: This assertion is directly contradictory to the Classical view that the economy self-corrects. It is important to understand that *both* positions are correct. Keynes' analysis is justified in the short run whereas the Classical analysis is correct in the long run.

Money is not neutral: In common with the Classical economists, the Keynesians believe that money supply changes do impact on aggregate demand but, unlike them, the Keynesian emphasis on short-run matters leads them to the conclusion that changes in aggregate demand due to monetary policy actions *do* affect production and employment.

Keynes and the Multiplier: Perhaps the concept of the **expenditure multiplier** (m) is the single most distinctive aspect incorporated by Keynes into *The General Theory*. Fortunately, it is quite intuitive.

THINK IT THROUGH: Having received good news and feeling more optimistic than usual, you suddenly increase your spending by $1,000. By how much will the economy's equilibrium income level change as a result?

As with much in economics, the answer is "It depends!" In this case, it depends on the size of the expenditure multiplier.

There is a positive relationship between income and consumption—higher income, more spending. According to Keynes, as the income received by households changes, consumption also changes, although not by as much. If we receive an increase in salary, then we will spend most of it but we will save some of it. The *marginal propensity to consume* (MPC) is the fraction of any additional income that is consumed and the *marginal propensity to save* (MPS) is the fraction of any additional income that is saved. Ignoring taxes at the moment, if our salary increases by $1,000, and we spend $900 and save $100, then MPC is 0.9 and MPS is 0.1. Together, MPC and MPS must sum to 1.0—all extra income received must be either spent or saved.

MPC + MPS = 1.0

Table 5-1 shows the multiplier process in an economy in which MPC is 0.9 and MPS is 0.1. The process begins with Round 1, when Andrew suddenly increases his investment expenditures by $1,000 and buys a new computer for his firm from Brenda's Bytes. Any element of expenditures—consumption, investment, government purchases, or net exports—could initiate the process, but we will assume that it is investment.

The new spending creates $1,000 of extra income for Brenda. With an MPC of 0.9 and an MPS of 0.1, she decides to spend $900 and save $100. In Round 2, Brenda spends $900 on a new carpet for her home that she buys at Claire's Carpet Closet. Claire's income now rises by $900 and she decides to save 10 percent ($90) and spend 90 percent ($810). In Round 3, Claire spends $810 on clothes at Della's Boutique, causing Della's income to rise by $810. Della will save 10 percent ($81) and, in

Table 5-1. The Multiplier Process

Round	New expenditure	=	New income	=	New consumption	+	New saving
Round 1	$1,000.00	=	$1,000.00	=	$900.00	+	$100.00
Round 2	$900.00	=	$900.00	=	$810.00	+	$90.00
Round 3	$810.00	=	$810.00	=	$729.00	+	$81.00
Round 4	$729.00	=	$729.00	=	$656.10	+	$72.90
Round 5	$656.10	=	$656.10	=	$590.49	⊢	$65.61
	.		.		.		.
Total	$10,000.00	=	$10,000.00	=	$9,000.00	+	$1,000.00

Round 4, spend 90 percent ($729), and so the process continues, each time with progressively more of the initial injection of spending power leaking into saving. It ends only when all of the initial $1,000 spent by Andrew has been transferred to saving.

At the end of the process, the initial $1,000 injection of spending power has been multiplied into a $10,000 increase in income—a tenfold increase. In this example, the value of the expenditure multiplier is 10. There has been an initial (autonomous) increase in spending of $1,000, and a subsequent increase in spending of $9,000, induced by the increases in income.

The multiplier's strength depends on how rapidly the injection of extra spending leaks away or, put differently, how long the "earning/spending" process endures. If, for example, Brenda had saved all of the extra $1,000 she received, then the process would have stopped dead and no additional income would have been generated. The larger is the marginal propensity to save (and the smaller the marginal propensity to consume), the smaller is the expenditure multiplier. In fact, in this simplest version, the formula for the expenditure multiplier (m) is

$m = 1/MPS$

We can use the circular flow diagram to help us to visualize the "earnings/spending" process affects the size of the expenditure multiplier, as shown in Figure 5-16.

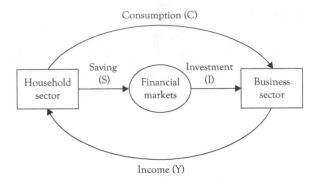

Figure 5-16. The circular flow diagram and the expenditure multiplier.

As income is generated and transferred from the business sector to the household sector, some portion of the additional income leaks away as saving, but the remainder is used for consumption spending, generating even more income. As we can see, the larger the leakage into saving (that is, the greater the marginal propensity to save) the more quickly the process will come to an end and equilibrium will be achieved.

Comment: Saving is simply nonconsumption so households may choose to keep their unspent funds under the mattress but, as shown in Figure 5-16, we shall assume that saving is funneled to the financial sector.

THINK IT THROUGH: If saving is merely nonconsumption, then how can investment possibly take place? Keep in mind that if households cut back in consumption, choosing to save more, then firms will experience rising inventory levels—and inventory accumulation counts as part of investment. No financial market involvement is required.

The expenditure multiplier resides at the heart of the Keynesian demand-driven model. If, for example, the multiplier's value is 10, this means that a relatively small initial change in government spending could trigger a large change in aggregate demand and have a significant impact on economic activity. Similarly, tax or monetary policy actions designed to influence consumption or investment spending would have substantial effects. The larger is the multiplier the more potent is the policy.

This raises a further issue. A sudden (autonomous) change in *any* element of aggregate demand (consumption, investment, government spending, or net exports) will provoke the multiplier effect—its influence is not restricted to the province of the policymakers.

If the expenditure multiplier's value is 10, and there is an autonomous change in expenditure (ΔE_A) of 100, then the overall change in equilibrium real GDP (income) will be 1,000.

$$100 \times 10 = 1,000$$

In general,

$$\Delta E_A \times m = \Delta y$$

Think again about movements in the position of the AD curve. If, for example, investment spending increases autonomously by 100, perhaps because of "animal spirits," then the AD curve will shift to the right by 100. But that is not the end of the story—the multiplier process will generate additional spending (and income) beyond the initial 100. If the expenditure multiplier is 10, then spending will be induced to increase by an additional 900. The overall increase in the aggregate demand curve can be decomposed into two aspects—the autonomous change (100) and the induced change (900) as shown in Figure 5-17.

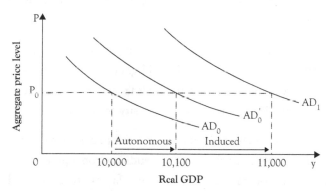

Figure 5-17. Autonomous and induced components of a shift in the AD curve.

How large is the multiplier? Having an accurate answer is an important issue for policymakers. In our economy, the personal saving rate is very low—perhaps 5 percent at most. Based on this, we might expect the value of the expenditure multiplier to be 1/0.05, or about 20. In fact, the multiplier's value for the American economy is estimated to be about 2. Clearly, our model is lacking some important details!

One aspect of this is that businesses and governments also save. National saving is the sum of private saving by households and businesses and public saving by the government. Unfortunately, although business saving (in the form of undistributed corporate profits, for instance) is usually positive, public saving is almost always negative because of government deficits. Currently, gross saving is about 15 percent of the value of national income and, arguably, the *marginal* propensity to save is somewhat higher.

The multiplier is weakened by any leakage that reduces the strength of the flow of funds from income to spending. National saving is one such leakage but there are others—income taxes, for example, or funds flowing out of the country to buy imported goods. Accordingly, the formula might be better thought of as

m = 1/Marginal Propensity to Leak

Accordingly, let us refer to the multiplier whose formula is 1/MPS as the "simplified" expenditure multiplier, recognizing that additional real-world leakages will reduce its size.

THINK IT THROUGH: A $100 increase in your salary is unlikely to translate into a $100 increase in your spending. Higher taxes and other deductions will reduce the amount. The greater the leakages are—voluntary or involuntary—the smaller the marginal propensity to spend.

There is a second, related but distinct, issue to consider—the size of the effect of an autonomous change in expenditures on equilibrium income. In this chapter, we have already met two factors that would diminish not the size of the multiplier *per se*, but the magnitude of its impact on equilibrium income. The crowding-out effect is one, and another is the operation of prices—the price dampener.

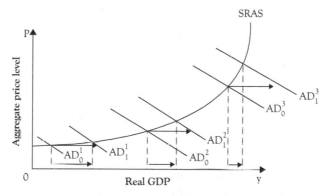

Figure 5-18. The slope of the SRAS curve and the strength of the multiplier.

The Price Dampener: In *The General Theory*, Keynes assumed that prices were constant. In terms of Figure 5-7, Keynes assumed that the economy was operating on the horizontal portion of the SRAS curve— a fair assumption during the Great Depression but hardly the typical case. Usually, as aggregate demand increases in response to an increase in spending, the aggregate price level increases and, because of the wealth, real interest rate, and foreign trade effects, aggregate demand is reduced. As can be seen in Figure 5-18, for a given shift in the AD curve (in each case from AD_0 to AD_1), we can see that the steeper the SRAS curve and the greater the increase in the aggregate price level, the smaller the impact of the autonomous spending increase. Collectively, we will call the operation of these three effects the *price dampener*.

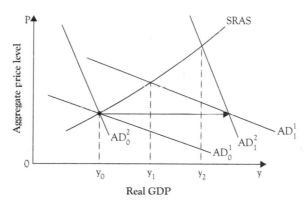

Figure 5-19. The slope of the AD curve and the strength of the multiplier.

In addition, as shown in Figure 5-19, the flatter the AD curve, the weaker the impact of the autonomous spending increase. With strong wealth, real interest rate, and foreign trade effects causing the AD curve to be quite sensitive to changes in the aggregate price level, the less the equilibrium level of output will change for a given change in the positive of the AD curve. If the economy's AD curve is similar in slope to AD^1, then the expansionary effect will be less significant than if it is similar to AD^2.

Finally, in the long run, because of the vertical LRAS curve, the price dampener reduces the impact of the expansion on equilibrium income level to zero!

Policy Views: The policy views of the Keynesians have already been discussed but, in summary, they believe that short-run demand-side fiscal and monetary stabilization policies are effective and, given the weakness of the self-correcting mechanism, ought to be pursued.

Review: This has been a long and complex chapter. We have introduced the ADAS model and discussed some of its long-run and short-run implications. Following this, we have considered the Classical (supply-side) view and the Keynesian (demand-side) view of the workings of the economy and how it may be controlled. As we leave this chapter, it is important to realize that each position is valid within its own terms of reference and has the support of a great many economists and policymakers. Which position we favor, if either, reveals as much about our own preferences as it does about the economy itself.

CHAPTER 6

The Government Sector

Fiscal Policy and Short-Run Stabilization

By the end of this chapter you will be able to:

1. Describe the economic functions of government in a market economy.
2. Define the federal deficit (surplus) and explain how its relationship to the federal debt.
3. Identify the tools of fiscal policy.
4. Describe how the inclusion of the government sector affects the ADAS model.
5. Explain how autonomous changes in government spending and net taxes affect output, unemployment, and inflation.
6. Assess the effectiveness of fiscal policy actions and some of the problems in the implementation of fiscal policy.
7. Explain how the incorporation of tax rates will influence the expenditure multiplier.
8. Explain the effects of automatic stabilizers on economic fluctuations.

If an opinion pollster were to ask you what you thought the proper role the government should be in the operation of the economy, then what would be your response? How far-reaching ought the government's control be? Clearly, the rival communist system of state-controlled production and distribution has largely withered away, with even China embracing capitalism but, within capitalism itself, what is the appropriate position for the public sector?

Chapter Preview: The basic logic in this chapter is the same as in Chapter 5, in the sense that we continue to use the ADAS model. The primary focus is short run. We begin by looking at the economic scope and functions of the government and then examine the tools it has at its command to conduct fiscal policy actions to achieve short-run stabilization of the economy.

In our model so far, we have assumed that net taxes are lump sum, that is, that they don't change as the level of economic activity changes. However, in this chapter we shall see that automatic stabilizers (such as the federal income tax system) do, in fact, alter with the level of economic activity and, in so doing, are yet another factor that reduces the size of the expenditure multiplier.

The Government Sector: Its Size and Functions

The Functions of Government

President Calvin Coolidge once famously stated, "the business of America is business" but, if pressed, most of us would admit that we need some degree of government intervention in the economy to facilitate the conduct of that business.

Legislative Function: At the very least, we need an organization to provide and enforce a stable set of rules for commerce. Among its functions, the government establishes a legal framework within which commercial and other transactions take place. At the most fundamental, as Adam Smith contended in *The Wealth of Nations, laissez-faire* capitalism thrives on self-interest and private property rights but, without laws and a legal system guaranteeing those rights, capitalism's power would be stunted. Even in a free-market economy, we need an organization to establish the rules of the game, to ensure that those rules are followed, and to sanction those who infringe them.

Arguably, a government need not stray beyond the legislative/judicial role. However, government has adopted other roles to foster a competitive environment and to make up for defects in the private market system. These functions include regulation of anticompetitive forces, provision of public goods, control of externalities, correction of undesirable free-market consequences, and macroeconomic stabilization policy.

Regulatory Function: Capitalism operates best when feeling the spur of competition so, if a company grows powerful enough to control a market and operate against the interest of its customers or its competitors, then a case may be made for the regulation of that company in order to enhance competitive forces. This is a major message of Smith's *The Wealth of Nations*—because the "invisible hand" of self-interest directs *laissez-faire* markets to do what's best for society, liberalization of trade is beneficial. Large monopolistic entities, such as the East India Company, or the Hudson Bay Company, cramp the strength of free enterprise and ought to be controlled.

Provision of Public Goods: Sometimes, markets fail to produce the mix of goods to meet the needs of society. *Public goods*, such as a lighthouse, are underprovided by the free market because a key characteristic of a public good is that, if it is provided to one user, then no other user can be excluded from its benefits. Clearly, there is a temptation on the part of would-be consumers to hold back until someone else buys and then receive the benefits "for free" but, if all customers follow this approach, then less than the socially optimal amount of the good will be produced because producers will receive insufficient revenue. This is known as the *free-rider problem*. Contrast this with a *private good* such as heart surgery, where the benefit is received only by the purchaser of the good. Those who do not buy can be excluded from the benefits—there is no free-rider problem with private goods. If you don't buy, you don't get.

In the case of public goods (lighthouses, national defense, the interstate system), the government provides the good to citizens and finances the outlay by imposing taxes—this method of compulsion is far distant from private choice but it is seen as necessary to guarantee the socially optimal level of provision of these goods.

Control of Externalities: In the quest for profits, private firms have exhibited the unfortunate tendency of ignoring the results of their actions on nonmarket participants. An entrepreneur's self-interest leads to her having few qualms about her factory's emissions causing acid rain in another state or country. In a *laissez-faire* world, if others suffer, then let it be. *Externalities*, costs or benefits imposed on nonmarket participants by the production or consumption of a good, certainly do disrupt the ability of the free market as a whole to provide the most desirable mix of goods and services for society. If we believe that water or atmospheric pollution by factories or mountaintop removal mining by coal companies imposes environmental costs on third parties, then we may feel justified in curtailing those commercial activities. Similarly, if driving after drinking, texting while driving, or tailpipe emissions are viewed as detrimental to society's well-being, then we may wish to impose restrictions on consumers.

Correction of Undesirable Free-Market Consequences: Working properly, the free market may cause outcomes that often are considered socially undesirable. Should we, for instance, allow those who are very productive and talented to keep the full reward from their efforts? Although many would assent to the proposition, the issue becomes less clear if we reverse it: Is it socially desirable (or fair) that those with handicaps or few skills should be reduced to lifelong poverty because of an inability to earn or learn? Government has assumed the controversial role of redistributor of income and wealth. Our progressive income tax system, for instance, is crafted *with the intent* of taking dollars from high-income earners and transferring them to the poor, the hungry, and the unhealthy.

Consumer choice is a cornerstone of free markets, but the government may decide that is better equipped than the private sector to judge what is good (or not good) for its citizens. The classic restrictive example is Prohibition, but sin taxes on so-called demerit goods (or "bads") such as cigarettes and alcohol, and restrictions on prostitution and pornography are other cases. On the other hand, the government may encourage cultural activities or use tax benefits to promote private donations to charities.

Macroeconomic Stabilization Policy: The 1946 Employment Act charged the government with the duty of maintaining relatively stable prices, preventing substantial fluctuations in economic activity and employment, and fostering an environment conducive to economic growth.

In the face of declining demand, self-interest may lead a producer to close a textiles mill and lay off his workers. Although this action is in his own best interest, it can have detrimental effects on his employees and the local community and, through the knock-on operation of the expenditure multiplier, further adverse external effects may be experienced throughout the economy. Accordingly, the government may seek to stimulate demand, proactively or reactively, to keep the economy on an even keel.

The Size of Government

In the fourth quarter of 2012, federal, state, and local government expenditures on consumption and gross investment (G) accounted for 19.6 percent of GDP, or about $3 trillion. The federal government was responsible for about two-fifths of the total, while state and local governments spent the remainder.

This is not the complete picture of government involvement in national expenditures, however, because this value only includes expenditures by federal, state, and local governments on *final* goods and services. Federal government defense and nondefense expenditures account for only about one-third of Washington's budget. Government transfer payments, such as Food Stamps, veterans' disability benefits, and Social Security checks, are excluded from expenditures (G) because transfer payments are not made in exchange for final goods and services. The influence of these transfer payments is reflected mainly in personal consumption expenditures (C), when Food Stamps are used to buy groceries or Medicaid benefits are used to defray the cost of health care by those with low incomes. Of the major categories of federal government outlays, the bulk (about 60 percent) is transfer to households or other institutions (with some subsidies thrown in). Interest payment on the national debt amounts to roughly 10 percent of outlays. The bottom line is that the government's influence on spending extends far beyond its own purchasing activities. The controversy in March 2013 about the severity of the effects of sequestration—the forced across-the-board budget cuts—highlighted that government expenditures do impact the private sector.

A Comment on the Deficit and the Debt

The **federal deficit** (or surplus) is the difference between this year's federal government receipts and this year's outlays. The deficit is traditionally represented as G – T, where G is **government expenditures** and T is **net taxes**, or taxes minus transfers. If outlays exceed receipts then there is a deficit and this adds to the **federal debt**, which is the total amount owed by the federal government to the public as a consequence of this, and previous, deficits. A surplus reduces the size of the debt. The estimated deficit for 2012 is just over one trillion dollars whereas the federal debt is in excess of 16 trillion dollars.

Citizens eye mounting deficits and debt with apprehension, but the view among orthodox economists has been more sanguine—a mounting national debt is nonthreatening as long as the ability to repay it is rising equally fast. However, since the surplus years of the Clinton administration (when tax rates were increased and expenditures cut), the debt has risen, as a percentage of GDP, from about 70 percent to in excess of 100 percent in 2012. During the George W. Bush administration, cuts in the average tax rate and unexpected war-related expenses restored deficits, and the deficit rose sharply during the early part of the Obama administration because of stimulus spending, slumping tax revenues, and ongoing war-related expenditures.

THINK IT THROUGH: Are deficits a "bad thing?" There is no single unambiguous answer to this question! When the United States entered the Second World War and accumulated deficits during the struggle to defeat Nazi domination, few would argue that the nation's efforts should have been curtailed in order to balance the books. In addition, with so many workers unemployed, tax revenues declined during the Great Depression—either cutting government spending or increasing tax rates as a consequence would seem counterproductive.

The majority view in economics is that the goal should be to balance the budget over the business cycle—deficits in years of famine and surpluses in years of plenty.

Fiscal Policy: Influencing the Economy by Spending and Taxing

Fiscal policy and monetary policy are the two broad avenues of economic influence. We shall consider monetary policy in Chapter 7. In each case, however, the overarching short-run objective is economic stabilization and the control of particular economic variables of concern, typically output, unemployment, and inflation. Because there are compelling reasons to believe that demand-side fiscal policy is not effective in the long run, the focus for the remainder of this chapter will be short run. In addition, although fiscal policy actions may impact the economy's capacity to produce (in other words, the economy's supply side), historically, the primary thrust of fiscal policy has been manipulation of aggregate demand and it is on this aspect that we will concentrate. Policies that are best characterized as "supply-side" will be discussed in Chapter 9.

The Tools of Fiscal Policy

Fiscal policy has three main tools: government expenditure (G), taxation, and transfer payments. Together, taxes and transfers are termed *net taxes* (T). Initially, to simplify matters, we shall assume that taxes are "lump sum" in nature, that is, tax revenues are not related to income and that the aggregate price level is constant—that is, there is no price dampener effect.

THINK IT THROUGH: Can you think of examples of taxes that are "lump sum" in nature—not affected by income level?

Property taxes on cars or homes, taxes on business equipment, or real-estate taxes imposed on a per lot basis irrespective of size are examples. A poll tax (or head tax) charging a fee per person would be a further example, such as the notorious community tax—a lump-sum payment per adult resident—that was imposed by Margaret Thatcher in Britain in the 1980s. In economies with poor record keeping or with an underdeveloped financial system where monetary transactions are absent or poorly reported, lump-sum taxes can be a convenient way of establishing tax liability.

Fiscal policy affects the economy through changes in aggregate demand. Ignoring net exports, the components of aggregate demand are consumption (C), investment (I), and government purchases (G).

$$AD = C + I + G$$

An *expansionary* policy is intended to increase the level of economic activity and create jobs by increasing aggregate demand whereas a *contractionary* policy is meant to reduce the level of economic activity, presumably to combat inflation, by reducing aggregate demand.

Expansionary fiscal policy: Because government spending is one of the components of aggregate demand, an autonomous increase in government spending will have a direct impact on aggregate demand, shifting the AD curve to the right and increasing the level of economic activity. Net taxes are not directly part of aggregate demand but still influence spending because, if net taxes are reduced, then households will receive more after-tax income and consumption spending will increase. (It is also possible that business taxes may be cut in order to encourage investment.) A decrease in net taxes is an expansionary policy.

The effect of an autonomous policy change in net taxes is weaker than that of an equivalent change in government spending. An autonomous increase in government spending of 100 and an autonomous decrease in net taxes of 100 will each shift the AD curve to the right, but the increase in government spending will have the larger effect because it will increase aggregate demand dollar for dollar. The decrease in net taxes, however, will not increase aggregate demand dollar for dollar. If households receive an increase in after-tax income of 100, then consumption spending will increase, but some portion of the extra income will be saved. Saving is not part of aggregate demand. If, for example, the marginal propensity to consume is 0.8 (and the marginal propensity to save is 0.2), then aggregate demand will increase by only 80 as a result of the tax cut.

We learned in Chapter 5 that the effect of an autonomous change in a component of aggregate demand is multiplied through the economy by the operation of the expenditure multiplier (m), as shown in the formula

$$\Delta E_A \times m = \Delta y$$

If the marginal propensity to save is 0.2, then the value of the simplified expenditure multiplier (1/MPS) is 5. Given an autonomous increase in government spending of 100, if the multiplier is 5, then the AD curve will shift rightward, initially by 100 from y_0 to y'_1 (the autonomous shift), but ultimately by 500, from y_0 to y'_1, as it is induced to rise through the multiplier process, as shown in Figure 6-1.

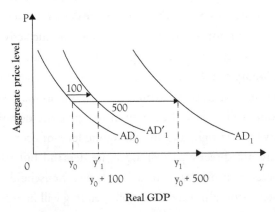

Figure 6-1. *Initial and ultimate shifts in the AD curve of an increase in government spending.*

A decrease in net taxes has a similar, if weaker, effect. An autonomous decrease in taxes of 100, given a multiplier of 5, will make the AD curve shift rightward, initially by 80 from y_0 to y'_1, as consumption spending increases autonomously by that amount, but ultimately by 400, from y_0 to y_1, as shown in Figure 6-2.

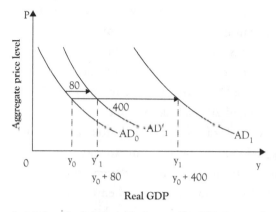

Figure 6-2. Initial and ultimate shifts in the AD curve of a decrease in net taxes.

The Keynesian "transmission mechanism" for changes in government spending is summarized in Figure 6-3.

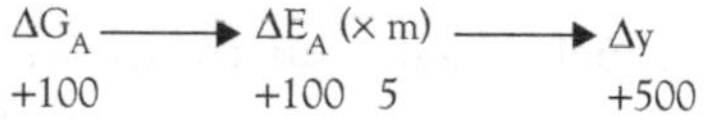

$$\Delta G_A \longrightarrow \Delta E_A \ (\times m) \longrightarrow \Delta y$$
$$+100 \qquad\quad +100 \quad 5 \qquad\qquad +500$$

Figure 6-3. The Keynesian fiscal policy transmission mechanism for government spending.

An autonomous increase in government spending (ΔG_A) of 100 flows directly as a positive autonomous change into expenditures (ΔE_A). The initial change in expenditures is multiplied by the "earning/spending" process, with income (Δy) ultimately expanding by 500 (still assuming that MPS is 0.2).

The Keynesian "transmission mechanism" for changes in net taxes is summarized in Figure 6-4.

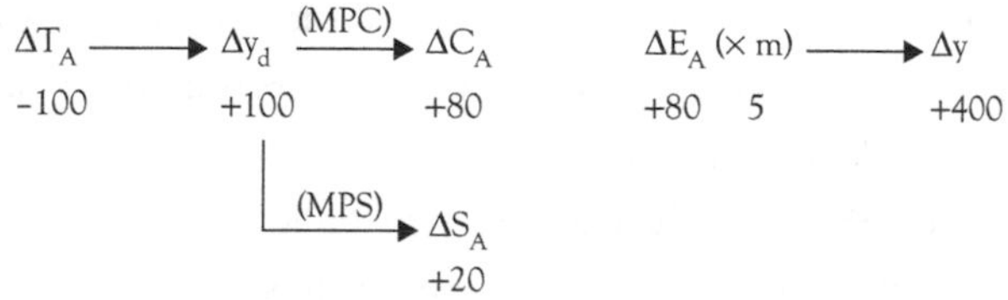

$$\Delta T_A \longrightarrow \Delta y_d \xrightarrow{(MPC)} \Delta C_A \qquad \Delta E_A \ (\times m) \longrightarrow \Delta y$$
$$-100 \qquad\quad +100 \qquad +80 \qquad\qquad +80 \quad 5 \qquad\qquad +400$$
$$\Big|\xrightarrow{(MPS)} \Delta S_A$$
$$+20$$

Figure 6-4. The Keynesian fiscal policy transmission mechanism for net taxes.

An autonomous decrease in net taxes (ΔT_A) of 100 increases after-tax or disposable income (Δy_d) dollar for dollar. Part of the increase in disposable income will be spent and part will be saved—how much each element changes depends on the marginal propensity to consume and the marginal propensity to save. If MPC is 0.8, then consumption (ΔC_A) will increase by 80 and saving (ΔS_A) will increase by 20. Consumption is a component of expenditure; therefore there is an autonomous increase in expenditures (ΔE_A) of 80. The initial change in expenditures is multiplied by the "earning/spending" process, with income (Δy) ultimately expanding by 400. The autonomous change in saving of 20 is a leakage and does not contribute to the process. Ultimately, all of the additional after-tax income will leak away into saving and the process will come to an end.

Contractionary fiscal policy: If the government wishes to dampen down the level of economic activity, then the fiscal policy tools can be reversed. Cuts in government spending, hikes in taxes, or reductions in transfer payments will all reduce expenditures autonomously, shifting the AD curve to the left.

A balanced-budget change: Every so often, there are calls for a balanced budget, which would require changes in government spending and net taxes to be equal. Would this constraint negate fiscal policy? In theory, no, but, in practice, fiscal policy would become far more cumbersome.

Keeping the values from the previous example, with MPS equal to 0.2, the multiplier 5, and assuming that the government's budget initially is in balance, let us examine the effect on equilibrium output of an autonomous increase of 100 in both government purchases and net taxes. At first glance, it might appear that the two changes would cancel each other out but this is incorrect.

The increase in government spending would make expenditures rise autonomously by 100, but the increase in net taxes (which would cut household income by 100) would have a weaker contractionary effect, reducing consumption spending by 80 and saving by 20. The net effect of the two policy actions would be to cause an autonomous increase in expenditures of 20. Given the size of the multiplier, the aggregate demand curve would shift to the right by 100. Equal (balanced-budget) increases in government spending and net taxes are expansionary whereas equal decreases are contractionary.

The transmission mechanism for this balanced-budget example is summarized in Figure 6-5.

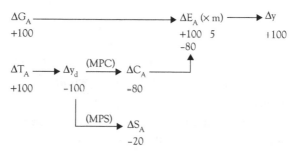

Figure 6-5. The Keynesian balanced-budget transmission mechanism.

THINK IT THROUGH: In the balanced-budget example, we saw that an equal increase of 100 in government spending and net taxes resulted in an overall increase of 100 in income (Dy). Must the final expansion in income (Dy) equal the initial autonomous change?

In the simple Keynesian model described in this chapter, yes, but, in general, no! We have assumed away many real-world economic features. Investment, for example, is assumed not to change as the economy expands—hardly likely. We have ignored the influence of the price dampener and the crowding-out effect. The implementation of fiscal policy is more complex than it might seem.

Problems with Discretionary Fiscal Policy

As represented earlier, fiscal policy seems attractive. Given a recession, a precise increase in government spending or decrease in net taxes should propel the economy smoothly to full employment. Similarly, given excessive inflation, a corrective contractionary action should set right the situation.

The real world is not so simple. There are problems that are applicable to any sort of discretionary policy and others that are specific to fiscal policy. First, the general problems.

General Problems in Implementing Stabilization Policy: We have made several important assumptions in constructing our economic model, assumptions that, if they do not hold, would make the conduct of policy far more complex. Several significant problems arise.

Time lags exist and are variable: Any policy response involves delays—delay in the recognition that a problem exists (the recognition lag); delay in the construction and implementation of policy (the administrative lag); and delay in the operation of the policy within the economy (the operational lag).

The *recognition lag* occurs because it takes time to detect the presence of an economic problem that will require action. Any economy suffers temporary surges and stalls in activity. Let us suppose that, today, the economy starts to slip into a recession. We will have no clue until economic data are published in a month's time. Even then, policymakers will wait for more data before concluding that this is, indeed, an economic slowdown requiring action. This lag may be exacerbated if politicians are loath to admit to economic problems or because of gridlock.

Once a problem is recognized, policy options must be considered, negotiated, and implemented—the *implementation lag*. Again, real-world political conditions would lead us to expect significant delays in hammering out and passing effective proposals.

Finally, once a policy is enacted, the effects may be slow to reach the economy—the *response lag*. A road-building project, for instance, may take months to plan and years to complete. As President Obama once remarked "There are no shovel-ready projects."

Stabilization Policy and the Great Recession: The Great Recession began in December 2007, following the bursting of the housing bubble, which itself was a major and easily observable economic event. Despite this, and although some commentators were remarking on a possible recession in January 2008, there was no political consensus that there was a *significant* economic problem for several months. The Economic Stimulus Act (passed in February 2008) was intended to prevent a *future* recession, not to correct a current one. This mild stimulus was wholly inadequate—policymakers had failed to recognize the extent of the down-turn. Further, the tax rebates for low- and middle-income families did not reach families immediately—several weeks elapsed while the economy sank—although, when the rebate checks were received, however, house-holds did respond as predicted by spending the additional dollars.

The Emergency Economic Stabilization Act (October 2008) created the Troubled Asset Relief Program (TARP) largely as a response to the subprime mortgage crisis and the global financial crisis rather than to the recession *per se* but, to the extent that it was a response to the recession, it had taken almost a year for Congress to react.

Finally, in February 2009, *fourteen months* after the recession's onset, Congress passed the American Reinvestment and Recovery Act, designed to pump almost $800 billion into the economy but the recession ended in July 2009, *before the bulk of those funds could be spent.*

Policymakers face the challenge of hitting a moving target, while using a weapon of dubious reliability or accuracy. Milton Friedman referred to the challenge of achieving policy accuracy in the face of poor information and time lags as the "fool in the shower" problem, with policymakers repeatedly over- and underestimating the impacts of policy measures in a rapidly evolving situation.

The full-employment output level is not known: If we do not know the output level that will guarantee full employment then, even if we do know the current state of the economy, the ability to implement effective policy actions is limited. Even the concept of full employment is elastic, with estimates changing over time.

The marginal propensity to consume is not constant: When we cal-culated the "simplified" expenditure multiplier, we made two important assumptions—that each individual would spend the same fraction of any additional income received and that that fraction (MPC) was known to policymakers. Evidence suggests that the MPC of low-income households exceeds that of high-income households and that the general willingness to spend extra income is affected by whether the additional income is believed to be a temporary change or a permanent one—a temporary bonus or rebate is more likely to be saved, a permanent one more likely to be spent.

The expenditure multiplier is not constant: To the extent that the size of the multiplier is open to doubt—and we saw in Chapter 5 that this is so—the ability of policymakers to determine the appropriate policy response is impaired.

The price dampener is not constant: The effect of the price dampener depends on the interplay between the slopes of the aggregate demand curve and the short-run aggregate supply curve and, as we saw in Chapter 5, the supply curve becomes steeper as full employment is approached, making the price dampener stronger and the effect of policy weaker.

Specific Problems in Implementing Fiscal Policy: The preceding points are relevant for any type of stabilization policy, but there are several other specific issues that can weaken fiscal policy effectiveness.

The crowding-out effect: If an expansionary fiscal policy action causes increased government borrowing and higher interest rates, then the public sector expansion may crowd out private sector investment and consumption spending. The reduction in private sector spending reduces the potency of the fiscal policy action and, to the extent that it is unpredictable, adds a layer of uncertainty to the policy.

Capital flight: An expansionary fiscal policy that boosts demand may also set up the expectation of higher taxes in the future and greater inflation. If so, businesses have an additional incentive to move operations offshore to shelter themselves from increased tax bills and rising production costs. This flight of capital and the consequent reduction in job opportunities has a further dampener on fiscal policy.

The future tax effect: The effect of a tax change on household spending may be influenced by whether or not households believe the tax change to be permanent or temporary. If consumers respond differently to a permanent change than to one that is perceived as short-lived then the effectiveness of a given policy is rendered less reliable. For example, if consumers believe that a tax cut will be ongoing then, believing that their after-tax income has increased permanently, they will tend to spend more vigorously. If, on the contrary, the tax cut is thought to be temporary and likely to be followed up by a compensating tax increase in the future, and that, therefore, the overall effect on after-tax income will be slight, then the impact of the tax cut on consumer spending will be smaller.

THINK IT THROUGH: If we believe that households do respond differently, based on their *perception* of a change in tax policy, then a tax cut enacted by a "credible" Administration will have a different (more profound) effect than the identical tax cut enacted by an Administration that is distrusted or suspected of perpetrating a quick fix that will soon be reversed. In government then, as in the business world, trust in fair dealing is crucial. Given the progressively low, and declining, regard in which policymakers are held by the public, the future tax effect suggests that fiscal policy actions will become less potent and more unreliable.

The ratchet effect: There must be some reason why the federal government has run deficits almost every year since the beginning of the 1960s. To be sure, there have been wars that have placed demands on the public purse, but persistent red ink would seem to be a symptom of something other than a belligerent world. Significantly, following the collapse of the Soviet Union, there was talk of a "peace dividend," but the deficits continued, with relief coming in the later Clinton years because of increased taxes (in 1993 and 1997) and increased tax revenue flowing from the prosperity caused by the dot-com bubble.

It seems to be quite a challenge for politicians, reliant, as they are, on voter popularity for reelection, to pursue unpopular but necessary spending policies—cutting back on programs that have been set up to stimulate the economy after the need for stimulus has abated, removing "entitlements" that cannot be afforded, reducing defense spending when the nation is not at war, and suppressing the vote-attracting benefits of "pork"—and raising tax rates and the tax base or reducing tax-payer deductions when such measures are appropriate. In short, it could be argued that the politicians who establish our economic policy have a self-interested desire to ratchet up and preserve deficit-increasing programs—Santa Claus is better liked than Scrooge. The promise of cuts in programs and higher tax collections is a formula that remains unlikely to promote success on the hustings or to attract many campaign contributions.

Assessment of fiscal policy effectiveness: Although our ADAS model might lead us to believe that fiscal policy is capable of precise economic surgery, the real-world evidence strongly suggests that it is a rather blunt instrument, useful more for causing broad shifts in the economy than for "fine tuning." In addition, poor forecasting and sluggish monitoring of economic data hamper policy effectiveness. Taken in combination with a faith in the speed and strength of the economy's self-correcting mechanism, a number of economists have discounted the usefulness of discretionary fiscal policy except in times of severe crisis, although, given the asymmetrical nature of the mechanism, corrective fiscal policy during recessions remains a viable if unpredictable option for most economists.

Automatic Stabilizers: Nondiscretionary Stabilization

The government has fiscal policy tools at its disposal that it can choose to deploy during economic downturns or upswings in order to stabilize the economy. The economy also has nondiscretionary **automatic stabilizers** that lessen the swings in GDP as the economy moves through the business cycle. Revenue and expenditure programs or policies established in the federal budget that adjust in magnitude as the level of economic activity changes are examples of automatic stabilizers.

Automatic Stabilizers During a Recession

During a recession, when incomes are falling and greater numbers of workers are on the unemployment rolls, more transfer payments are pumped into the economy in the form of unemployment compensation and welfare, partly replacing the lost wages and salaries—spending falls less than it otherwise would have.

In a situation of declining employment and income, income tax liabilities also decrease. Ours is a mildly *progressive* income tax system and acts as a stabilizer.

A digression on tax systems: Tax systems may be progressive, proportional, or regressive. To understand the differences, we must define two new concepts—the average tax rate and the marginal tax rate. The *average tax rate* is the fraction of every dollar earned that is paid in tax. If you earn $100,000 and send IRS $10,000, then your average tax rate is 10 percent. The *marginal tax rate* (MTR) is the fraction of each *additional* dollar earned that is paid in tax. If you accept some secondary employment, worth $50,000, and your total tax liability increases from $10,000 to $20,000, then your MTR on the extra $50,000 is 20 percent—tax has risen by $10,000 whereas income has risen by $50,000.

With a *progressive* system, the marginal tax rate increases as income increases—we are pushed into progressively higher tax brackets—and the average tax rate also increases. The marginal and average tax rates remain unchanged with a *proportional,* or "flat tax," system—the Social Security tax (until a specified income value, at least) is proportional. With a *regressive* system, as income increases, the marginal and average tax rates decrease. Such a system is destabilizing for the economy.

This can be deceptive. A 5 percent sales tax levied by a state may seem to be a flat tax but is, instead, regressive, as the following example shows.

A regressive tax: Let us suppose that Smith earns \$40,000 annually and Wesson earns twice as much. The state of West Dakota imposes a 5 percent sales tax on all purchases. Earning \$40,000, Smith spends all of his income and saves none—he pays \$2,000 in taxes, with an average tax rate of 5 percent. In contrast, Wesson, earning \$80,000, is able to set aside \$8,000 in a savings account. These funds are not subject to the sales tax and Wesson's tax liability is 5 percent of \$72,000, or \$3,600. His average tax rate is 4.5 percent. The average tax rate decreases as income increases—a hallmark of a regressive tax system.

To the degree that federal income taxes are progressive whereas state and local sales, excise, and property taxes are regressive, the federal tax system operates as an automatic stabilizer but the state and local systems do the opposite!

Automatic Stabilizers During an Upswing

Automatic stabilizers function just as much during economic expansions as they do during downturns. With rising demand and spending, the progressive income tax system siphons off increasingly larger amounts of wages and salaries, dampening down the rate of expansion. Unemployed workers, finding jobs, see their new earnings offset by losses in unemployment benefits. The upswing in the economy is diminished.

Assessment of Automatic Stabilizers

Automatic stabilizers are a two-edged sword, having both attractive and unattractive features. Ignoring the issue of disincentives caused by a progressive tax and transfer system, automatic stabilizers keep the economy stable—a good thing if the economy is close to full employment, but unfortunate if it is not, because policy packages have to be stronger in order to overcome the inertia due to stabilizers. A reasonable body of evidence demonstrates that automatic stabilizers, in fact, do reduce the severity of business cycles although, on their own, they are unable to reverse them.

THINK IT THROUGH: In the aftermath of the Great Recession, with unemployment obstinately high and with unemployment benefits gone, many unemployed workers who had become "discouraged" applied for disability benefits. These benefits unintentionally served to prop up income and spending and to reduce the likelihood of a "double-dip" recession.

The Expenditure Multiplier Revisited

The Tax-Rate Dampener: In Chapter 5, we defined the expenditure multiplier (m) as 1/MPS, noting that the size of the multiplier in the American economy (roughly 2.0) seemed at odds with our knowledge of the marginal propensity to save, even if saving is taken to mean national saving rather than only personal saving. We broadened the multiplier definition to

m = 1/Marginal Propensity to Leak

The propensity to save more as income increases is one source of leakage; the progressive income tax system is another, drawing off spending power from the economy as income expands through the MTR and automatic stabilizers in general. We can add the MTR to our original definition of the expenditure multiplier as follows

m = 1/(MPS + MTR)

The more sharply tax brackets increase with income, the smaller the multiplier will be. We shall call this effect the *tax-rate dampener*. In this more complex model, the tax-rate dampener diminishes the size of the expenditure multiplier. We shall extend our understanding of the expenditure multiplier in Chapter 7 but, for now, we extend the circular flow diagram we first met in Chapter 3 as shown in Figure 6-6.

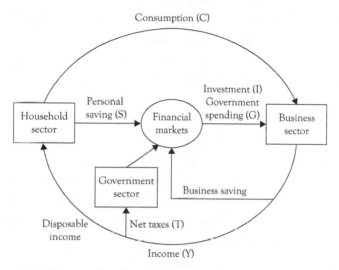

Figure 6-6. The circular flow diagram with a government sector.

As we can see, the introduction of the government sector permits an additional major leakage in the "earnings/spending" process, in the form of tax payments. The diagram assumes that imbalances between net tax receipts and government spending (usually deficits) are dealt with in financial markets, as the government competes for funds with the private sector, with the consequence being the crowding-out effect we discussed earlier. Indeed, there is growing evidence that the expenditure multiplier has dwindled in strength over the years, with some recent estimates suggesting a multiplier value of less than 1.0 for some fiscal policy actions. Certainly, President Obama's stimulus package in 2009 has offered little evidence that a sizeable injection of spending would cause a rapid economic recovery, despite following hard on the heels of the Bush Administration's Emergency Economic Stabilization Act of 2008, TARP, and historically low interest rates.

Some fiscal policies are more powerful than others—as our model predicts, government spending changes wield a stronger influence than tax changes. Among spending programs, the multiplier effect of increasing food stamps is more powerful than that of increased federal aid to state governments. The impact of tax changes was even more muted. But, all in all, the consensus of recent research is that fiscal policy actions have only mild influence on overall economic behavior.

Negative fiscal multipliers: Critics of discretionary fiscal policy even go so far as to suggest that fiscal policy actions are counter-productive, leading to fiscal multiplier effects that are negative in the long term! How might this paradoxical result occur?

Let us suppose that Washington increases grants to the states and that this increase in government spending has a small stimulatory impact in the short run. The policy has added to the deficit and, so the argument goes, the shortfall will have to be recouped at some point in the future, probably with higher taxes. The increase in taxes, though, will have a negative impact on the level of economic activity and, if the negative effect is sufficiently strong, the net effect of the initial increase in government spending will be negative.

As 2012 drew to a close, the economy's attention was focused on Washington's efforts to resolve the issue of the so-called fiscal cliff—the threatened across-the-board spending cuts that would be implemented if action was not taken to bring the federal budget under control. The spending cuts were proposed in 2011 to control the swelling deficit (the Budget Control Act). In addition, in the absence of explicit action, Bush-era expansionary tax cuts were scheduled to expire at the end of 2012.

Considering just the Bush tax cuts, the relevance of this to negative fiscal multipliers was that, if, the taxes had been allowed to expire, then this action could have pushed the still-sluggish economy into a "double-dip" recession. If, conversely, the taxes were not allowed to expire then there would be a need for some offsetting tax hikes or spending cuts elsewhere in the budget. In either circumstance, the economy would have faced a long-term contractionary effect. As it turned out Congress and the president opted for a compromise, raising some taxes while extending unemployment benefits. The issue of limitations on government spending was deferred for two months until sequestration was triggered in March 2013. Further disruptions threatened over the government's debt ceiling remained unresolved.

THINK IT THROUGH: How did the economy react to Washington's brinks-manship over the debt and deficit issues? Do you feel that last-minute policy-peddling is beneficial for or harmful to the business sector's ability to accomplish effective strategic planning?

Review: We have incorporated the government into our ADAS model in this chapter. The essential architecture of the model is unchanged from Chapter 5, but there is richer detail. Because, by its nature, demand-side fiscal policy is short run in impact—having no special ability to shift economy's long-run performance—this chapter has dwelt on short-run stabilization issues. Although its effective implementation faces particular challenges, discretionary fiscal policy can influence the short-run fortunes of the economy. Nondiscretionary (automatic) stabilizers, while not able to reverse a change in the economy, can reduce the severity of economic fluctuations.

CHAPTER 7

The Financial Sector

Money Matters and Interest Rates

By the end of this chapter you will be able to:

1. Identify three functions that money performs in the economy.
2. Distinguish among barter, commodity money, and fiat (token) money.
3. Define two different measures of the U.S. money supply (M1 and M2).
4. Describe the process of money (deposit) creation. Define and explain the importance of the deposit multiplier.
5. Describe how equilibrium is achieved in the money market.
6. Identify three monetary policy tools and describe how they are changed to adjust the money supply in the pursuit of policy objectives.
7. Explain the impact of the interest sensitivity of money demand on the effectiveness of monetary policy.
8. Explain the impact of the interest sensitivity of investment and consumption spending on the effectiveness of monetary policy.
9. Describe how the monetary dampener reduces the size of the expenditure multiplier.
10. Outline how monetary policy can "accommodate" fiscal policy and enhance its effectiveness.

Unless you are quite unusual, the topic in the first part of this chapter will pose one particular problem for you. Our subject is "money" and, almost certainly, your preconceived image of money will differ from any definition of money that you will meet in this chapter! Even the very narrowest definition of the money supply (M1) includes traveler's checks, for instance, whereas a somewhat broader definition (M2) includes items such as certificates of deposit. No definition of money includes credit cards. As we begin this chapter, think about the roles that money plays in the economy, and, based on these roles, try to find a suitable definition for money.

Chapter Preview: In this chapter we consider how the financial sector influences the economy. First, we must determine what money is and what it does. Following this, we examine the market for money and how the financial authorities may manipulate it in order to affect the broader economy.

Functions and Definitions of The Money Supply: What Money Does and What Money Is

In this section, we look at how and why money evolved, define money, and consider the functions that money performs in a modern society.

A Brief Evolutionary History of Money

In early human history, there was no need for money. As hunter-gatherers, primitive humans foraged in extended family groups, living hand to mouth. As herders, though, they may have encountered other groups and, desiring to trade some surplus stock, they would have bargained and traded goods for goods. *Bartering* in this way is cumbersome because it requires a *double coincidence of wants*—you must want what I have and I must want what you have. If one of the two "wants" is absent, then trade can't occur.

THINK IT THROUGH: Even ignoring the problem of finding a trading partner with a double coincidence of wants and negotiating a satisfactory deal, the barter system is inefficient in the sense each trader must hold a substantial range of trade goods in expectation of the day when a visitor arrives with just that item that is most desired. One would not wish to pass up an opportunity because of a lack of tradable goods. Accordingly, we would expect a barter economy to have a fairly significant amount of production that is underutilized.

Clearly, as farming grew in importance and as families stopped being self-sufficient and realized that there were gains to be derived from specialization and trade, a better system than barter was required to facilitate that trade. The first step was the introduction of a good that not only was valuable in its own right but also was acceptable as a means of payment—a *commodity money*. Commodities such as gold or silver, tobacco or pelts, shells or beads, have all been used as a means of payment. The Aztecs and Maya used cocoa beans—the commodity was acceptable because of its intrinsic value and because the understanding was that, if the recipient had no use for more cocoa beans than he already had, then they were universally acceptable as payment for a good that he wanted.

Characteristics of a "good" money: Like any type of money, to be effective as a "good" money, commodity money requires particular characteristics—it must be portable and divisible (gold is good, goats are not), durable and comparable (cocoa beans are good, cows are not), and restricted in supply.

THINK IT THROUGH: In *The Hitchhiker's Guide to the Galaxy*, Douglas Adams describes the Golgafrinchams choosing the leaf as their currency. The leaf is a poor choice because, with so many leaves available, inflation becomes rife, prompting them to burn down the forests! In addition to the difficulties involved in restricting supply, because the leaf is not intrinsically valuable, durable, or comparable, the Golgafrinchams would have been wiser to have opted for one particular type of leaf that is durable, difficult to substitute or counterfeit, and valuable in its own right—tobacco, for instance.

Gold (or silver) is a good candidate as money, especially if its quality can be "guaranteed" by being formed into coins with an official stamp of approval. Like leaves though, the value of gold (or silver) depends on supply and, when supply increases sharply (the California gold rush, the Klondike), the value of the metal decreases and inflation ensues.

The final evolutionary step (so far) has been the development of fiat or token money. *Fiat money*, such as a dollar bill, has little intrinsic value—it is worth a dollar only because the financial authorities say it is worth a dollar. Because, on the rare occasions when the metal content of silver and copper coins has risen above the face value of the coins themselves and opportunists have sought out those coins and melted them down, it is in the best interests of the financial authorities to make sure that our tokens are intrinsically worthless.

Fiat money bestows a greater ability on the issuing authority to control the supply of currency. In addition, the value of resources tied up in the money stock is less—contrast the difference in the value of resources needed to mine and refine an ounce of gold and the value of those needed to run off its current price of $1,775 in bank notes. Because the use of fiat money also bestows a greater ability to overproduce currency, with the attendant destabilizing inflationary consequences and loss of confidence, financial authorities typically strive to protect the integrity of their currency.

THINK IT THROUGH: Public acceptability of a currency is key to its success. If citizens lose confidence in the integrity of their nation's money, then its function as a facilitator of trade is impaired. This is why a government will go to such great lengths to instill confidence in its currency, and why counterfeiting is such a serious crime—it not only jeopardizes "restricted supply," but it also undermines confidence. During the First Gulf War, the American-led forces dropped bundles of counterfeit banknotes throughout Iraq—financial warfare designed to disrupt the economic mechanism.

The Trial of the Pyx: Every year since 1282, the coins of the British Royal Mint have come under independent scrutiny by a jury to guarantee that they conform to standards of diameter, metal composition, and weight. In early times, when the temptation and ability to debase gold and silver coins was greater, the Trial was held quarterly. The point of the Trial is simple—to reassure users of British currency that, although it may no longer be "as good as gold," it is at least as good as money should be. With currency, confidence counts for a great deal.

Functions of Money

Money fulfills three major economic functions—it is a medium of exchange (or means of payment), a store of value, and a unit of account. As we discuss each one, consider the injurious effect of inflation.

Medium of Exchange: For most of us, the primary function of money is to buy the things we need. Money maybe can't buy us love, but it can buy most other things. By specifying that goods and debts can be settled legally with a transfer of "money," barter's clumsy double coincidence of wants is avoided. Money is the oil that makes the economic engine run smoothly.

Inflation damages this function of money because, if prices rise, the supplier of a real good such as corn may be unwilling to accept monetary payment, preferring to revert to the certainty of barter. If money is the oil in the engine, then inflation is a contaminant.

Store of Value: When we get our paycheck, it is unlikely that we will spend all of it immediately. Some portion will be retained and we expect that portion to maintain its value. In this sense, money operates to transfer potential purchasing power across time. We can accumulate funds received in previous months to be used when we go on vacation—our expectation is that the money will store its value until it is needed. Money is not unique in this function—any asset that retains its purchasing power is a store of value.

Inflation impairs this function of money too. As prices rise, the dollar in your wallet shrinks in value. It may become wiser to hold your wealth in another form that is retaining its purchasing power more effectively— real estate, collectible baseball cards, or stock. In such circumstances, *liquidity* (the ease and cost of converting an asset into purchasing power) must be considered. A particular asset may be a hedge against inflation but if, when you need the spending power, you find it difficult or expensive to convert that asset into cash (in other words, if it is fairly "illiquid"), then the convenience of money may be the better option. Cash is unique in the sense that it is perfectly liquid—it is purchasing power embodied.

Unit of Account: Money is what we use to keep score—the dollar is our yardstick and its use in virtually all of our transactions gives transparency and ease of comparison between options, such as items on a menu or salaries of executives. Complex aggregations—GDP, for instance, or a sales rep's monthly performance—are simplified by being measured in dollars. We can judge the financial success of movies by comparing their gross receipts at the box office. This convention is convenient and fairly reliable, but inflation is detrimental to comparisons, especially when comparisons over time are attempted. Certainly, *Gone with the Wind* or *The*

Sound of Music were huge box office successes but because ticket prices in 1939, or even in the 1960s, were so low, neither movie dents the list of "all-time" top grossing movies.

Definitions of Money

In the previous section, it was stated that cash is perfectly liquid. While this is true, it is wrong to assume that "money" is also perfectly liquid. Although cash is part of the nation's money supply, it is *only* a part and, in fact, not even the largest part. There are several widening definitions of money but we shall be content with the two most frequently seen definitions—M1 and M2.

M1: M1 (or "narrow" money) focuses on the "medium of exchange" function of money, counting those financial instruments that we use to purchase goods and services. M1 includes currency (notes and coins) held by the public outside banks and the value of the public's checking accounts inside banks. Checking accounts (usually just over half of the value of M1) comprise demand deposits and other checkable deposits (such as "negotiable order of withdrawal," or NOW, accounts). Traveler's checks (a tiny portion of M1) are used for purchases so they are also included.

M1 = currency held by the public outside banks + checkable
     deposits + traveler's checks

THINK IT THROUGH: This phrase "held outside banks" is significant. If a dollar bill were always "money" irrespective of who holds it then, by depositing a dollar bill into my checking account, I would cause the money supply to increase—the value of my checking account would rise by one dollar but "cash" would remain unaffected. To prevent this miscounting, as the dollar bill slides over the counter and is received by the banker, it ceases to be part of the money supply. My deposit will change the composition of the money supply (currency down, deposits up) but not its size. This is an important point and we shall return to it.

THINK IT THROUGH (MORE): "What about credit cards? I use my credit card to pay for restaurant meals, hotel rooms, airline flights, and so on. If money is what we use as the medium of exchange, then surely my Visa card must be included!"

Credit cards do not feature in any definition of the money supply. The reason is simple. When you use a credit card, the card company is extending a loan to you. The transaction is not completed until you pay off the credit card account—typically with a payment from your checking account. Payments made using a *debit* card are monetary transactions, since the debit card accesses your checking account.

M2: **M2** (or "broad" money) focuses more on the "store of value" function of money, including items that most of us would be unlikely to classify as "money," such as certificates of deposit. M2 includes everything in M1 plus savings accounts, money market accounts, money market mutual funds, and "small" time deposits (that is, certificates of deposits of under $100,000). The assets in M2 are less liquid than the assets in M1—there may be a "penalty for early withdrawal"—but they are still quite readily convertible into spending power.

As a rule of thumb, M2 is usually somewhat more than four times larger than M1. In August 2012, M1 was $2,333 billion whereas M2 was just over one trillion dollars. (If you're interested, you can find more information on the composition of the money supply at federalreserve.gov.)

The Money Creation Process: Prudence versus Profit

In this section we explore how money is created (or destroyed, if the process is reversed). During the process of receiving deposits and extending loans in pursuit of profit, bankers discovered that they had the capacity to create spending power for their customers. This ability is both attractive and dangerous—attractive because money creation can generate profits; dangerous because it can lead to inflation and, possibly, bankruptcy. Following a wave of bank collapses and a crisis of confidence in the banking sector at the turn of the twentieth century, it was felt that a regulator was required to inject prudence into banking matters and so, in 1913, the Federal Reserve System (the "Fed") was established.

The "Fed": The Fed sits at the heart of the financial system. It performs many functions but, for us, the main ones are that it sets limits (reserve requirements) on how aggressively banks can lend out their depositors' funds and it determines and implements monetary policy. The Fed is the banks' bank—just as the public can deposit funds in or borrow funds from Bank of America, so Bank of America can deposit funds in or borrow funds from the Fed. The Fed may act as a "lender of last resort" for a bank in trouble that is "too big to fail."

The Money Creation Process: Simplifying Assumptions

Let us simplify the model by looking at the narrow money supply and assuming that it includes only *currency* (CC) or *notes and coins held by the public outside banks*, and *demand deposits* (DD). We will ignore other checkable deposits and traveler's checks. The money supply (M) is

$$M = CC + DD$$

Further, we assume that, at the start of the process, all banks are fully "loaned up," that is, every bank in the system has loaned to their maximum extent—there are no loans to be had anywhere, at any price. Also, we assume that all banks have the same reserve requirement. To explain: When you deposit a $100 banknote into your checking account, your bank's balance sheet is affected in two ways. First, its *assets* (the things the bank owns) increase by $100 as it now holds the $100 bill—more on the significance of this later. Second, its *liabilities* (the things the bank owes) increase by $100 because you have a claim worth $100 against the bank—it has a demand deposit liability that it is obliged to repay. Your bank could lend out all of the $100 deposit that it has received from you—lending, after all, is how banks earn revenue. However, there is a tug-of-war between profit and prudence. The more the bank lends, the more revenue it earns, but the more it lends, the more likely it is to have insufficient funds available when depositors wish to withdraw their funds as cash. Clearly, there is some compromise between profit and prudence and, history has shown, bankers sometimes miscalculate, lending so freely that they are unable to meet their obligations to depositors and must declare bankruptcy.

THINK IT THROUGH: If you are of a certain age, you may well have an image in your mind of James Stewart and *It's a Wonderful Life*. The banking problem that Stewart's character faced in that movie it the one we're considering now.

To impose prudence, the Fed sets a *reserve requirement* that each bank must retain a fraction of its demand deposits in reserve. If the **required reserve ratio** or *liquidity ratio* (rr) is 10 percent then, if a bank has one million dollars in demand deposit liabilities, it may lend out $900,000 of those deposits but it is required to hold $100,000 in reserve.

THINK IT THROUGH: Is the reserve requirement the same for all banks? In fact, it is not. Currently, it is 10 percent for institutions with checkable deposits in excess of $71.0 million, 3 percent for institutions with deposits between $11.5 million and $71.0 million, and zero for smaller institutions. Although the cutoff points vary over time, the ratios are fairly stable.

THINK IT THROUGH (MORE): If reserve requirements are in place to guard against banks being unable to meet their obligations, it would seem plausible that a larger bank (with more assets and a broader geographical base) would be more likely to ride out a panic than would a small local bank with few assets. If so, then shouldn't the more stringent requirement be placed on the smaller banks? And, if so, why is it not?

This argument is reasonable—smaller banks are more likely to succumb to "runs" or other adverse conditions and, therefore, ought to meet higher standards. The reason that the opposite is true is because it has long been felt that it is advantageous to have competitive local "grass roots" banks. The preferential treatment permits them to lend more aggressively and to survive in the face of large predatory banks that reap the benefits of economies of scale and that would probably otherwise undercut them.

Banks are required to hold a fraction of their demand deposit obligations "in reserve." A bank's total reserves (R) may be held as *vault cash* or as *deposits at the Fed*. For instance, as you deposit your $100 bill and it slides across the counter to the banker, it becomes part of the bank's vault cash. If the bank subsequently deposits the $100 bill into its account with the Fed, then it is reclassified as "deposits at the Fed." In either form, the $100 bill counts as bank reserves. If the required reserve ratio is 10 percent, then $10 must be held as required reserves (RR) but, because the other $90 are excess reserves (ER), they may be loaned out.

To summarize, a bank's total reserves may be held either as vault cash or as deposits at the Fed. Some portion of these reserves is earmarked as *required* reserves but any other reserves are *excess* reserves and are available to be loaned out.

$$R = RR + ER$$

At the start of the money creation process, we assume that all excess reserves have been loaned out—in other words, banks have only required reserves left on hand.

Our final assumption is that those who borrow funds from banks will then spend the loan and that the subsequent recipients of those dollars will redeposit them in the banking system—in other words, there are no *currency drains*.

Table 7-1 shows the money creation process in an economy in which the required reserve ratio is 0.1 (10 percent). In our example, the process, which could be initiated in several ways, begins when Andrew suddenly deposits $1,000 into his bank (Bank A).

Bank A's reserves increase by $1,000, of which $100 are required reserves (which can't be loaned out) and $900 are excess reserves (which can be loaned out). The bank loans $900 to Peter. Usually, the loan will be in the form of an increase in the borrower's checking account but, for simplicity, we will assume the bank gives Peter cash. Bank A's (excess) reserves are gone but it has a loan asset with Peter instead—it now has the $1,000 deposit liability, $100 in required reserves, and $900 in loan assets.

THINK IT THROUGH: The "change in excess reserves" column in Table 7-1 contains two steps, the first indicating the initial increase in excess reserves, the second assuming that all excess reserves have been loaned out as cash.

Peter spends the $900 at Brenda's store and she deposits the funds in her bank (Bank B). Bank B has $900 in deposits from Brenda—$90 in required reserves, and $810 in excess reserves. Bank B lends $810 to Eric. Bank B's excess reserves fall to zero, but it still has the $900 deposit, $90 in required reserves, and $810 in loan assets.

Table 7-1. The Money Creation Process

Bank/depositor		New demand deposits	=	Change in reserves (R)	=	Change in required reserves	+	Change in excess reserves	=	Change in loans/borrower
A/Andrew	=	1,000.00	=	1,000.00	=	100.00	+	900.00 /0	=	900.00/Peter
B/Brenda	=	900.00	=	900.00	=	90.00	+	810.00 /0	=	810.00/Eric
C/Claire	=	810.00	=	810.00	=	81.00	+	729.00 /0	=	729.00/Thelma
D/Della	=	729.00	=	729.00	=	72.90	+	656.10 /0	=	656.10
E	=	656.10	=	656.61	=	65.61	+	590.49 /0	=	590.49
...	=	...	=	...	=	...		...		...
Total	=	10,000.00	=	10,000.00	=	1,000.00		0		9,000.00

Eric uses the proceeds of the loan to buy a new carpet at Claire's Carpet Closet. Claire deposits $810 in her bank (Bank C). Bank C's reserves increase by $810, of which $81 are required reserves and $729 are excess reserves that can be loaned out. When Bank C lends $729 to Thelma, its excess reserves fall to zero, but it still has $810 deposit, $81 in required reserves, and $729 in loan assets. When Thelma spends the cash in Della's Boutique, Della's subsequent deposit will increase the money supply by $729.

And so on. The process continues, each time with progressively more of Andrew's initial injection of reserves leaking into required reserves. It ends only when all of the initial $1,000 deposited by Andrew has been transferred to required reserves and is no longer available to lend out. At that point the process must stop.

At the end of the process, Andrew's initial $1,000 demand deposit has been multiplied into a $10,000 increase in demand deposits—a tenfold increase. In this example, the value of the **deposit multiplier** (d) is 10. There has been an initial (autonomous) increase in deposits of $1,000, followed by a subsequent increase in deposits (by Brenda, Claire, Della, and so on) of $9,000.

THINK IT THROUGH: For the banking system, the $10,000 expansion in demand deposit liabilities is balanced on the asset side of their balance sheet by $1,000 of required reserves and $9,000 of loan claims.

The size of the deposit multiplier is determined by the required reserve ratio (rr) because, on each cycle of the "lending/spending/depositing" process, a specified fraction of the deposited funds must be withdrawn from the process. The formula for the deposit multiplier (d) is

$$d = 1/rr$$

The greater the required reserve ratio (that is, the greater the amount of reserves that banks are required to retain and not lend out), the smaller the deposit multiplier.

We have found that a $1,000 increase in bank reserves can lead to a tenfold expansion in demand deposits, courtesy of the deposit multiplier:

$$\Delta R \times d = \Delta DD$$

As we shall see later in this chapter, this relationship between changes in available reserves for banks and changes in demand deposits is the key to understanding how monetary policy functions.

A Small Point: We know that demand deposits have increased by $10,000, but has the money supply also increased by $10,000? In this example, no, it hasn't!

Recall that the money supply (M) is

$$M = CC + DD$$

When Andrew deposited $1,000 that started off the process, currency held by the public decreased by $1,000, so the net increase in the money supply is only $9,000. (If the increase in bank reserves is initiated in a way that doesn't reduce currency—for example, a purchase of bonds by the Fed from the banking system—then the offsetting change will not occur, and the money supply will increase tenfold. Because of this, the deposit multiplier is frequently, if inaccurately, known as the "money multiplier.")

As you will recognize, the deposit creation process is quite similar to that described for the expenditure multiplier in Chapter 5. To get an intuitive feel for the deposit expansion process, you can use a diagram similar to the one presented there. In this case, the public is split into borrowers and depositors, but otherwise the argument is the same. Here, the leakage occurs when banks retain funds as required reserves.

In reality, other leakages reduce the size of the deposit multiplier. Such leakages include borrowers or depositors preferring to hold funds as currency (*currency drains*) instead of passing them on to the next step in the process, or banks choosing to hold excess reserves instead of loaning them out. The deposit creation process and the leakages that reduce its strength are depicted in Figure 7-1.

Each time a member of the public deposits funds into his or her checking account the money supply increases and more reserves are received by banks to continue the process.

THINK IT THROUGH: Is the size of the deposit multiplier relatively stable? How might it vary in response to changing economic conditions?

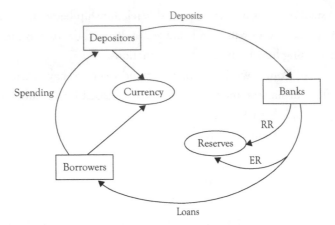

Figure 7-1. Financial sector circular flow diagram.

We should expect the deposit multiplier to vary with such factors as the business cycle and the degree of optimism in the economy. During "good times," banks, eager to lend to the many creditworthy applicants they encounter, will reduce the amount of funds retained as excess reserves, and the deposit multiplier will move closer to its maximum value. However, during recessions, with greater risk of default, banks will become more cautious, holding back more funds as excess reserves, and the deposit multiplier will decline. Historically, banks have maintained low levels of excess reserves but, during the Great Recession, they accumulated significant excess reserves and this behavior made the deposit multiplier sink far below its theoretical value.

In this section, we have discovered that there is a "multiplier" relationship between commercial bank reserves and demand deposits, and that changes in bank reserves can fuel changes in the money supply.

The Market for Money: Money Supply, Money Demand, and the Interest Rate

In this section, we construct a model of the money market. In this market, the interest rate can be thought of as the "price" of money. We shall analyze the factors that influence the quantity of money demanded as the interest rate changes and the factors that affect the demand for money but, first, we shall examine the supply side of the market.

The Supply of Money

We have already done the heavy lifting in understanding the behavior of the quantity of money supplied as the interest rate changes. In general, there is a positive relationship between the interest rate and the quantity of money supplied, as shown in Figure 7-2.

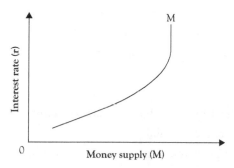

Figure 7-2. The supply of money.

First, when the interest rate—the reward for lending—increases, banks will lend out more aggressively by reducing the amount of excess reserves they retain. As excess reserves are reduced and as more loans are generated, the quantity of money in circulation (in truth, the quantity of demand deposits) will increase. At the same time, when the interest rate increases, there will be a reduction in the currency drains that reduce the strength of the money creation process— members of the public will reduce their holdings of currency as the reward increases for holding funds in the form of bank deposits. Both of these factors combine to cause the financial sector to process reserves more actively as the "price" of money increases and, therefore, the money supply curve (M) is upward-sloping.

THINK IT THROUGH: At some interest rate, all currency drains and holdings of excess reserves will be reduced to zero and, at that interest rate, the deposit multiplier will have achieved its maximum value. Further increases in the interest rate will have no effect on the quantity of money supplied—the money supply curve will become vertical.

Factors that can shift the position of the money supply curve. The nation's money supply (CC + DD) depends on the **monetary base** (also known as *high-powered money*), which is composed of currency held by the public (CC) and bank reserves (R). The currency component of the money supply has a one-to-one relationship with the currency component of the monetary base but, we know, demand deposits have a multiplied value relative to reserves so the monetary base supports a quantity of money larger than itself.

If the level either of currency or of reserves changes, or if the value of the deposit multiplier changes, then the size of the money supply will change. If, for example, the required reserve ratio is reduced then the money supply curve will shift to the right. If the level of bank reserves is reduced, then the money supply curve will shift to the left. It is unlikely that currency held by the public will change significantly so, from now on, we will ignore that possibility.

In summary, given the interest rate, the money supply curve will shift in response to a change in the quantity of bank reserves or a change in the size of the deposit multiplier.

The Demand for Money: Liquidity Preference

We have established that money fulfills several important functions, chief among them being as a medium of exchange. As economic agents, we have two competing objectives—we seek liquid assets in order to buy the goods and services we desire but we also wish to allocate our financial assets in order to receive earnings from them.

There is a negative relationship between the interest rate and the quantity demanded of money, as shown in Figure 7-3.

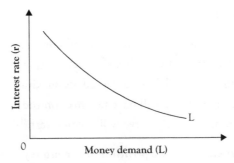

Figure 7-3. The demand for money.

The negative slope of the demand for money curve (L) can be explained in several ways, but perhaps the simplest explanation is to observe that the higher the interest rate, the greater the opportunity cost of holding currency or demand deposits that yield little or no interest. The higher the interest rate, the more attractive it becomes to seek interest-bearing and less liquid assets elsewhere in the financial sector.

Factors that can shift the position of the money demand curve. The position of the money demand curve will shift in response to changes in factors such as the level of economic activity (real GDP), the aggregate price level, and the technology of financial markets.

The demand for money will increase as the level of economic activity increases—more transactions will cause an increase in the demand for funds to finance them. The money demand curve will increase (shift to the right) during economic upswings and decrease (shift to the left) during recessions.

If real GDP remains unchanged, but the aggregate price level increases, then the demand for money to finance transactions will increase—the money demand curve will shift to the right.

Developments in the technology of financial markets such as debit cards, ATMs, and online banking have made it easier and cheaper to convert illiquid assets into cash. Accordingly, with reduced transactions costs, the public has become more willing to hold lower money balances than in the past.

THINK IT THROUGH: In the approach to the millennium, the "Y2K" panic caused a spike in the demand for money, as pessimistic members of the public, afraid that computer problems would prevent them from accessing their accounts, withdrew funds from their bank accounts. In anticipation of this mass action, the Fed increased the supply of reserves, thereby easing the strain placed on banks.

Equilibrium in the Money Market

Combining money supply (M) and money demand (L), we can analyze how the money market achieves the equilibrium interest rate.

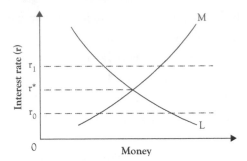

Figure 7-4. Equilibrium in the money market.

Consider Figure 7-4. Let us suppose that the initial interest rate is r_1 and that the quantity of money demanded is low relative to the quantity supplied—the public has more money balances than it desires. In this situation, individuals will try to decrease their money holdings by increasing their holdings of bonds or by transferring funds to other interest-bearing assets.

Consider the market for bonds. Standard demand and supply analysis tells us that as a result of the increase in the demand for bonds, the price of bonds will increase. The influx of money into the bond market signals to issuers of bonds that this is now a seller's market and that they can attract funds from borrowers at a lower interest rate than had previously been necessary—there is a negative relationship between the price of bonds and the market interest rate. As the price of bonds rises, the interest rate declines. Because of this decline in the interest rate, there is an increase in the quantity demanded of money (a movement *along* the money demand curve) and a decrease in the quantity of money supplied (a movement *along* the money supply curve).

If the initial interest rate is r_0, then the quantity of money demanded is high relative to the quantity supplied—there is a shortage of money balances. To get the money they desire, individuals will transfer funds from interest-bearing assets—they will sell bonds. An increase in the supply of bonds will drive down bond prices and (given the negative relationship between bond prices and interest rates) push interest rates higher. The increase in interest rates will result in a decrease in the quantity of money balances demanded and an increase in the quantity of money supplied.

THINK IT THROUGH: What causes the increase in the quantity of money supplied as the interest rate increases? As the interest rate increases, the reward received by banks for lending is raised, encouraging them to lend more vigorously and to reduce their holdings of excess reserves while, simultaneously, currency drains by the public will be reduced. The deposit multiplier will increase in size and, given the reserves in the system, the quantity of demand deposits will expand.

If there is either a surplus or a shortage in the money market, then we would expect to see adjustments in the interest rate that would move the market toward the equilibrium interest rate (r^*).

Single-Shift Cases: As we did in Chapter 2, let us apply demand and supply analysis to the money market. We are given four bits of information and asked to predict their consequences on the interest rate and the quantity of money in circulation. The four pieces of information are as follows:

Case 1. There has been an increase in the aggregate price level.
Case 2. The quantity of bank reserves has increased.
Case 3. The economy is experiencing a recession.
Case 4. The reserve ratio has been increased.

First, in each case, determine if there has been a change in the demand for money or a change in the supply of money. In each case, has the specified curve increased or decreased? Predict the effect on the equilibrium interest rate and the quantity of money.

The changes in Cases 1 and 3 affect the demand for money. In Case 1, rising prices provoke a greater demand for the medium of exchange whereas, in Case 3, the sluggish economy, suffering from a reduced level of transactions, will cause a decrease in the demand for money. The effects of Case 1 are shown in Figure 7-5.

The initial money demand and money supply curves are L_0 and M_0, respectively, and the equilibrium interest rate is r_0. The increased demand for money shifts the money demand curve right to L_1. Given the initial interest rate, there is now an excess demand for money and the public will respond to the shortage of liquidity by selling (liquidating) noncash assets such as bonds. The increased supply of bonds will cause the price of

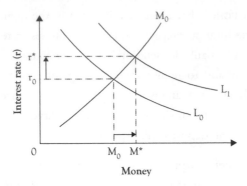

Figure 7-5. An increase in the demand for money.

bonds to decrease and, given the negative relationship between them, the interest rate will increase until equilibrium is achieved, at r^*.

The changes in Cases 2 and 4 affect the supply of money. In Case 2, the increased quantity of bank reserves will result in greater lending activity and money creation as banks seek to lend out excess reserves, shifting the money supply curve to the right, whereas, in Case 4, the money supply curve will shift to the left because the higher reserve requirement will reduce the size of the deposit multiplier, meaning that a smaller quantity of loans can be supported than was previously the case. (Note that, in Case 4, the quantity of reserves themselves has *not* been affected.) The effects of Case 2 are shown in Figure 7-6.

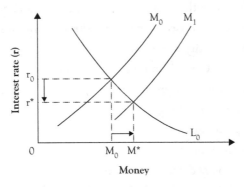

Figure 7-6. An increase in the supply for money.

As before, the initial money demand and money supply curves are L_0 and M_0, respectively, and the equilibrium interest rate is r_0. The increased supply of money shifts the money supply curve right to M_1. At the initial interest rate, an excess supply for money now exists and the public will respond to the unwanted liquidity by transferring funds to assets such as bonds. The increased demand for bonds will drive up the price of bonds and the interest rate will decrease until equilibrium is restored, at r*.

In this section, we have constructed a model of the money market, explaining the shapes of the money demand and money supply curves and specifying important variables that can cause those curves to shift position.

Monetary Policy: Influencing the Economy Through the Financial Sector

The Federal Reserve influences the overall economy by manipulating activities in the financial sector. How does it achieve this goal? First, we must address a theoretical issue—does the Fed use the money supply as its policy instrument of choice or does it use the interest rate? In the past, the focus was on adjusting the money supply but because the money supply is hard to quantify on a day-to-day basis, there has been a progressive shift in focus toward targeting a key observable interest rate—**the federal funds rate**.

As we have seen, banks find it convenient to hold a portion of their reserves as "deposits at the Fed" and, while many of these deposits are required reserves, others are not required reserves and these funds can be loaned out. It is possible that a bank may find itself with insufficient reserves to cover its required obligations—if so, then it must borrow to meet its reserve requirement. One option for an institution in such a position is to borrow reserves directly from the Fed and, in this case, the interest rate charged by the Fed is known as the **discount rate**. Alternatively, a bank with deficient required reserves could borrow on a short-term basis (usually overnight) from a bank that has surplus balances of *federal funds*—if so, then the interest rate charged is the federal funds rate.

In recent years, the Fed has found that targeting the federal funds rate is an effective method of signaling its stance on monetary policy. In practice, the Fed targets a range of values for the federal funds rate, adjusting its actions to maintain the actual market rate within that range.

If the actual range is higher than what the Fed wishes, then the Fed will buy bonds from institutions. This action has the effect of increasing the reserves of the participating institutions because they are exchanging bonds (which are not counted as reserves) for increased deposits at the Fed (which do). As a result, the number of banks with surplus reserves increases whereas the number with insufficient reserves and with a need to borrow federal funds is reduced—the federal funds rate decreases.

If the actual federal funds rate is felt to be too low, then the Fed will reverse the action—selling bonds at an attractive price to banks. The banks receive bonds (nonreserve assets) and give up some of the reserves that they have deposited at the Fed. The supply of federal funds is reduced while the demand for such funds is increased, causing the federal funds rate to increase.

Tools of Monetary Policy

There are three major tools of monetary policy and we have already touched on each of them, directly or indirectly. The tools, in ascending order of frequency of use by the Fed, are the required reserve ratio, the discount rate, and open-market operations. Be aware that other central banks, which have access to similar policy options, may not employ them with the same frequency or in the same proportions as the Fed. Japan, for instance, has been using quantitative easing since the 1990s and the People's Bank of China favors the use of the discount rate.

Consider once more the relationship between reserves and demand deposits and, by extension, the money supply:

$$\Delta R \times d = \Delta DD$$

Required reserve ratio: At its simplest, the deposit multiplier is the reciprocal of the reserve ratio. If the Fed cuts the reserve requirement, then the existing quantity of bank reserves will be capable of supporting a greater quantity of demand deposits than before. By freeing up reserves that previously had been required reserves and allowing them to be loaned out to borrowers, a decrease in the reserve ratio permits the money supply to increase.

Conversely, if the Fed wishes to clamp down on the money supply, one option is to increase the reserve requirement. This will convert reserves that had been excess reserves into required reserves and reduce the ability of banks to lend. In such a scenario, banks may not have sufficient excess reserves on hand to convert into required reserves and, in order to satisfy the new requirement, would probably have to borrow reserves from the central bank.

THINK IT THROUGH: The required reserve ratio is an extremely powerful tool of monetary policy but it is used rarely by the Fed. The requirement was reduced from 12 percent to 10 percent in 1992 (but, even then, more to support bank profitability following the 1990–1991 recession than as an action intended to influence interest rates) but it has not been changed since. Changes (especially increases) in the reserve ratio are potentially disruptive to commercial bank balance sheets, which attempt to match new loans with maturing ones. Changing the rules in mid-game seems unfair, and forcing banks to find reserves to meet a higher requirement would present a challenge, almost certainly compelling banks to "call" loans (that is, to require repayment of loans that have been set up as repayable on short notice) and to borrow from the Fed at the discount window.

Discount rate: The discount rate is the interest rate charged by the Fed to borrowing institutions. Borrowing from the Fed expands the borrowing bank's excess reserves and its capacity to lend and the discount rate can be seen as the cost of acquiring these reserves. A decrease in the discount rate reduces the cost of excess reserves and, given the market interest rate, increases the profitability from lending to the public. A decrease in the discount rate, therefore, ought to encourage the banking sector to indulge in additional borrowing from the Fed and lending to the public, thus increasing the money supply.

When the discount rate is changed, there is a second effect in play that influences the size of the deposit multiplier and, through it, the money supply. The discount rate may be thought of as the penalty for miscalculating reserve obligations. If the rewards from lending are high, then bankers will lend vigorously and will trim down their excess reserves until, perhaps, they have insufficient reserves to meet their obligations. At that point, they would have to borrow. If, on the one hand, the cost of borrowing from the Fed is low relative to the rewards from lending to the public, then institutions are more likely to reduce their excess reserves, causing the size of the deposit multiplier to rise toward its maximum value. If, on the other hand, the discount rate is relatively high, then institutions are more likely to play it safe and, by keeping a larger cushion of excess reserves, reduce the size of the deposit multiplier and, therefore, the money supply.

In short, an increase in the discount rate will cause the money supply to decrease whereas a decrease in the discount rate will encourage an expansion in the money supply.

Open-market operations: The primary tool of monetary policy is open-market operations. Open-market operations occur when the Fed (in practice, the Open Market Desk in the Federal Reserve Bank of New York) enters the bond market and buys or sells securities. These transactions may be with financial institutions or with individuals or firms outside the financial sector. In any case, the results are similar— a Fed purchase of bonds increases the quantity of reserves available to the financial sector and expands the money supply whereas a Fed sale of bonds reduces the quantity of reserves and reduces the money supply.

Consider what happens to the reserves of Bank A when the Fed approaches it with an offer to buy $5 million worth of its bond holdings. The bonds held by Bank A are not part of its reserves, being neither vault cash nor deposits at the Fed. However, when the deal takes place, Bank A's balance sheet will show a $5 million reduction in bonds and a $5 million increase in deposits at the Fed, because the Fed will pay for the bonds by crediting Bank A's Fed account. The upshot of the transaction is that Bank A's reserves have increased by $5 million and it now has funds available to lend out. We would expect to see an increase in the money supply when the Fed buys bonds in the open market.

Learning Tip: As you work to master the intricacies of monetary policy, there are a couple of tricks that can help. The discount rate and reserve ratio move in the same direction—an expansion in the money supply can be achieved by reductions in either, for example. With respect to open-market operations, when the Fed (**B**)uys bonds the money supply grows (**B**)igger, and when the Fed (**S**)ells bonds the money supply grows (**S**)maller.

A Cautionary Comment: On the face of it, it looks as though monetary policy actions are neatly symmetrical, with equal purchases and sales of bonds by the Fed having equivalent but opposite impacts on reserves and, from there, the money supply. However, the Fed is more likely to be successful at contracting the money supply than it is at expanding it. This distinction is summed up in the phrase "You can't push a string" meaning that, although bankers may be compelled to reduce their lending, they can't be compelled to increase their lending. In an economy with a bleak outlook, in which the Fed might hope for greater extension of credit, bankers may quite simply balk.

A Further Caution: In addition to the forgoing comment, the self-interested actions of bankers may intensify the effects of business cycles. During a recession, for example, bankers, more cautious than usual, may lend less energetically and accumulate additional excess reserves, causing the deposit multiplier to decline. This decline will cause a decrease in the money supply and higher interest rates than would otherwise have been the case. As we shall see next, rising interest rates will intensify the economic slowdown by discouraging private sector spending.

The Impact of Monetary Policy

Thinking back to our discussion of fiscal policy in Chapter 6, we know that an "expansionary" policy is one whose purpose is to encourage economic expansion—higher aggregate demand, more jobs—whereas the intent of a "contractionary" policy is to slow down an overheating economy's inflationary pressures. Where the fiscal policy transmission mechanism was short and direct—increase government spending to increase aggregate demand, for example—the monetary policy transmission mechanism has many more links and, therefore, more opportunities to fail.

The Monetary Policy Transmission Mechanism: We already have some of the links in hand. We know that the Fed can increase bank reserves by buying bonds from financial institutions (or from the private sector) or by reducing the discount rate. Also, we know that the size of the deposit multiplier can be influenced by changes in the required reserve ratio or the discount rate. The Fed's policy tools can affect the money supply and, therefore, the interest rate.

If, for example, the money supply is increased and the interest decreases, then the costs borne by businesses wishing to borrow financial capital in order to increase investment will be reduced, and previously unprofitable projects will become feasible. Lower borrowing costs increase investment. Moreover, reduced borrowing costs will encourage additional borrowing by households on "big-ticket" items such as cars, furniture, and household appliances. In short, a decrease in the interest rate will energize two major components of aggregate demand and will have an expansionary effect on the economy.

The monetary policy transmission mechanism for a policy using open-market operations is summarized in Figure 7-7.

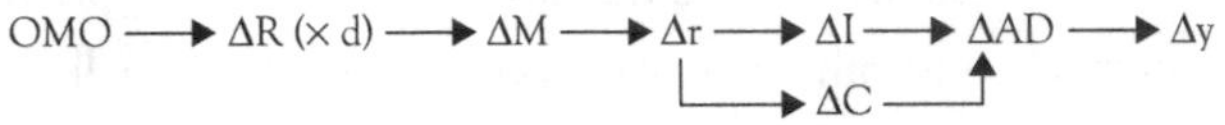

$$OMO \longrightarrow \Delta R\,(\times\,d) \longrightarrow \Delta M \longrightarrow \Delta r \longrightarrow \Delta I \longrightarrow \Delta AD \longrightarrow \Delta y$$
$$\longrightarrow \Delta C \longrightarrow$$

Figure 7-7. The monetary policy transmission mechanism.

Let us suppose the Fed wishes the economy to expand and, as is typically the case, uses open-market operations, buying bonds. If the Fed buys bonds (OMO), then bank reserves will increase (ΔR) and, given the size of the deposit multiplier (d), the money supply will increase (ΔM). The increase in the money supply will depress interest rates (Δr)—the cost of borrowing. With reduced borrowing costs, businesses and households will borrow more heavily, reduce saving, and spend more. Investment and consumption spending will increase (ΔI, ΔC), driving up aggregate demand (ΔAD) and real GDP (Δy).

Cautions: This looks fairly cut and dried, but several cautions must be raised.

The Interest Sensitivity of Money Demand: One key link in the process is how sensitive demanders of money are to interest rate changes. If money demand is fairly sensitive to changes in the interest rate then, for a given change in the money supply, the change in the interest rate will be quite small, and the effectiveness of the policy will be stunted. This case is shown in Figure 7-8.

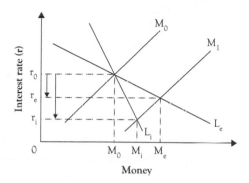

Figure 7-8. Interest sensitivity of money demand.

Relatively, the more vigorously money demanders respond to a change in the interest rate, the flatter the money demand curve. In our diagram, the flatter money demand curve, L_e, is more interest-sensitive than L_i. Given the increase in the money supply from M_0 to M_1, and with sensitive (or, in economists' terminology, *elastic*) money demand curve L_e, when the interest rate responds, it falls, but not by much (from r_0 to r_e). If, conversely, money demand is relatively insensitive (*inelastic*) to interest rate changes, then the money demand curve will be quite steep, as shown with inelastic demand curve L_i. Here, with the same increase in money supply, the decrease in the interest rate (from r_0 to r_i) is stronger. The stronger the interest-rate response, the more powerful the effect of a given policy action—monetary policy is more effective the less interest-sensitive is the demand for money.

Following the Great Recession, and particularly in the latter part of 2012, with interest rates driven down by Fed policy to historically low levels, there was renewed talk of a potential *liquidity trap* for the United States' economy and for others. A liquidity trap occurs if the money demand curve becomes horizontal—as can be seen from Figure 7-8, changes in the money supply would become wholly ineffective in such a situation. Money supply changes would have no effect on interest rates. Once a theoretical curiosity, respected economists have argued that the Japanese economy wallowed in a liquidity trap during its "lost decade" at the end of the past century.

THINK IT THROUGH: What could cause the money demand curve to be horizontal? Essentially what is happening is that any money that is pumped into the system is instantly snapped up and hoarded by the public. If interest rates are very low, then there is no strong advantage to holding interest-bearing assets that are less liquid and more risky than cash and, therefore, cash becomes the preferred asset.

As the Japanese discovered, for an economy captured in a liquidity trap, the standard monetary policy focus on manipulating short-term interest rates is ineffectual. The Japanese responded by shifting their monetary policy emphasis to *quantitative easing*, a path revisited by the Fed in the aftermath of the Great Recession. We consider quantitative easing later in this chapter.

The Interest Sensitivity of Investment and Consumption: A further key, and controversial, link in the monetary policy transmission process is to do with the responsiveness of businesses and households to changes in short-term interest rates. The assumption of an expansionary policy is that, by cutting the cost of borrowing during an economic downturn, there will be an upswing in new investment projects (new businesses created and existing businesses expanded) and additional purchasing by households, and that the size of that upswing will be predictable. If the assumption is not valid, however, then the policy's effectiveness is jeopardized.

Time Lags: As with fiscal policy, monetary policy is hampered by lags between the emergence of a problem and its cure. While the recognition lag is the same as for fiscal policy, and the implementation lag is likely to be shorter, it has been argued, by Milton Friedman among others, that the response lag—the time between an interest rate change and its impact on the actions of businesspeople and households—may be "long and variable," adding to the general air of uncertainty involved in policy matters.

The Monetary Dampener: Finally, we must consider the effect of a feedback from the real sector of the economy to the financial sector. We shall call this feedback the *monetary dampener* and, like the "dampeners" we have encountered in previous chapters (the price dampener, the tax-rate dampener) its presence reduces the size of the expenditure multiplier

(m) and, from there, the effectiveness of both monetary and fiscal policy. It should be noted that, although the following example begins with an expansionary monetary policy action, the monetary dampener is present even in the absence of a policy action.

Given an economy thought to require a stimulus, let us suppose that the Fed buys bonds, boosts bank reserves, expands the money supply from M_0 to M_1, and reduces the interest rate from r_0 to r_1, as shown in Figure 7-9.

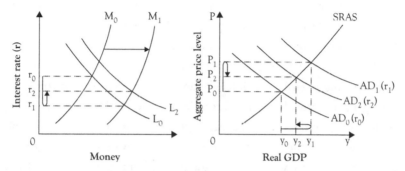

Figure 7-9. An expansionary monetary policy action.

If all goes according to plan, investment and consumption spending increases, raising aggregate demand through the operation of the expenditure multiplier from AD_0 to AD_1. This is what we have seen in our past analysis but now we can consider the effect of the monetary dampener. As aggregate demand increases, both real GDP and the aggregate price level increase, to y_1 and P_1, respectively. As we have established, an increase in one or both of these variables will cause a rightward shift in the demand for money curve, as shown in Figure 7-9, with the movement from L_0 to L_2. This increase in money demand chokes off and then partially reverses the desired decrease in the interest rate, which ends up at r_2. Consequently, the hoped-for expansion in investment and consumption is lessened and the rightward shift in aggregate demand is offset to some extent and aggregate demand comes to rest at AD_2. The monetary dampener reduces the size of the expenditure multiplier, acting as an automatic stabilizer that weakens the potency of policy actions.

THINK IT THROUGH: Verify the effect of the monetary dampener in the case where consumption spending suddenly increases because of an increase in optimism within the household sector. You should find that the equilibrium interest rate will increase, retarding the expansion in private spending.

A Defense of Monetary Policy: From the preceding paragraphs, you may have begun to query the effectiveness, or even the wisdom, of monetary policy. However, monetary policy can be enacted quickly and fine-tuned precisely, and, in practical terms, given the frequent political gridlock regarding the construction of fiscal policy, credit for the historically low inflation rates achieved over the past quarter century may be reasonably laid at the door of the Fed.

In addition, fiscal and monetary policies work through different channels, so the effectiveness of policy can be enhanced if a complementary blend of fiscal and monetary policy can be coordinated.

Policy Coordination: An expansionary fiscal policy drives up interest rates. The more sensitive to interest rate changes the private sector is, the stronger is the crowding-out effect of fiscal policy and the less effective is such a policy, but, for the same reason, the *more* effective is monetary policy—the greater the interest-sensitivity of the private sector, the greater is the impact of a given change in the money supply. Accordingly, faced with an expansionary fiscal policy that, as a by-product, increases interest rates and produces crowding-out, the Fed can enhance the effectiveness of the fiscal policy by expanding the money supply through open-market purchases, thereby neutralizing the pressure on interest rates and forestalling the crowding-out effect.

In summary, through a coordinated effort, the Fed can heighten the potency of fiscal policy by "accommodating" actions.

The Great Recession and Recent History

During the first few years of the new century, there was a boom in housing prices and in the stock market. The Fed was unsuccessful in calming down the "irrational exuberance" of the markets and, with the addition of questionable financial products and practices, the economy crashed in 2007, resulting in bailouts of firms that were considered "too big to fail" and the introduction of the Troubled Asset Relief Program (TARP), the takeover of housing lenders Fannie Mae and Freddie Mac by the U.S. Treasury, and tightened restrictions in the financial sector through the passage of the Dodd–Frank Act of 2010. Let us consider the Fed's policy of *quantitative easing*.

Quantitative Easing (QE): Quantitative easing was first introduced in Japan in the 1990s in the absence of feasible conventional monetary policy options. For similar reasons, the Fed initiated quantitative easing in 2010 because previous policy actions had driven short-term interest rates, such as the federal funds rate, close to zero and orthodox monetary policy actions were severely constrained. Quantitative easing involves the manipulation of longer-term interest rates.

There is, of course, not one single "interest rate" but rather a family of rates. Long-term rates, such as mortgage rates, are based on current short-term rates and expectations about how those short-term rates will change in the future and, in normal times, the Fed can influence long-term rates by acting on short-term rates. However, with short-term rates close to zero and expected to remain there, the Fed turned to quantitative easing to influence long-term rates and the overall economy. In practice, the current (2012) policy—buying mortgage-backed securities and decreasing the riskiness of banking sector balance sheets in an effort to increase the money supply—is a turn away from targeting the interest rate and a rehabilitation of the importance of the *quantity* of money in the system.

In Chapter 4, we examined the *proportional form* of the quantity theory, which states that

percentage change in M + percentage change in V
= percentage change in P + percentage change in y

In a liquidity trap, with individuals eagerly holding onto money balances, the velocity of circulation decreases but, with a stagnant economy, real GDP grows only slowly. Consequently, the Classical critique of quantitative easing is simple—quantitative easing runs the risk of igniting inflation as well as spending.

In addition, as we know from demand and supply analysis, the increase in the supply of a good can be expected to decrease its price. Similarly, an increase in the supply of dollars can be expected, other things remaining equal, to decrease the value of the dollar relative to other currencies—the exchange rate. A depreciation in the value of a nation's currency can have significant macroeconomic effects on variables such as exports and imports and it is to the international sector that we turn in Chapter 8.

Review: In this long and intricate chapter we began by considering the meaning and functions of money, and then examined the ability of the central bank to manipulate the money supply and interest rates and, through that manipulation, the level of activity in the macroeconomy. We have found that monetary and fiscal policy acting in coordination can be more effective than if they operate in isolation.

CHAPTER 8

The International Sector

Trade and Finance

By the end of this chapter you will be able to:

1. Use comparative advantage to show how countries can gain from specialization and trade.
2. Given a particular two-country, two-good situation, determine which country will trade which good and indicate the feasible range for the terms of trade.
3. Given a particular two-country, two-good situation, and specific terms of trade, use consumption possibility frontiers to demonstrate that trade can be beneficial.
4. Evaluate common arguments in favor of trade restrictions.
5. Distinguish between a quota and a tariff.
6. Use demand and supply analysis to outline the costs involved in the imposition of a tariff.
7. Use demand and supply analysis to describe the determination of the international value of the dollar. Explain how each determinant plays a role in the process.
8. Explain the reasoning behind the purchasing-power parity theory.
9. Incorporate imports and exports into the ADAS model and explain how imports affect the size of the expenditure multiplier.
10. Outline the effects of the exchange rate on the effectiveness of monetary and fiscal policy.

In 1981, the Japanese auto industry announced a voluntary limitation on the number of cars sent to the United States. This "voluntary export restraint," which was welcomed by the Reagan administration, lasted until 1994. In this chapter, we shall analyze the economic effects of this apparently benevolent restriction on car sales by the Japanese.

Chapter Preview: In the present chapter, we shall pull together several topics that we have met previously and integrate them into our model of the macroeconomy. In Chapter 1, we first encountered the production possibility frontier diagram and used it to depict several economic issues, including the benefits of trade and the sources of economic growth. In this chapter we shall develop that early analysis to help us consider more fully the gains for trade and, in Chapter 9, we shall turn to a deeper consideration of economic growth.

In Chapter 2, we used demand and supply analysis to examine consumer and producer surplus and the gains that flow from markets. We shall employ this insight to lend further support to our conclusion that trade can be mutually beneficial. Demand and supply will also help us to discover how exchange rates are determined.

International Trade: The Principle of Mutually Beneficial Trade

In 1817, David Ricardo introduced the world to the Law of Comparative Advantage—first, an explanation of the pattern of trade between nations and, second, an argument in favor of trade liberalization, because Ricardo demonstrated that trade could be mutually beneficial. Respected economist Paul Samuelson has described the Law of Comparative Advantage as "the most beautiful idea in economics."

Since the trailblazing days of David Ricardo and Adam Smith, economists have generally expressed confidence in the ability of free and fair trade to provide the most advantageous outcome for the greatest number of individuals. It may seem perverse, therefore, that the practice of international trade has had such a long history of restrictions. In this section, we shall first review and expand the model of trade we started in Chapter 1 and then consider arguments for and against free trade.

The Law of Comparative Advantage

Let us suppose that we have two countries—Germany and France—that produce two goods, barrels of beer (B) and wheels of cheese (C). Further, we shall assume that there are no trade restrictions between the two countries, that transportation costs are insignificant, and that the two countries have production possibility frontiers that exhibit constant costs. The production possibility frontiers are shown in Figure 8-1.

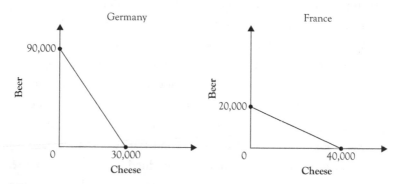

Figure 8-1. Production possibility frontiers for Germany and France.

From Chapter 1, we know that the slope of a production possibility frontier depicts the opportunity cost of producing more of one good in terms of the other good. If the production possibility frontier is a straight line, then because the slope of the frontier is constant, the opportunity cost is also constant. Our diagram shows that, at maximum, Germany can produce 90,000 barrels of beer (and no cheese) or 30,000 wheels of cheese (and no beer) whereas, at maximum, France can produce 20,000 barrels of beer (and no cheese) or 40,000 wheels of cheese (and no beer).

In our example, if Germany decides to specialize entirely in the production of cheese (producing 30,000 wheels of cheese), then the opportunity cost is the 90,000 barrels of beer that otherwise could have been produced—each wheel of cheese "costs" three barrels of beer. If France specializes entirely in the production of cheese (producing 40,000 wheels of cheese), then the opportunity cost is the 20,000 barrels of beer forgone. In France, therefore, each wheel of cheese "costs" a half of a barrel of beer. We can conclude that the opportunity cost of cheese is lower in France—France has a comparative cost advantage in the production of cheese.

Reversing the argument, if Germany specializes in beer production (producing 90,000 barrels), then the opportunity cost is the 30,000 wheels of cheese that otherwise could have been produced—each barrel of beer "costs" one-third of a wheel of cheese but, if France specializes entirely in beer production (producing 20,000 barrels), then the opportunity cost is the 40,000 wheels of cheese forgone. In France, each barrel of beer "costs" two wheels of cheese. The opportunity cost of beer is lower in Germany—Germany has a comparative cost advantage in the production of beer.

As we saw in Chapter 1, this is a general result—if the production possibility frontiers have differing slopes, then the opportunity costs must be different and each country must have a comparative cost advantage in the production of one of the two goods. It is not possible for either country to be cheaper at producing both goods. Only if the slopes of the frontiers are equal—meaning that the costs are equal—will no advantage exist.

Having established that Germany's comparative cost advantage is in beer production and France is in cheese production, Ricardo would recommend that each country play to its strength and specialize in the good in which it has the advantage. Each country should retain that portion of its domestic production that it desires and trade the remainder—its surplus—for the good in which it had the disadvantage. Following this strategy, Ricardo stated, ought to result in mutually beneficial trade. Can we prove Ricardo's assertion?

The Terms of Trade: To keep this simple, Ricardo assumed that traders barter, exchanging goods for goods. The **terms of trade** is the technical term for the "price" or the "barter rate of exchange," such as when one wheel of cheese is traded for two barrels of beer.

Let us suppose that the terms of trade are one wheel of cheese (C) trades for three barrels of beer (B), or 1C = 3B. Put differently, one barrel of beer trades for one-third of a wheel of cheese, or 1B = 1/3C. If so, then Germany, which specializes in beer production, cannot gain from trade. Why? Because Germany's cost of production of beer (one barrel of beer costs one-third of a wheel of cheese) is identical to its selling price, the terms of trade. If the "cost" and the "price" are the same—no gain!

France, however, would gain from trade. France's opportunity cost of producing a wheel of cheese is one-half of a barrel of beer and it can exchange each unit of cheese for three barrels of beer. Because it can produce cheese at a "cost" that is lower than the "price" at which it can sell its cheese, France gains from trade.

In this situation (1C = 3B), because France would gain from trade and Germany wouldn't lose, trade should proceed.

Now, suppose that the terms of trade are one wheel of cheese (C) trades for one half of a barrel of beer (B), or 1C = 1/2B. Put differently, one barrel of beer trades for two wheels of cheese, or 1B = 2C. Here, Germany will gain from trade because the opportunity cost of its specialty, beer, is less than the terms of trade, but France would neither gain nor lose, because the opportunity cost of cheese production in France is identical to the terms of trade.

In such a situation (1C = 1/2B), because Germany would gain from trade and France wouldn't lose, trade should proceed.

The Limits to the Terms of Trade: We have identified the *limits to the terms of trade*. These limits are the values at which one country will gain from trade while the other will not lose. In our example, one limit is 1C = 3B (Germany gains) and the other limit is 1C = 1/2B (France gains). As we shall see, if the terms of trade stray beyond these limits, then trade will break down but, before examining that point, let us consider what determines the limits to the terms of trade.

France specializes in cheese and its opportunity cost for a wheel of cheese is half a barrel of beer (1C costs 1/2B), whereas Germany specializes in beer and the opportunity cost there of a barrel of beer is one-third of a wheel of cheese or, put differently, the German opportunity cost of a wheel of cheese is three barrels of beer (1C costs 3B). The limits to the terms of trade are determined by the respective opportunity costs in the two countries.

Going Beyond the Limits to the Terms of Trade: What if, somehow, the terms of trade moved beyond either limit? What would happen then?

Suppose that the price of cheese rose from three barrels of beer (1C = 3B) to four barrels of beer (1C = 4B) or, put differently, the price of each barrel of beer fell to one-quarter of a wheel of cheese (1B = 1/4C). In this situation, with cheese highly priced, the French would be quite happy to produce cheese. The beer-producing Germans, however, would be less content because, if they produced beer (at a cost of one-third of a wheel of cheese) they would have to sell it for a lower price (one-quarter of a wheel of cheese). They would not produce beer. As there are only two goods, if the Germans do not produce beer then they must produce cheese. This is feasible, in the sense that the German cost of cheese production is three barrels of beer, but the international price of cheese is higher, at four barrels of beer. Germany should produce cheese.

Trade, therefore, breaks down! With both countries bringing only cheese to the market, there is nothing to trade it for. If there were more than two countries and one was sufficiently low cost in beer production (the Czech Republic, perhaps), then trade could continue but, with only two countries, the basis for trade is removed.

THINK IT THROUGH: Using the other limit (1C = 1/2B) for reference, determine a value for the terms of trade that lies beyond that limit, such as 1C = 1/5B. Verify for yourself that, in this case, both France and Germany will find it preferable to produce beer and that trade between them will cease.

A mechanism exists to restore trade. If both France and Germany produce only cheese, then it is likely that consumers will be weary of their endless diet of cheese (the demand for cheese will decrease, causing a surplus) while there will be a heightened desire for beer (the demand for beer will increase, causing a shortage). Relatively, the price of cheese will decrease and the price of beer will increase—the terms of trade will move in favor of beer. We should expect that, typically, the terms of trade will lie at one or other of the limits to the terms of trade or, more likely, at a value between the limits.

A mutually beneficial value for the terms of trade: If the terms of trade are established somewhere between the limits, for example, with one cheese trading for one beer (1C = 1B), then we can demonstrate that trade will be mutually beneficial.

Consider cheese-producing France. The opportunity cost to France of producing a wheel of cheese is one-half of a barrel of beer (that's the amount of beer France gives up in order to produce its cheese). France can trade the cheese for one barrel of beer. By trading, France has gained a barrel of beer at a cost of one-half of a barrel of beer—France wins!

The same conclusion is true for beer-producing Germany. The opportunity cost to Germany of producing a barrel of beer is one-third of a wheel of cheese—the amount of cheese Germany forgoes in order to produce its beer). Germany can trade its barrel of beer for one wheel of cheese. By trading, Germany has gained a wheel of cheese by giving up one-third of a wheel of cheese—Germany wins!

In short, any terms of trade value that lies between the limits to the terms of trade will produce mutually beneficial trade, just as Ricardo predicted. The closer to one limit the actual terms lie, the greater the advantage to one trading partner and the less to the other, but the underlying proposition still holds—both parties gain by specializing and trading according to comparative advantage. Table 8-1 summarizes our discussion on the terms of trade and the gains from trade.

Table 8-1. Terms of Trade and the Gains from Trade

Terms of trade	Values for terms of trade	Results
Beyond the limit to the terms of trade	1C > 3B	France produces cheese
(trade breaks down)	1B < 1/3C	Germany produces cheese
At one limit to the terms of trade	1C = 3B	France gains from producing cheese
(one country gains from trade)	1B = 1/3C	Germany breaks even
Between the limits to the terms of trade	1C = 1B	France gains from producing cheese
(mutually beneficial trade)	1B = 1C	Germany gains from producing beer
At one limit to the terms of trade	1C = 1/2B	France breaks even
(one country gains from trade)	1B = 2C	Germany gains from producing beer
Beyond the limit to the terms of trade	1C < 1/2B	France produces beer
(trade breaks down)	1B > 2C	Germany produces beer

THINK IT THROUGH: Two countries with similar costs have little scope for advantageous trade but the gains from trade are likely to be greater for countries the more dissimilar are their opportunity costs.

The Consumption Possibility Frontier: The discussion in the previous section contains a fair amount of math but it is possible to reach the same conclusion, both parties gain by specialization and trade, by using a graphical method—the consumption possibility frontier.

A *production* possibility frontier shows how much it is possible for a country to produce, given its current resources and technology. In an entirely analogous way, a **consumption possibility frontier** (CPF) shows how much it is possible for a country to consume, given its current resources and technology. For a country that does not indulge in trade, its consumption possibility frontier and its production possibility frontier are identical—alone on his island, Robinson Crusoe can consume no more than he can produce.

Let us use the value between the limits to the terms of trade (1C = 1B) that we have shown to yield mutually beneficial results for France and Germany, and recast the analysis in terms of consumption possibility frontiers.

For Germany, specializing in the production of beer, one consumption option is to produce 90,000 barrels of beer, not trade, and consume them all. In that case, Germany's consumption bundle would be 90,000 barrels of beer and no cheese. This is point A in Figure 8-2.

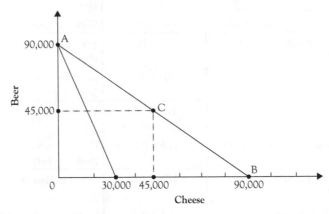

Figure 8-2. Germany's consumption possibility frontier.

A second alternative is to produce 90,000 barrels of beer and trade them all for cheese, at a rate of one beer for one cheese, allowing Germans to consume 90,000 wheels of cheese and no beer. This is point B in Figure 8-2.

A third alternative is to produce the 90,000 barrels of beer and keep 45,000 barrels and trade the other 45,000 barrels for cheese, at a rate of one beer for one cheese, allowing Germans to consume 45,000 barrels of beer and 45,000 wheels of cheese. This is point C in Figure 8-2.

In this way, we can build up all of Germany's possible consumption alternatives. Except for "no trade" point A, which lies on the production possibility frontier, trade expands Germany's consumption possibilities beyond what it can achieve without trade.

The consumption possibility frontier starts at point A, depicting the situation where Germany is specializing in beer production. The slope of the consumption possibility frontier is determined by the terms of trade. If the terms of trade move in Germany's favor, with a barrel of beer exchanging for a greater amount of cheese, then the frontier will pivot outward from point A, with point B representing a growing quantity of cheese. If, however, the terms of trade move against Germany, then the frontier will pivot inwards from point A, with point B representing a dwindling quantity of cheese. If the terms were such that at one barrel of beer exchanged for only one-third of a wheel of cheese, then Germany's consumption possibility frontier would coincide with its production possibility frontier—there would be no gains from trade. Why? Because 1B = 1/3C is the limit to the terms of trade at which Germany does not gain. Check Table 8-1 to verify this conclusion.

We can construct France's consumption possibility frontier in a similar fashion, as shown in Figure 8-3. Note that point B is the endpoint at which the French consumption and production possibility frontiers meet—this is because France specializes in cheese production. Further, observe that the consumption possibility frontiers have identical slopes— they *must* have, because the slope of the consumption possibility frontier is determined by the terms of trade that are shared by the two countries.

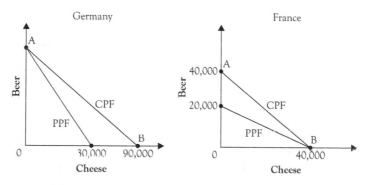

Figure 8-3. Gains from trade demonstrated using consumption possibility frontiers.

"But," you may object, "there's a problem here. If this is a two-country, two-good world, the analysis suggests that Germany can consume 90,000 wheels of cheese at point B. But, if only France produces cheese, and it can produce a maximum of 40,000 wheels of cheese, how can Germany get 90,000?"

Clearly, Germany can't get 90,000 wheels of cheese. If we included a third (cheese-producing) country, then the problem might be solved but, having set up our model as a two-country world, we must offer a more satisfactory answer. First, given that it is improbable that Germany will press for the maximum possible quantity of cheese because the nation is likely to desire some beer as well, we could suggest that that area of the German consumption possibility frontier is unlikely to come into play. But, because it could come into play, we must consider what would then happen.

A high demand for cheese coupled with an insufficient supply will cause the price of cheese (in terms of beer) to increase—in other words, the terms of trade will move in favor of the French. The German consumption possibility frontier will pivot inwards—90,000 barrels of beer no longer will be able to be traded for 90,000 wheels of cheese. At the same time, the 90,000 barrels of beer that the Germans wish to trade are being met by a French demand for only 40,000 barrels. The surplus of beer will cause the price of beer to decrease (in terms of cheese). This effect is merely the flip side of the increase in the price of cheese.

The upshot is that there is a mechanism present in the market that will adjust the terms of trade to an appropriate rate of exchange in order to remove shortages and surpluses. As long as the terms of trade lie between the limits to the terms of trade, the German and French consumption possibility frontiers will lie beyond their respective production possibility frontiers. Our basic point remains: Levels of consumption can be achieved with trade that cannot be achieved without trade—trade is mutually beneficial.

Arguments Made for Protectionism

From the preceding discussion, there would seem to be scant reason for opposing free trade but Ricardo (and Adam Smith before him) developed such strong arguments in favor of unrestricted trade precisely because there were powerful opponents of free trade. Protectionist arguments persist to this day, despite pressure from the General Agreement on Trade and Tariffs (GATT) in 1947, and the establishment, in 1995, of the World Trade Organization (WTO), which has become the world's main forum for promoting and facilitating freer trade among nations.

Are We On The Production Possibility Frontier?: First, a technical point. We must note that our conclusion—that trade guided by comparative advantage can be beneficial—depends on the assumption that each economy has full employment, because our opportunity cost calculation is determined by the slope of the production possibility frontier. If that full-employment assumption is not true—and in the short run it quite frequently is not—then the economy must be operating inside the frontier and the argument for free trade on the basis for comparative advantage evaporates because our opportunity cost calculations are valid only along the frontier itself. A nation struggling through a recession might still find it to be in its own best interests to restrict imports and create homegrown jobs. It is certainly true that, when nations experience recessions, they tend to play the protectionist card.

In Chapter 5, we found that each economy has a "self-correcting" mechanism that will cause it to operate at full employment in the long run. However, given that the economy is, or tends to be, fully employed in the long run and that, on that basis, free trade is advantageous, there endure several deeply entrenched arguments supporting trade restrictions, with the general argument in favor of protection resting on the observation that efficient foreign competition will result in job loss for domestic workers, lost production, and national disruption. Particular arguments for protection from foreign competition include the "infant-industry" argument, appeals regarding national security, and the "cheap foreign labor" complaint. Some of these arguments are simply false, and others are valid but misused. Let us evaluate each of these protectionist justifications in turn.

"Infant-Industry" Argument: This justification for trade restrictions claims that recently established industries may not be large enough to benefit from economies of scale and, hence, will temporarily be at a cost disadvantage relative to larger foreign competitors. Protection should be offered in order to allow such industries to achieve their full potential.

On the face of it, this argument has some merit but only if private venture capital is unavailable for some reason because if, in the long term, the industry will be profitable (which, after all, is the premise of the argument) then private resources will be attracted through capital markets. However, if any form of intervention is justified, government loans are more appropriate than trade restrictions.

National Security: In our two-good, two-country model, if one good is "guns" and the other is "butter," then an argument may be advanced that each country, guided by prudence, ought to produce some guns. Again, this view has some merit, the difficulty being where to draw the line between production that is important for national security and production that is not.

THINK IT THROUGH: Suppose the government announces that it will protect only goods that are essential for national defense. Choose a locally produced good or, if you prefer, chewing gum. Can you devise reasons to support the chosen good's claim for protection? The more creative your arguments, the more difficult they will be to refute.

"Cheap Foreign Labor": This is a frequent but flawed argument. First, wages reflect productivity so, if a nation's workers receive relatively low wages, then it is because their productivity is comparatively low. American workers receive higher wages because they are more productive, perhaps through superior training, a greater quantity and quality of capital, a stronger work ethic, or better health. In terms of GDP per hour worked, American workers are almost three times more productive than Mexican workers, for instance.

Second, trade is based on *comparative* advantage. Even if American workers are more productive and more highly paid across the board, as long as there are industries where the superiority is less marked, then specialization and trade will be beneficial. One could claim that the reason that the United States is shedding textiles jobs is because American workers in hi-tech industries are so very productive!

THINK IT THROUGH: Nations often accuse each other of unfair trade practices as a justification for some form of retaliation in order to "level the playing field." Such practices include predatory dumping (flooding a market with underpriced goods with the intent of destroying the domestic industry) and currency manipulation (where an exporting nation reduces the value of its currency and, therefore, increases the value of the currency of the importing nation). Although these practices can disrupt the pattern of trade, the appropriate response nowadays is not to retaliate with protectionist policies, but to place the matter before the World Trade Organization, the body set up to arbitrate such international trade disputes.

Demand and Supply Analysis of Trade Benefits and Restrictions

In Chapter 2, we introduced the concepts of consumer and producer surplus within a demand and supply context. We will now use this insight to analyze gains from trade.

Comment: You may wish to review the section in Chapter 2, "A New Way To Look at Demand and Supply," before proceeding.

The Market for Oil: Figure 8-4 shows the domestic market for oil in the United States.

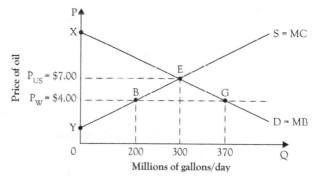

Figure 8-4. The market for oil.

Without imports, let us suppose that the equilibrium price of gasoline (P_{US}) is $7.00 per gallon. The equilibrium quantity (Q_{US}) is 300 million barrels per day. The consumer surplus—the difference between the market price and the demand (or marginal benefit) curve—is the triangle P_{US}XE. The producer surplus—the difference between the market price and the supply (or marginal cost) curve—is the triangle P_{US}YE. The total economic surplus for the economy is the combined area, XYE. (This is exactly the analysis we conducted in Chapter 2 with Figure 2-25.)

Assume that the world price of gasoline (P_W) is $4.00 per gallon. If the domestic market is opened up to permit imported gasoline, then the domestic price of gasoline will be driven down to the global price level. Domestic production will decrease from 300 million gallons to 200 million gallons and quantity demanded will increase to 370 million gallons—170 million gallons will be imported.

How will this change affect the economy's total economic surplus? Producer surplus will shrink to P_WYB—American oil producers will certainly oppose the change—but consumer surplus will expand to P_WXG. The area, BEG, represents the net gain for the economy. Although some individuals lose, trade is generally beneficial.

Immigration: Before we move on, let us consider the American labor market, as shown in Figure 8-5.

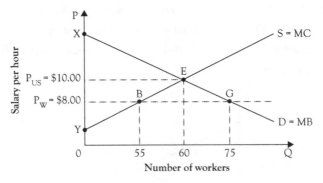

Figure 8-5. The market for labor.

In the absence of foreign labor, let us suppose that the equilibrium salary for low-skilled workers (P_{US}) is $10.00 per hour. The equilibrium quantity of workers employed (Q_{US}) is 60 million. The consumer surplus—the difference between the market price and the demand (or marginal benefit) curve—is the triangle P_{US}XE. This requires a little thought—the demand curve is the demand for labor by *employers*, so the triangle P_{US}XE is the surplus for employers. The producer surplus—the difference between the market price and the supply (or marginal cost) curve—is the triangle P_{US}YE. Again, we must be careful, because the supply curve represents the supply of labor by homegrown *American workers* and the area P_{US}YE is the benefit accruing to them when foreign labor is excluded. The total economic surplus for the economy is the combined area, XYE, as in the previous example.

Assuming that the hourly wage (P_W) is only $8.00 for workers employed outside the United States, there is an incentive for 20 million foreign workers to enter the American labor market. The domestic wage rate will be driven down to $8.00. Producer surplus (for American workers) will decrease to $P_W YB$—American workers will certainly oppose the liberalized immigration as a threat to their jobs and standard of living—but consumer surplus (for employers) will expand to $P_W XG$. The net gain for the economy is represented by the area, BEG. Although some individuals lose, liberalized labor markets are generally beneficial.

Voluntary Export Restraint (VER): Since the 1994 Uruguay Round of trade negotiations, voluntary restraints on exports have been discouraged, in order to foster freer trade between nations and to prevent deadweight losses for importing countries. As mentioned in our chapter opener, one famous example, initially welcomed by the United States, was the restriction Japanese automakers placed on their car exports to the United States in the early 1980s. Consider Figure 8-6.

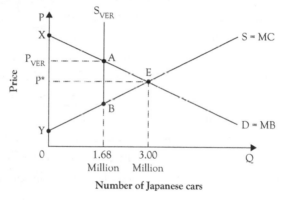

Figure 8-6. Japanese voluntary export restraint.

The diagram shows the American demand and supply situation for imported Japanese cars in the early 1980s. At the time, gas prices were high and small, reliable compact cars were an attractive purchase. Because American car makers were slow to respond, Japanese companies found an enthusiastic market with, perhaps, two million cars traded at a price, P^*. The consumer surplus for American purchasers of Japanese cars is shown by the area P^*XE; producer surplus for Japanese carmakers is P^*YE, and the total economic surplus is XYE.

Fearing punitive import taxes (tariffs), the Japanese voluntarily restricted shipments of cars to 1.68 million—in effect causing the supply curve to become vertical at that quantity, as shown by S_{VER}. The price of Japanese imports rose to P_{VER}, by some estimates a 15 percent price hike. Japanese producer surplus increased to $P_{VER}ABY$ but American car buyers lost—their surplus declined to $P_{VER}XA$. The major winner, however, was the domestic car industry, which, because of the reduced competition, was able to retain high prices while gaining additional customers. Note that the competitive need for American carmakers to innovate was dulled by the Japanese action.

A **quota**, a maximum import limit imposed by an economy, functions in a similar fashion to a voluntary export restraint, and similar welfare-reducing distortions occur, but with the additional threat of retaliation.

Tariffs

So far in this chapter we have employed a variety of techniques to present the argument that free trade offers benefits to economies and we have evaluated some of the frequent protectionist arguments against free trade. It is true that barriers to trade have been reduced over the years, but restrictions still survive and the most prominent is the tariff. A **tariff** is a tax imposed on imports. It has the effect of raising the price of the imported good, blunting any price advantage the import may have over domestic substitutes. It also has the attractive feature—for the government that imposes it—of generating tax revenues while preserving the jobs of voters. Consider Figure 8-7, which depicts the market for steel in the United States.

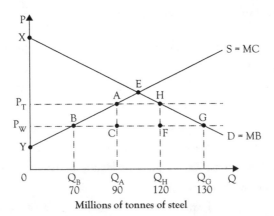

Figure 8-7. The effects of a tariff.

Because the world price (P_W) is lower than the domestic price, the United States is producing 70 million tonnes (Q_B), demanding 130 million tonnes (Q_G) and, therefore, importing 60 million tonnes ($Q_G - Q_B$). The domestic producer surplus is P_WYB and the consumer surplus is P_WXG.

In 2002, the Bush administration imposed a temporary tariff on steel, ranging from 8 to 30 percent. Canada and Mexico, as members of NAFTA, were exempt, as were some other steel-producing countries. The reason given for imposing the tariff was protection against an alleged detrimental surge of foreign-produced steel that had bankrupted more than 30 domestic producers. To simplify matters, we shall assume a single tariff (T) that raises the price of steel in the American market to P_T.

As a consequence, the quantity supplied by domestic producers increases from Q_B to Q_A, a gain of 20 million tonnes—the producer surplus increases by $P_W P_T$AB. The quantity demanded by domestic purchasers decreases from Q_G to Q_H, a loss of 10 million tonnes—the consumer surplus decreases by $P_W P_T$IG.

It would seem that the imposition of the tariff has caused a deadweight loss of BAHG, but this conclusion fails to include the third player—the government. Although imports have decreased, they still amount to 30 million tonnes ($Q_H - Q_A$) and the government receives tax revenue amounting to CAHF. The deadweight loss caused by the tariff is shown by the two remaining triangles, namely ABC and FGH.

THINK IT THROUGH: It is worth noting that the tariff revenues taken by the government, represented by the area CAHF, are best thought of as a redistribution toward the government and away from the consumers of imported goods, not as a tax that is being levied on and paid for by foreign producers. When Washington imposes a tariff, it is the consumer surplus of American citizens that is being reduced.

Comment: In the real-world case, the WTO found that no surge in imports had occurred and that the tariffs were therefore illegal. The European Union threatened retaliatory measures and the WTO authorized a two billion dollar sanction. The tariffs were removed.

Summary: The main point to be taken from the preceding discussion is that unrestricted trade is allocatively efficient. Trade restrictions engender deadweight losses because scarce resources are misdirected to inefficient lines of activity. Although trade may result in temporary unemployment in particular sectors, and that unemployment might prove socially disruptive, the preferred response ought to be to encourage displaced resources to seek out those activities in which they hold the comparative advantage.

International Finance: Exchange Rates and the Value of the Dollar

In Chapter 2, we began an analysis of the international currency market. There, we found that the dollar can increase (appreciate) or decrease (depreciate) in value.

A Brief Review of What We Learned in Chapter 2

The international demand for dollars is a *derived demand*—dollars are demanded, not for themselves, but for what they can buy—American exports. Other things remaining equal, an appreciation in the value of the dollar leads to a decrease in the quantity demanded of dollars (by foreigners) because, from the viewpoint of foreign buyers—as the dollar strengthens and the foreign currency correspondingly weakens— American goods become more expensive. With American goods less attractive, there is a decrease in the quantity demanded of dollars needed to buy those goods.

The quantity of dollars supplied (by Americans) is also affected by the exchange rate. As the dollar appreciates in value (and the foreign currency depreciates), foreign goods become easier for Americans to buy—the strong dollar stretches further—and to buy the increased quantity of such goods, which require payment in the local currency, more dollars must be supplied. With foreign goods more attractive, there is an increase in the quantity supplied of the dollars needed to buy the foreign currency in which those goods are price-tagged.

THINK IT THROUGH: A large part of these currency exchanges is invisible to American purchasers because the dollar is such a well-known and generally acceptable currency. Certainly, foreign companies that have a healthy trade with the United States are frequently willing to accept payment in dollars and then, with a fee added on, make the currency conversion themselves. Companies, such as Amazon and Paypal, allow buyers to designate their preferred currency for international transactions. Credit card purchases in Paris, Moscow, or Shanghai convert local currency purchases into dollars and report them as such on the next statement. But, although we may be barely aware of international exchange activities, those transactions still continue.

In Chapter 2, we concluded that the international market for dollars can be represented as shown in Figure 2-22 (reproduced here as Figure 8-8), with the dollar's value increasing if either the demand for dollars increased (because of an increased foreign demand for American exports) or if the supply of dollars decreased (because of a decreased American demand for foreign goods).

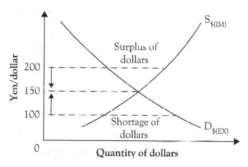

Figure 8-8. Equilibrium in the international market for dollars.

The flow of exports and imports is not the only factor influencing the international value of the dollar, however. We are now in a position to consider more fully the factors that determine the exchange rate.

Determinants of the Exchange Rate

We can identify two major factors that can influence the international price of the dollar, over and above the levels of exports and imports— relative international interest rates, and relative international price levels. In general, relative interest rate changes have a fairly rapid impact on exchange rates as financial capital flows swiftly across international borders, whereas changes in international price levels operate more slowly.

Relative international interest rates: Diversification—not keeping all one's eggs in the same basket—is a basic dictum of investors. To spread the risk, an investor should hold a variety of assets, such as U.S. Treasury bonds and bonds issued by the Bank of Japan. Each bond pays an interest rate—let us suppose 2 percent for the Treasury security and 5 percent for the Japanese bond. On any given day, both American investors and Japanese investors will be purchasing Treasury bonds and Japanese bonds. A Japanese wishing to buy a U.S. bond requires dollars and an American wishing to buy a Japanese financial instrument requires yen. Investors may be willing to accept a lower interest rate on the Treasury bond because of the desire to diversify or, perhaps, because U.S. bonds are perceived to hold a lower risk than Japanese bonds.

Let us suppose that international flows of funds between the two countries to buy bonds have stabilized but now the interest rate of Treasury bonds increases from 2 percent to 3 percent. U.S. bonds are relatively more attractive (and Japanese bonds are relatively less attractive), than formerly and, therefore, the demand for U.S. bonds will increase but the demand for Japanese bonds will decrease.

As Japanese demand for U.S. bonds increases, the demand for dollars to buy those bonds will also increase—an increase in the relative interest rate on U.S. securities causes an appreciation in the value of the dollar. Simultaneously, as American demand for Japanese securities is reduced, the demand for yen to buy those securities is also reduced and—the other side of the same transaction—the supply of dollars to buy the yen is reduced, also causing an appreciation in the value of the dollar.

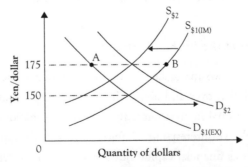

Figure 8-9. The effects of an increase in U.S. interest rates.

An increase in the relative interest rate of U.S. bonds increases the demand for dollars from $D_{\$1(EX)}$ to $D_{\$2}$, and decreases the supply of dollars from $S_{\$1(IM)}$ to $S_{\$2}$, causing a dollar appreciation, as shown in Figure 8-9.

Here is the solution to the trade conundrum that was broached earlier—how is it possible for the United States to run a persistent balance of trade deficit? The demand curve $D_{\$1(EX)}$ represents the demand for American exports whereas the supply curve $S_{\$1(IM)}$ represents the demand for American imports. At the new exchange rate ($1 equals 175 yen), imports exceed exports—there is a trade deficit, shown by the line segment AB. One reason we have been able to sustain our trade deficit is because foreign lenders have been willing to buy our IOUs (bonds).

THINK IT THROUGH: Earlier, in Chapter 2, we developed a rule of thumb regarding shifts in demand and supply curves, namely, "One factor shifts one curve and it shifts it only one time." In the current case, this rule is infringed because one factor—a change in an interest rate—has caused *both* curves to shift position. This is quite unusual in most markets but, as we shall see, to be expected in exchange markets.

Relative international price levels: One of the oldest of economic laws is the "law of one price," or **Purchasing-Power Parity**. This law states that a price of a good, such as a sack of rice, should be roughly the same in different countries. Transportation costs or sales taxes may interfere but, if such costs are negligible, then competitive forces should equalize prices. If rice is cheaper in North Dakota than in South Dakota, then entrepreneurs will have an incentive to buy low in North Dakota and sell high in South Dakota. The increased demand in North Dakota and the increased supply in South Dakota will force prices closer.

If the American price level increases relative to that of Japan, then Japanese goods will become more attractive to American purchasers whereas Japanese purchasers will become less keen on buying American-produced goods. The demand for imports will increase, causing an increase in the demand for yen and an increase in the supply of dollars. However, the Japanese demand for U.S. exports will decrease, causing a decrease in the demand for dollars. Working together, both factors will result in a depreciation in the value of the dollar.

Put differently, if the United States' inflation rate increases, then we should expect the dollar to weaken.

The purchasing-power parity theory argues that changes in relative price levels drive the exchange rate. An economy with a rapidly rising aggregate price level (i.e., a relatively high inflation rate) should expect to see its currency depreciate in value. And, in the long run, what causes the aggregate price level to increase? Recalling our discussion of the Quantity Theory in Chapter 4—overenthusiastic expansions in the money supply! Purchasing-power parity contends that an economy whose currency is losing value over time is experiencing this result because its aggregate price level is rising relative to those of its trade partners. According to purchasing-power parity, if Canada and the United States traded only with each other, and if the Canadian price level were twice as high as that of the United States, then the Canadian dollar would be worth half of an American dollar.

THINK IT THROUGH: What would happen if carpets were priced at "600 dollars" on the Canadian side of the border (in Fort Erie) but at "300 dollars" on the American side of the border (in Buffalo), and each American dollar was exchangeable for one Canadian dollar? Canadians would drive to Buffalo to buy carpets, exchanging 300 Canadian dollars for 300 American dollars. The demand for American dollars would increase, causing the American dollar to appreciate in value. This process would continue until the incentive for Canadians to travel to Buffalo disappeared—when the American dollar became twice the value of its Canadian counterpart.

There are some flaws in the theory, however, when applied in the real world. Driving to another country to buy a carpet may be inconvenient, time consuming, and expensive. Products may not be identical and local taxes may be a complication. In addition, the economy's overall price level reflects the price of services as well as goods, but services (haircuts, for example) are difficult to "export." For these reasons, the law of one price should be seen as a description of a general tendency for the behavior of exchange rates rather than a hard and fast rule.

Before continuing, it is worth reiterating that a "weak" dollar, just like a "strong" dollar, is a mixed blessing—good news for some, bad news for others.

International Trade and the ADAS Model

We are now ready to add the foreign sector into our macroeconomic model. **Net exports**, the difference between a country's exports and its imports (EX – IM), are included in aggregate demand. Our complete formula is

$$AD = C + I + G + (EX - IM)$$

An increase in exports or a decrease in imports will shift the aggregate demand curve to the right, causing the economy to expand and creating jobs. Given the exchange rate, the level of demand for exports is determined by foreign factors. Typically, as our trading partners prosper, our exports grow—a recession in Europe, or a slowdown in Japan, is bad news for American exporters.

Similarly, the volume of our imports is largely determined by our own domestic conditions. As our income increases and we prosper, we import more. In other words, there is a marginal propensity to import. The *marginal propensity to import* (MPM) is the fraction of any additional income that is spent on imported final goods.

The Marginal Propensity to Import and the Expenditure Multiplier: Like the marginal propensity to save (MPS) and the marginal tax rate (MTR), the marginal propensity to import is a leakage of spending power from the circular "earnings/spending" process that we first encountered in Chapter 3 and have subsequently refined. In those earlier chapters, we found that the size of the expenditure multiplier was affected by the degree of leakage from the circular flow—the greater the leakage, the smaller the multiplier. The same conclusion is valid when the foreign sector is incorporated into the model—the greater the marginal propensity to import, the smaller the expenditure multiplier. The purchase of foreign goods involves an outflow of spending power from the domestic economy and our willingness to buy imported goods as the economy expands can be seen as a *trade dampener* on the multiplier. In fact, we can modify the expenditure multiplier formula to include the marginal propensity to import as follows:

$$m = 1/(MPS + MTR + MPM) = 1/\text{Marginal Propensity to Leak}$$

The complete circular flow diagram is presented in Figure 8-10.

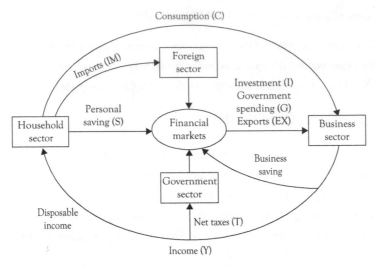

Figure 8-10. The complete circular flow diagram.

If a nation runs a balance of trade surplus (its exports exceed its imports) then the earnings gained can be used to increase the nation's net wealth, either by acquiring more holdings of foreign assets (government or private) or by buying back domestic assets that have been held by foreigners. A surplus nation such as China might buy U.S. Treasury debt, real estate in California, ownership in American corporations, or pay off some of its own previously incurred liabilities. By contrast, a nation with a balance of trade deficit faces a reduction in its net wealth in order to pay for the extra expenditure, achieved by selling off assets owned overseas or at home.

Macroeconomic Policy in an Open Economy

Fiscal and monetary policymakers face additional challenges when operating in an open economy. As we have seen, the size of the expenditure multiplier is reduced because of the leakage of income overseas. Let us assume that the economy is in recession and that the government wishes to stimulate it with expansionary fiscal or monetary measures. How will policy actions influence the balance of trade and the exchange rate?

Fiscal Policy, the Balance of Trade, and the Exchange Rate: An expansionary fiscal policy calls for increases in government spending or cuts in taxes. Such a policy will increase aggregate demand, causing increases in both real GDP and the aggregate price level. As the economy grows more prosperous, imports will expand. Further, as the domestic price level rises, foreign goods will become increasingly attractive. Combined, these effects will cause a deterioration in the balance of trade and a depreciation in the exchange rate. However, with more transactions and an increasing price level, the demand for money will increase, pushing up the interest rate—the *monetary dampener* effect that we met in Chapter 7. The higher interest rate will make domestic investments more attractive for foreigners and, therefore, there will be an upward pressure on the exchange rate.

Conclusion: We should predict that an expansionary fiscal policy will cause a deterioration in the balance of trade, but will have an indeterminate effect on the exchange rate, at least in the short run. In the longer term, the rising domestic price level may cause a decline in the value of the currency.

Monetary Policy, the Balance of Trade, and the Exchange Rate: An expansionary monetary policy involves an increase in the money supply (probably through open-market operations) and downward pressure on interest rates, even with the offsetting presence of the monetary dampener. Again, such a policy will increase aggregate demand. The subsequent increase in real GDP will stimulate imports, as will the increase in the domestic aggregate price level. The balance of trade will deteriorate, as will the exchange rate. Because the net effect of the policy on interest rates is to make them decline, there is a greater incentive to invest overseas, causing a further downward pressure on the exchange rate.

Conclusion: We should predict that an expansionary monetary policy will cause a deterioration in the balance of trade, and that the currency will depreciate.

Application: China—A Currency Manipulator?

During the presidential race of 2012, both candidates accused China of being a "currency manipulator." In fact, this charge was first leveled at the emerging Chinese economy as far back as 1992. Let us consider two questions: "How can China manipulate its currency?" and "Why would China wish to manipulate its currency?"

How can China manipulate its currency?: A nation may keep its currency's value low either by decreasing the demand for it or by increasing the supply of it. Alternatively, the manipulator could target a rival currency and drive up its value by increasing the demand for it. If China, for example, wishes to keep its currency (the yuan) low in value relative to the dollar, then it could pump yuan into international currency markets, exchanging them for the dollars necessary to purchase dollar-denominated U.S. government debt. The supply of yuan increases, as does the demand for dollars and the Chinese accumulate holdings of U.S. debt and dollars. By mid-2012, China was by far the largest foreign holder of U.S. government debt.

Why would China wish to manipulate its currency?: A nation may wish to manipulate its currency to "peg" it, that is, to keep it stable relative to that of an important trading partner, thus reducing uncertainty about the cost of international transactions. There is good evidence that, from 1994 to 2010, China engaged in this practice—the yuan/dollar exchange rate scarcely moved during that period.

The thrust of the accusations of currency manipulation is, however, not so much that the yuan's value was stable but that the yuan was *undervalued*. A cheap yuan (and expensive dollar) makes Chinese goods relatively cheap for American purchasers, increasing China's competitiveness, whereas prospective Chinese purchasers of American goods are discouraged. In addition to merchandise, a cheap currency is a boon to services—China is the world's third most-frequent destination for tourists, for example. Allowing a currency appreciation would diminish these competitive advantages.

Review: Although our macroeconomic model has been expanded to incorporate the international sector, the basic ADAS structure remains intact. We have established that international trade can be beneficial and have examined common arguments for protectionism. In addition, we have expanded the analysis of exchange rates that we began in Chapter 2, and considered how the presence of international transactions modifies the conduct of fiscal and monetary policy.

CHAPTER 9

Economic Growth and Lasting Lessons

By the end of this chapter you will be able to:

1. Outline the rationale of modern supply-side policies and evaluate the effectiveness of such policies.
2. Define economic growth and identify the three sources of economic growth.
3. Interpret the information presented by an aggregate production function.
4. Describe the causes of diminishing marginal productivity.
5. Describe the insights of endogenous growth theory.
6. Outline the issues involved in achieving sustainable long-run growth.
7. Discuss the "lasting lessons" of macroeconomics.

In 1728, Johnathan Swift, satirist and author of *Gulliver's Travels*, sowed an intellectual seed that bore fruit in a Washington D.C. restaurant two and a half centuries later. Swift noted that imposing higher duties on imports caused government revenues not to increase, but to decrease because, with higher penalties, there was a stronger incentive to avoid payment through smuggling and other tactics. His insight into increasing taxes and decreasing revenues—as he put it, that two plus two equal not four but one—was repeated by David Hume and, most influentially, by Adam Smith in *The Wealth of Nations*.

In 1974, the American economy was wracked with inflation and President Ford had launched the WIN (Whip Inflation Now) cam paign that included proposed tax increases designed to soak up income that might otherwise be spent, aggravating inflationary pressures. In a high-level meeting with senior White House officials, economist Arthur Laffer argued that raising tax rates would be counterproductive because excessively high tax rates would generate fewer revenues, not more. He sketched the so-called *Laffer Curve*—modern supply-side economics was born.

Chapter Preview: This chapter shifts the primary focus of our discussion from the short run to the long run and from demand-side concerns to supply-side ones. Many of the debates over economic policy can be seen as boiling down to differences of opinion regarding the relative effectiveness of demand-side and supply-side actions. We shall begin by exploring supply-side policy prescriptions and then move on to look at the sources of long-run economic growth.

Supply-Side Economics: Defeating Unemployment and Inflation Simultaneously

The roots of modern supply-side economic thought run deep. Because of their confidence in the preeminence of the long run, the Classical economists and their successors have largely subscribed to the view that the government sector ought to be small, balanced, and noninterventionist. Short-run stabilization policy is not for them. As George W. Bush stated, "Stay the course," a view in sharp distinction to the Keynesian dictum that "In the long run we're all dead."

We examined Classical economics in Chapter 5—modern supply-side economics is one of its more recent manifestations. The underlying belief in the potency of markets, incentives, and self-interest to create wealth and prosperity is pure Adam Smith.

The Supply-Side Rationale

Supply-side policies are crafted to increase the incentives to supply labor, to save, and to invest more in capital and, thereby to nurture potential output, shifting the long-run aggregate supply curve and, therefore, the short-run aggregate supply curve, to the right, as shown in Figure 9-1.

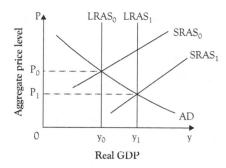

Figure 9-1. The rationale behind supply-side policies.

By so doing, the aggregate price level will be driven down, from P_0 to P_1, reducing inflationary pressures, while additional job opportunities will be created. With more robust economic activity and an expanding tax base, tax revenues can grow and transfers shrink, allowing budget deficits to be tamed, despite (or because of) reductions in tax rates.

Incentives and Self-Interest: Adam Smith argued that self-interested individuals, driven by incentives and as if directed by "an invisible hand," will produce that mix of goods and services that most fully satisfies the needs of society—in other words, self-interest, operating through liberalized markets, is allocatively efficient. To be sure, there are roles for government, as a regulator of markets and as a provider of so-called public goods including national defense, but the private sector is the main engine of production. The more effectively that engine is allowed to run, the more productive the economy will be.

By reforming the tax code, so that productive individuals could keep more of what they earned, the supply-siders argued that more resources would be supplied—more resources are supplied as taxes are reduced and rewards are increased. With higher take-home pay, more workers would be willing to work more hours; with less tax on interest earnings, households would be encouraged to save more; with incentives to invest (investment tax credits) and a greater reward for successful entrepreneurship (lower taxes on profits), more business ventures would be encouraged to flourish.

Trust in Private Market Efficiency: Although reforming the tax code is a centerpiece of supply-side economics, the rationale is not restricted to this one tactic. Any impediment to production, such as burdensome regulations on businesses, high interest rates due to government deficits (the crowding-out effect), or inflexibilities in resource or financial markets, are likely to be viewed unfavorably.

THINK IT THROUGH: As a candidate, Ronald Reagan promised cutbacks in environmental regulations. During his presidency, when supply-side economics held center stage, the economy experienced deregulation in the agricultural, transportation, and financial sectors. The minimum wage remained virtually unchanged throughout the Reagan years and, therefore, in real terms, declined in value. Can you see how each of these policies is in agreement with the supply-side stance?

The Laffer Curve: If supply-side policies could achieve the twin goals of controlling inflation and alleviating unemployment but could do so at the cost of sharply higher government deficits, then their appeal would be diminished. However, the Laffer Curve, depicted in Figure 9-2, seemed to offer a rationale for expecting such policies to be deficit-reducing.

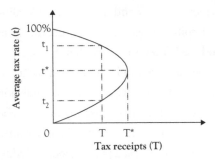

Figure 9-2. The Laffer curve.

The Laffer Curve diagram shows tax receipts on the horizontal axis and the average tax rate on the vertical axis. Clearly, if the tax rate is zero, then no tax receipts will be collected. Similarly, if the tax rate is 100 percent, then, again, no tax receipts will be collected, because of the profound disincentive to work and massive noncompliance. There must be a tax rate (t^*) between these two extremes at which tax revenues are maximized and if tax rates are higher than this level, then tax rate cuts will increase tax revenues while boosting incentives to work by allowing taxpayers to retain more of their salaries. Laffer believed that prior tax policies had pushed the tax rate beyond t^* to a point such as t_1. By reducing the tax rate from t_1 to t^*, Laffer contended that tax revenues would increase.

Policy Recommendations: The supply-side rationale supports reductions in personal and corporate tax rates and in the capital gains tax rate in order to increase the supply of labor and capital. With lower income tax rates, individuals' after-tax income is increased, providing a greater incentive to work.

Similarly, by cutting taxes on earnings from savings, the flow of funds into financial markets would swell, reducing interest rates and, therefore, the cost of investment. Further, by offering more generous investment tax credits, capital accumulation should increase, resulting in greater productivity. In addition, government regulation of private sector enterprise should be lessened.

Evaluation of Supply-Side Economics: Although an alluring theory, little empirical evidence supports the supply-side view. Supply-side effects, to the extent that they exist at all, seem dwarfed by demand-side changes. Income tax cuts, taken in the name of supply-side policy during the Reagan years, raised disposable income and, from there, stimulated the economy through shifts in aggregate demand.

Similarly, an investment tax credit, while it may increase productive capacity, also has the more immediate and stronger impact of increasing spending on investment.

THINK IT THROUGH: Certainly, a particular policy may have influence both on the supply side and on the demand side of the economy. Early in his administration, President George W. Bush proposed a tax cut, arguing that lower taxes would motivate workers to greater effort and entrepreneurs to greater investment—a "supply-side" argument. Before the tax cut was in effect, however, the economy suffered a recession, and the president shifted ground, contending that the tax cut would strengthen aggregate demand by boosting consumption spending!

Tax cuts aimed at increasing the supply of labor, or encouraging saving, seem less effective than those aimed at spurring business investment. On balance, such policies have at best a minor impact on productive capacity in the long run; although, because it certainly has been demonstrated that taxpayer behavior is influenced by changes in marginal tax rates, any future tax rate proposals must be assessed carefully. A side effect of policies that pursue growth by reducing capital gains taxes or corporate income taxes is the likely widening of income inequalities within society, as the successful thrive and the unsuccessful survive.

Finally, history's judgment has come down heavily against the Laffer Curve's prediction that tax rate cuts would increase tax receipts and shrink the budget deficit. In fact, referring to Figure 9-2, the evidence shows that, far from having a tax rate similar to t_1, the economy's rate was similar to t_2, meaning that reduced tax rates exacerbated deficit problems.

Although the supply-side economics experiment of the 1980s is generally judged a failure—respected economist and former head of George W. Bush's Council of Economic Advisors, Gregory Mankiw refers to it as "fad economics," a less unkind term than "voodoo economics"— its call for lower taxes and smaller, less interventionist, government still appeals to many and the upsurge in belief in the power of incentives, less regulation, and self-interest to shape our national destiny persists in the economic and political arenas. This may be the true legacy of supply-side economics—no longer can we focus exclusively on the demand-side effects of policy actions. As an example, it is significant that President Obama's American Recovery and Reinvestment Act (2009), although largely Keynesian and demand-side in approach, also allocated funding for infrastructure investment, technological improvements, and human capital enhancements—all measures that a supply-sider would advocate.

In further defense of supply-side economics, we should note the limitations on the effectiveness of orthodox Keynesian policy that were exposed during the Great Recession. Many economies, including the United States and the Europeans, adopted policy stances that were primarily Keynesian and, yet, more than 5 years after the onset of slowdown, those economies still exhibit sluggish economic performance with frail growth and persistently high unemployment. In Chapter 6, we identified some of the problems associated with Keynesian fiscal policy—declining and unpredictable fiscal multipliers, the crowding-out effect on the private sector of government borrowing, capital flight, the political disincentives incurred in fiscal discipline.

Sources of Economic Growth

In this section, we consider how economic growth occurs and how it may be sustained. Why do some countries grow more rapidly than others do? Is there an optimal environment that nurtures growth and, if so, can policy actions improve our chances of creating such an environment?

First, though, we must define terms—what is economic growth? We may define **economic growth** as the expansion in the quantity of goods and services produced by an economy as time goes by. For convenience, this is often measured in terms of real GDP (gross domestic product) and, frequently, because population changes over time, as *per capita* real GDP.

Achieving Growth

If asked how we could promote economic growth, we should reply, "Add resources, improve resources, and improve resource performance." Although reckoned by many to be a failure, supply-side economics offers some clues about improving growth performance by emphasizing the encouragement of labor and investment in capital.

"Add resources": We can learn from history. Great empires have grown by expanding their territories and exploiting the resources of their colonies and hinterlands. In the nineteenth century, for example, Britain ascended to the summit of world power through its single-minded acquisition of territory. France, Germany, the Netherlands, and Belgium followed suit. Earlier, Napoleon, and later, Hitler, sought to acquire additional human and natural resources for similar purposes.

The United States prospered by the Louisiana Purchase, the development of resources through successive Homestead Acts, and the purchase of Alaska from Russia. Successive waves of immigrants augmented the existing supply of labor as did, in the most brutal way, the slave trade. Additional resources—human, capital, and natural—promote growth.

In fact, we reached this conclusion in our first chapter, when we considered the production possibility frontier. As we saw there, the frontier—the boundary between what the economy can produce and what it cannot—expands as resources increase in quantity, improve in quality, or are combined more productively through advances in technology, as shown in Figure 9-3.

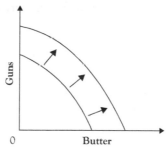

Figure 9-3. Economic growth.

Using the production possibility frontier as a guide, we can visualize economic growth as an outward shift of the frontier—we become able to produce more guns and more butter.

Adding more resources bestows a greater capacity to process—together, Robinson Crusoe and Man Friday can produce more than Crusoe alone. When the Dutch enclosed and drained the saltwater from the Zuiderzee, they successfully created a freshwater lake and 600 square miles of land—the new province of Flevoland.

A Digression on the Law of Diminishing Marginal Productivity: In 1798, an English clergyman, the Reverend Thomas "Bob" Malthus, published *An Essay on the Principle of Population*. Wildly controversial, it ran through six editions while he was alive and remains highly influential today. Malthus, and subsequent Classical economists, contended that constraints on the availability of farmland would limit the world's ability to feed its population, resulting in famine and disease. In the oil-strapped 1970s, The Club of Rome (a global think tank) published *The Limits to Growth*, making essentially the same point that, because of limitations in nonrenewable natural resources, sustained long-run economic growth is an unattainable dream.

If Malthus and his modern advocates are correct—that there is a limit to the quantity of key resources—then, as other resources, such as labor, are added to the productive effort, the productivity of these additional resources will decline until, eventually, no further gains in production can be eked out. Supporters of this view, that marginal productivity will decline, observe "you can't feed the world from a flowerpot."

We can see the effect of diminishing marginal productivity in the following diagram, which shows an aggregate production function.

A *production function* is a device (a graph or a mathematical formula) that relates the quantities of inputs to the quantity of output—either for

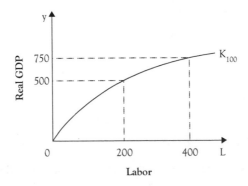

Figure 9-4. An aggregate production function with diminishing marginal productivity.

an individual firm or for the overall economy—an *aggregate production function* relates inputs and output at the overall level. In Figure 9-4, we have one variable input, units of labor, shown on the horizontal axis. All other resources (for simplicity, we will assume only capital equipment) are fixed in quantity—we have a given amount of machines (K_{100} in our example). Real GDP is shown on the vertical axis.

Note: The slope of the production function *is* the marginal product of labor. Recall that the slope of a line is "rise over run." Here, the "rise" is the change in output whereas the "run" is change in labor input.

As we add workers to our stock of machines, output will increase but, as the slope of the production function shows, the rate of increase decreases—marginal productivity declines. If, for example, we double the number of workers from 200 to 400, then output level will change from 500 to 750 units—increasing but not doubling.

Are such predictions—that we simply will "run out" of resources—a realistic view? Probably not. As we shall see, rapid accumulation of physical and human capital and technological innovation permit sustained expansions in labor productivity. There are creative ways around apparent constraints.

"Improve resources.": If, instead of adding more resources—more workers, for example—we keep the same quantity of resources but improve their quality, then we still should experience economic growth and the production possibility frontier will still shift outward. If a worker trains and acquires new skills, this acquisition is termed "human capital." If better nutrition or public health programs are introduced, or if literacy programs are made more widespread, then our given stock of workers will become more productive—healthy and educated workers can do more than sickly and illiterate ones. Education of any kind that increases the abilities of our labor force is an investment in human capital.

We can also increase the productivity of our workers by providing them with more capital or better capital—a secretary with a word processor is more productive than is a secretary with a typewriter. Cell phones and laptops, and the ability to use them, increase productivity. When compared with workers in other countries, American workers are highly productive, partly because of the greater quantity of our human capital—education and training, work ethic, level of health—and partly because of the greater quantity of capital available.

The impact of additional or improved resources on the economy's production function is shown in Figure 9-5.

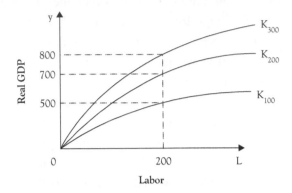

Figure 9-5. Shifting the production function.

In Figure 9-5, the 200 workers, using 100 units of capital, can produce 500 units of output. If additional capital is given to the same number of workers, we would expect increased production—graphically, the production function will swing upward (from K_{100} to K_{200}). However, the law of diminishing marginal productivity still applies—doubling the capital stock, from 100 to 200 machines, increases but does not double production. Adding a further 100 machines will have a still smaller positive impact on production, as shown by K_{300}. Additions to human capital or technological improvements will have a similar result—expansions in output, but at a decreasing rate of increase.

THINK IT THROUGH: The high school graduation rate in the United States is well over 80 percent, with more than 25 percent of the population earning at least a bachelor's degree. Entering the labor force, these workers embody significant knowledge and skills, especially when set against the legions around the world who are barely literate or who have never had the opportunity to complete grade school.

THINK IT THROUGH (MORE): Consider the massive stock of capital within the borders of the United States—including not just the privately owned factories, warehouses, and machines, but also the social capital, such as roads, airports, and docks. A corn farmer in Kansas has easy access to sophisticated tractors, computerized irrigations systems, and mechanization. Aerial spraying can control pests or crop disease and spare parts for machines are readily available, only a phone call away. This farmer's counterpart in Mexico has few of these options and, consequently, is less productive. In other, less developed, economies even dependable sources of fuel or water may be limited.

"Improve resource performance": Economic growth can also be fostered by technological improvements and innovation—using the same resources as before, but more effectively. Put differently, it is implausible that an economy will be able to sustain growth merely by increasing its resources—it must also find new and more effective ways of combining the resources it has.

Innovation is the discovery and application of more efficient production techniques or the development of new products. A better crop rotation system may boost agricultural yields, for instance, a better floor plan in a factory or improved management techniques may enhance production. Fresh insight may result in ways of combining or eliminating steps in a process, achieving the same or better results with less use of resources. The genetic modification of crops, controversial or not, is an example of innovation where a "new" product has been engineered.

THINK ABOUT IT: Consider the automobile of today and the car your grandparents drove. Today's car is assembled by highly mechanized robotic assembly lines with computers guiding the flow of resources. Much of the heavy and costly steel that used to weigh down the cars of yesteryear has been replaced with plastics and other composite materials that are lighter, stronger, and more durable. Under the hood, tiny computers direct the engine systems, monitoring and optimizing performance, causing less fuel to be needed, while a catalytic converter reduces tail-pipe pollutants (unless you have switched to an electric vehicle!). Mechanical breakdowns are rare and GPS allows you to reach your destination without error, saving time and, again, conserving fuel.

Perhaps the largest area where technological change has been felt is in the field of information technology. Today's college student can be far more productive than a student from her parents' generation, perhaps from the 1980s. The student in the 1980s had no Wikipedia—in fact, no Internet access at all as we recognize it today. There was no Google, and e-mail was still in its infancy. Finding resources in the campus library would require a physical search through a card catalog. There were no online classes. Graphing calculators were uncommon and expensive and, although word processers were available, they were still fairly unusual, while laptops in class were science fiction. The innovations of the digital age bestow on today's student learning advantages undreamed of by her parents.

So far, we have identified the broad sources of economic growth—more resources, improved resources, and better ways of combining resources. Given the limitations inherent in natural resources, in practical terms growth will typically spring from capital accumulation through investment in human and physical capital and from innovation and improvements and technology. We can model this process in Figure 9-6.

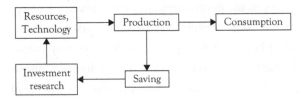

Figure 9-6. A simple model of economic growth.

This model indicates that production derives from the innovative combination of our resources and technology. That production then may be consumed or saved. Think of a farm producing corn. The more corn that is consumed, the less will be saved and, therefore, the less there will be available for next year's planting. Saving begets investment and investment augments the resources and technology available for future production. According to this model, there is a trade-off between consumption today and consumption tomorrow—the more corn we consume today, the less corn we will be able to consume in the future.

It is certainly true that the saving rate is a key predictor of successful growth—countries with high saving rates tend to grow more rapidly than those countries with low saving rates. Investment equips workers to do the job and to sustain productivity growth and, if saving is lacking, then either investment is stalled or funds must be attracted from foreign sources.

New (endogenous) growth theory: Until fairly recently, the orthodox view held that innovation was unpredictable and serendipitous—simply "happening" without economic rhyme or reason—and that, therefore, capital formation was the preferred engine for growth. However, even with capital accumulation, the threat of diminishing marginal productivity remains alive because, as we have seen in Figure 9-5, each successive addition to a growing stock of capital has a smaller impact on productivity, leading to renewed concerns about the viability of sustained growth.

Rather than changes in the quantity or quality of resources, *endogenous growth theory* emphasizes the role of innovation and technology in fostering economic growth and, importantly, that technological change is *not* a random event but the result of economic structures and incentives that create *knowledge capital*—the knowledge accumulated from experience, education, and research and development. Moreover, unlike a machine or a newly trained worker whose contribution to production is restricted to one office or factory, it is contended that knowledge capital is not bound by the law of diminishing marginal productivity because new knowledge bestows benefits throughout the economy. Whether this assertion—that knowledge bestows positive externalities that overcome diminishing marginal productivity—is valid remains unproven but endogenous growth theory has opened up for discussion the topic of how to promote innovation and, more broadly, what can be done to achieve higher growth rates.

Promoting Sustainable Growth

The Convergence Hypothesis: One of the implications of diminishing marginal productivity is that economies that have achieved high standards of living will tend to grow more slowly than those with lower standards of living because the introduction of additional resources should have a stronger impact on output in the "poor" country than those same resources will have in the "rich" country. In addition, "poor" countries, starting late, should be able to learn from, and avoid, the mistakes of "rich" countries by adopting only those production techniques and technologies that have been shown to be effective.

Although it is true that some nations have successfully transitioned from low to high per capita GDP performance—Japan and the other "Asian tigers" are obvious examples—numerous other countries have failed to catch up. Convergence is not guaranteed.

The question remains, "Why do some economies prosper while others languish?" Increasingly, the focus has been on the role of institutions in fostering or retarding growth. Underachieving countries frequently have weak financial and governmental institutions, corruption, and inadequate protection for lenders and investors, all of which discourage capital investment. With respect to human capital, an economy with a strong educational system and healthy workers will prosper relative to one with low educational standards and poor health provision. In addition, laggards often suffer from *capital flight* and a *brain drain*, as funds that could have been invested locally seek safer or higher returns elsewhere and as skilled workers emigrate to more lucrative or rewarding environments.

What are the conditions necessary for an economy to achieve and sustain a satisfactory rate of economic growth? We may identify two broad conditions—enhancements to saving and investment and to innovation.

Opportunities and Incentives to Save and Invest: Saving provides the funding for investment, so policies that encourage saving enhance investment. Replacing income tax with a national sales tax, although potentially regressive, would offer incentives to save rather than spend. Thinking of the crowding-out effect of government spending, reductions in government deficits would allow more, and cheaper, funds to flow to private investment projects. While considering supply-side policies earlier in this chapter, we found that modifications of the tax code to reward investment—capital gains taxes, investment tax credits, and corporate taxes—had fairly minor influence but, cumulatively, over the long term, provision of additional permanent incentives ought to establish bolder patterns of capital accumulation.

Let us not forget that education and training represent investments in *human* capital so growth is assisted by improvements in the quality of education and its availability. Pell grants, low-interest student loans, and federal funding for colleges all reduce the cost and increase the accessibility of education and, hence, all promote human capital investment and economic growth. Expanding online offerings has a similar effect—reducing the "cost" of attending college.

Opportunities and Incentives to Innovate: Innovation begins with invention of new technologies. Over time, waves of invention—such as the development of steam power and, most recently, computer chips and the Internet—have driven economies forward. Although a new technology may spring from a happy accident, it is more likely to come from a culture that supports basic research and development. The United States offers substantial support to R&D through funding of research programs at public universities and organizations such as NASA, Department of Defense, and the National Science Foundation. Rather than merely "more" education in general, recently there has been an increased emphasis on STEM education—science, technology, engineering, and math. Superior engineers, for instance, should develop superior technologies. Additional government support for private research comes from the tax code (for example, the Research and Experimentation Tax Credit, introduced in the early "supply-side" days), and robustly enforced patent laws, intellectual property rights, and trademarks. In itself, political stability and adherence to the rule of law cultivates the soil in which fresh ideas germinate.

Lasting Lessons

President Truman once quipped that he needed a "one-handed economist," because every time he asked for a policy recommendation the advisor's reply would be in the form "on one hand, this, but, on the other hand, that," resulting in no definite answer! There's a grain of truth in this story because economists can differ quite widely in their interpretation of a given situation.

Economics is an endlessly intriguing field of study, and one in which two plus two seldom add up to equal only four. Our views of policy effectiveness are colored by the relative emphasis we place on short-run outcomes and long-run outcomes, the role of government, and so on. Policy choices are buffeted by emerging new (and old) schools of thought. Currently, Keynesian demand-side views are in the ascendancy but, a few years ago, supply-siders had the ear of policymakers. Other opinions, such as the Austrian school, are lurking on the wings, waiting for their opportunity at stardom. Is it any wonder, then, that students of macroeconomics, looking for "the" answer, all too often come away from their course of study with a feeling of bafflement?

It is true, however, that macroeconomists have been patiently building a consensus and, although it is a hard-fought struggle, we can distill some durable lessons.

First, Adam Smith mostly had it right. Remarkably, many of Smith's views have come down to us largely intact and untarnished. To be sure, his emphasis was "supply side" and "long run" but, nevertheless, his faith in the benevolence of the "invisible hand" and the productive power of lightly regulated markets resonate today.

What lessons can we take away from our brief exploration of macroeconomics? Here are ten "big ideas."

Big Idea #1: *"There's no such thing as a free lunch."* Choices matter and trade-offs exist because of scarcity. When we choose an alternative, we give up all the other competing options—there is an opportunity cost and that is value of the next most-preferred alternative given up. In a world of limited resources, our actions have consequences, and no lunches are free.

Big Idea #2: *"Trade is beneficial."* More precisely, free trade voluntarily entered into can be mutually beneficial. Smith's *The Wealth of Nations* was a reaction against the restrictive trade policies of the time and his argument was that exchange benefits both partners. A generation later, David Ricardo provided the theoretical confirmation with the Law of Comparative Advantage. Is trade *always* beneficial? No—in times of high unemployment, for instance, the temptation to "save jobs" through protectionist policies may be compelling but, in general, freer trade generates gains that restricted trade denies.

Big Idea #3: *"Markets efficiently coordinate production and consumption."* Self-interest and incentives drive competitive markets to produce the mix of goods that is most preferred by society. Government's function is to act as a referee, facilitating transactions and standing by to levy sanctions when the market's rules are broken.

THINK IT THROUGH: By this point, it should not be surprising to you to learn that the overwhelming majority of economists support the legalization of marijuana. This is not because economists believe that marijuana smoking is a desirable activity (although they may!) but because, generally, prohibitions or restrictions on markets are felt to be undesirable, inefficient, and costly.

Big Idea #4: *"Sometimes markets fail."* As discussed in Chapter 6, there are cases where third parties are affected, positively or negatively, by market transactions. Markets are blind to such external effects and, therefore, government intervention is required. There is also scope for government intervention in situations where one party is capable of yielding undue power, or where free riders exist.

Big Idea #5: *"Fiscal and monetary actions primarily affect the demand-side of the economy and can influence output, employment, and the price level, but only in the short-run."* Demand-side (Keynesian-style) stabilization policies are a short-term fix with no lasting beneficial impact on economic performance but, if financed by printing money, can stoke inflation and, through the crowding-out effect, can impair the effectiveness of the private sector.

Big Idea #6: *"Demand-side fiscal and monetary actions involve a short-run trade-off between inflation and unemployment."* Expansionary policies may expand output and alleviate unemployment in the short run, but one consequence is higher rates of inflation. Put differently, one consequence of choosing to combat inflation with demand-side policies is that more households will suffer the stresses of unemployment.

Big Idea #7: *"In the long run, it's the rate of expansion in the money supply that determines the rate of inflation."* In general, the proponents of the Quantity Theory are correct. Over the long haul, the rate at which we print money sets the rate at which the aggregate price level rises—our inflation rate is largely a product of actions taken by the government and the Fed.

Big Idea #8: *"In the long run, there's no significant tradeoff between the inflation rate and either the unemployment rate or the level of production."* Except when hyperinflation results, printing more money, or less, has no major impact on our long-term standard of living because the long-run aggregate supply curve is vertical.

Big Idea #9: *"Economic growth is a supply-side phenomenon."* Demand-side policies have little influence on our long-term economic performance. Further, capital expansion and innovation are the keys to sustained growth. The choices we make about consumption and saving today set the stage for our ability to consume in the future.

Big Idea #10: *"The economy has a long-run self-correcting mechanism, although it may be weak."* As we saw in Chapter 6, markets will operate to push the economy toward full employment—in the long run. This does not mean, however, that there is no role for short-run stabilization policy when the economy is not at full employment. We may still feel that intervention to hasten the restoration of full employment is justified.

Parting Thoughts

Welcome to the final section of our book. If you've read all nine chapters, then you've been challenged and worked hard, and you've encountered many economic concepts that I hope you will carry with you through life. Economics is the study of the choices we make as we pass through life—the world is our laboratory and our concepts are useless if we fail to apply them to that life. Certainly, you should have a sharper awareness of the transactions that surround you, the news that meets you each morning, and your perspectives on personal and global events.

At the very beginning of our first chapter, you were asked to imagine being in a restaurant and consulting the menu of choices. Economics is all about choice. We must make choices as we strive to achieve the best outcomes possible in our own self-interest. Individually and as a society, we must make choices because, although we have unlimited wants, we have limited resources to meet those wants. Along the way, imperfections in the market mechanism or special considerations may make those choices difficult to realize, but the more aware we are of the imperfections and of the nature of the process itself, the more likely it is that our choices will serve us well.

My best wishes to you in the choices you make this day and in your future days.

Index

OTHER TITLES IN THE ECONOMICS COLLECTION

Philip Romero, The University of Oregon and Jeffrey A. Edwards,
North Carolina A&T State University, Collection Editors

- *Managerial Economics: Concepts and Principles* by Donald Stengel
- *Your Macroeconomic Edge: Investing Strategies for the Post-Recession World* by Philip J. Romero
- *Working with Economic Indicators: Interpretation and Sources* by Donald Stengel and Priscilla Chaffe-Stengel
- *Innovative Pricing Strategies to Increase Profits* by Daniel Marburger
- *Regression for Economics* by Shahdad Naghshpour
- *Statistics for Economics* by Shahdad Naghshpour
- *How Strong Is Your Firm's Competitive Advantage?* by Daniel Marburger
- *Game Theory: Anticipating Reactions for Winning Actions* by Mark Burkey

---

Announcing the Business Expert Press Digital Library

Concise E-books Business Students Need for Classroom and Research

This book can also be purchased in an e-book collection by your library as
- a one-time purchase,
- that is owned forever,
- allows for simultaneous readers,
- has no restrictions on printing, and
- can be downloaded as PDFs from within the library community.

Our digital library collections are a great solution to beat the rising cost of textbooks. e-books can be loaded into their course management systems or onto student's e-book readers.

The **Business Expert Press** digital libraries are very affordable, with no obligation to buy in future years. For more information, please visit **www.businessexpertpress.com/librarians**. To set up a trial in the United States, please contact **Adam Chesler** at *adam.chesler@businessexpertpress .com* for all other regions, contact **Nicole Lee** at *nicole.lee@igroupnet.com*.